D0757872

The Real
David Beckham

The Real David Beckham

An Intimate Biography

Gaynor Morgan

JOHN BLAKE

Published by Metro Publishing Ltd,
3, Bramber Court, 2 Bramber Road,
London W14 9PB, England

www.blake.co.uk

First published in hardback in 2004

ISBN 1 84358 120 5

British Library Cataloguing-in-Publication Data:

A catalogue record for this book is available from the British Library.

Design by www.envydesign.co.uk

Printed in Great Britain by Creative Print and Design

1 3 5 7 9 10 8 6 4 2

To my late Mum, 'My Rock',
and to my Dad, 'My Hero'
I will always love you.

ACKNOWLEDGEMENTS

To my Mum and Dad: for all your love and support throughout my life: I love you.

Love to my beautiful son Alex who is my inspiration: I hope that you will understand that it has helped me to write this book and put down all my past experiences, ready to start a new chapter in my life whilst always being a devoted mother to you.

To my dear brother Scott: we have been through some tough times together but thankfully have come out the other side a lot wiser and stronger.

To my friends who I have been lucky enough to find during my life who have always been there for me: Lisa Watts, Lizette Roberts, Robin and Julie Arnold, Sarah Wallace, Denise Welch and Mike Tait. A special thanks to Lisa and Mike, who have given me unconditional support whilst writing this book.

To everyone at Blake Publishing: John, Rosie, Michelle and Adam for their patience and support.

Thanks to all the photographers who provided me with pictures for this book: Damien McGillicuddy, Nick Jones, Jean Havilland, Joanne Ellis, Sandi Hodkinson, Maura Williams, Dave Nelson and Jason Van-Blerk.

Finally thanks to Carl Nagatis, who has shared with me his invaluable knowledge of writing and experience in journalism.

Gaynor Morgan
June 2004

Visit my website at www.gaynormorgan.com
Management - Can Associates

CONTENTS

INTRODUCTION

'The marriage was in trouble before my affair
with David so I am not to blame for the
breakdown of their relationship.'

**Rebecca Loos, speaking after her affair
with David Beckham was made public**

There are many different David Beckhams.

There is the national hero, arguably the best footballer
England has seen for three decades, a man whose every
movement on the pitch keeps the fans breathless, and
whose spectacular displays of virtuosity rarely disappoint.

There is the icon. Too often the word is used lightly, but
in David's case it is apt. He is a sign of our times, an
individual who encapsulates our modern preoccupation
with celebrity, but who achieves it hand in hand with
astonishing talent; a role model for young and old alike; a
man who sets trends.

There is also the David Beckham that I got to know. A young man who, despite having earned the adulation and respect of millions around the world, does not seem to be able to command the same adoration where he needs it most: at home.

And then there is the darker side of David Beckham: obsessive, demanding, uncompromising. They are essential assets in his field of endeavour, but they can serve him ill in other situations. We all have aspects of our personality that make others feel uncomfortable, and David is probably no exception.

I have set out to try and describe the real David Beckham. I believe I am qualified to do this for the same reasons that my relationship with him changed from one of casual friendship to one of intimacy. I have grown up with Manchester United, and I have grown up with celebrity. I am comfortable with them both, and I think David sensed that in me the first night we met. I was not overawed by the hype; I was interested in him as a human being, not a piece of media meat, and he reacted positively to that.

Looking back with the advantage of hindsight, I can see that it was almost inevitable that our relationship should have been taken to the level it was. During our time together and my experience of growing up in that environment, it was apparent that David was a man looking for something else. I would not say that he was caught in a loveless marriage – nobody looking from the outside can tell with any accuracy what exists between a man and his wife – but I can say beyond fear of contradiction that there was something missing in the seemingly fairy-tale union of Posh and Becks. When the revelations of his indiscretions with Rebecca Loos came to light, I was far from surprised. And when she states her view that she was in no way responsible for any breakdown in their marriage, I believe her. I know from my own experience that the marriage appeared to be faltering long before she came on the scene. With hindsight and with hearsay I now have no doubt that any dalliance, however insignificant, could have developed into something more than it actually did. It seemed that was what David wanted and, as I discovered, he is a man who is used to getting what he wants.

Like Rebecca, I do not believe for one minute that any one single person could feel responsible for the marital difficulties the Beckhams have encountered. But I do think that those difficulties can be traced back to the time we first met in a fashionable Manchester nightclub: it was then in my mind that the apparent first chinks in the seemingly impenetrable armour of the Posh and Becks phenomenon started to show.

Now that so many inaccuracies and half-truths have been told about this seminal cultural figure of our time, I want to set the record straight. Over a period of eighteen months, I grew to understand what it means to be David Beckham and, from my vantage point as the daughter of one of the most esteemed of David's predecessors at Manchester United, I want to paint a picture of the bizarre life inside what the footballer refers to as 'Bubble Beckham': the highs and the lows, the strains, the stresses, the magic and the mayhem.

I want to tell the truth about us.

I want to show you the real David Beckham.

CHAPTER ONE

THE MAGNIFICENT SEVENS

Among the more spectacular of David Beckham's growing set of tattoos, such as the guardian angel on his back which hovers over the names of his sons, and Michelangelo's statue of his namesake on his shoulder, there is a very simple set of roman numerals. These spell out 'VII', the number seven, with a Latin inscription underneath: 'Perfectio In Spiritu' (spiritual perfection). This is probably the most significant mark that he has chosen to bear permanently on his body. It commemorates his entry into a unique and legendary line of football players: those who have pulled on the number 7 shirt for Manchester United. For a long time there was nothing particularly special about that shirt, and not all the players who have worn it deserve to be called legends by any means. However, in the 1960s, the handsome but wayward Irishman George Best became the first in a line of players who have come to be known as the Magnificent Sevens, the often controversial but always exciting footballers who were adored by the fans on the packed Old Trafford terraces. One of David's own personal heroes when he was a small boy was Bryan Robson. United and England's 'Captain Marvel' dominated the midfield as a number 7. Eric Cantona, the enigmatic and controversial Frenchman, finally found an appropriately great stage for his own swaggering brand of football genius wearing that shirt, the collar turned up in the style that became his trademark.

I understand exactly how David Beckham felt when he could call the Manchester United number 7 shirt his own. My father, Willie Morgan, was one of the most illustrious players ever to wear that shirt, playing a total of 236 games for Manchester United. As the age of five I went to Old Trafford to see my father in a live game for the first time. Sitting in the special seats reserved for the players' families, next to Sir Matt Busby's children Sheena and Sandy (who remain close friends even to this day), it was an exhilarating experience, but a bewildering one. I watched my father run out on to the Old Trafford pitch with the magic number 7 on his back. The roar of the crowd from the terraces as they saw him was deafening, and they began to sing his name in a special chant, 'Willie Morgan on the wing', sung to the old boy scouts' tune of 'Ging Gang Goolie'. I was confused. Afterwards in the players' lounge, as we mingled with the families of United legends like Paddy Crerand and Denis Law, I raised a smile by asking why everyone was singing about my daddy. I hadn't yet learned that I would have to share him with thousands of others.

Later, when I was older and able to understand, my father explained to me many times the special power that the number 7 shirt possessed. 'A buzz goes round the crowd, Gaynor, whenever the number 7 gets the ball. Sixty thousand-odd people are expecting something special from you. And as the adrenalin hits you, you feel that you can do anything, you want to do something special, make something happen.'

Willie Morgan did not often disappoint the Old Trafford faithful. My father was a very good-looking, lean winger, with a mastery of the ball which left opposition defenders in his wake as he sped past them with a burst of acceleration, or beguiled them into a mistake with his trickery. Off the pitch he was a celebrity, a model and fashionable dresser in the unmistakable style of the seventies. His curly dark hair was cut short on top and fell on to his shoulders at the back in the most popular cut of the day. At a time when footballers were beginning to be compared with pop stars, my father was alive to the new trends and became the first footballer in the world to have his own organised fan club.

He played for United with distinction at the end of the 1960s and on into the 1970s, joining the club from Burnley as Sir Matt Busby's last signing in 1968 for a record fee of £117,000. A Scottish international star, capped twenty-one times for his country, he played in a United forward line that would rival Real Madrid's current *galacticos*, Raul, Ronaldo, Luis Figo, Zinedine Zidane and of course David Beckham. To buy that United line-up of Willie Morgan, Bobby Charlton, Denis Law, George Best and Brian Kidd today would take an astronomical sum that would be beyond the resources of any of the top clubs. Dad captained the Reds at the height of his career, and in 1972 he was voted the best winger in the world. He never regretted signing for Manchester United even though, following their victory in the European Cup in 1968, the team he joined was in decline. As my father puts it when asked, 'I chose the right club, but the wrong team.' For him, Manchester United will always be the greatest club in the world. I believe that David Beckham feels the same, even though in Real Madrid he has found another club steeped in tradition and with a great history of success.

It was with deep regret that Dad had to leave United when he was thirty years old because of a dispute with manager Tommy Docherty. However, that wasn't the end of my father's footballing adventures. He returned to Burnley, then moved to Bolton Wanderers where he was instrumental in helping the Lancashire club win the Second Division championship in 1978. For four years the summer closed season was spent commuting to the USA, playing in the North American Soccer League for Chicago Sting and Minnesota Kicks, in the heady days when it looked as though soccer was going to become a major spectator sport over there. He ended his career with Blackpool after twenty years as a professional footballer. In his testimonial brochure he listed his biggest disappointments: losing in so many semi-finals, going out of the World Cup while the Scots team was still unbeaten and never meeting Elvis.

One of the reasons I was to become so interested in David Beckham's career was precisely because he seems to share so many parallels with my father, although I guess David would be more concerned about not meeting his rap hero, Tupac Shakur, rather than Elvis. But I never thought, as David's fame grew, that I would eventually come to enjoy a special friendship with him.

It was my father who had first alerted me to David Beckham's potential to become a top player. It was 1995, and David Beckham had just broken through into the first team. We have a private box at Old Trafford, and had gone as a family to see a United game. 'See that lad, see him?' Dad exclaimed, his Scots accent still as broad as ever despite many years living in the north of England. 'After what I've just seen, I can tell you he's going to be somebody, Gaynor. This lad has really got what it takes to make his mark at Old Trafford.'

When it comes to football, my dad is very rarely wrong, so I looked with interest at the face of this future star. I had seen him before on television, a young man stuttering over his answers in an interview. Gangly and incredibly nervous, he looked as if he was trying to hide behind the long fringe of his floppy fair hair. He was shy, with an attractive but apologetic smile. There seemed to be nothing particularly memorable about him, and I told my dad as much. My father was not impressed by my verdict, and he was determined to change my opinion of Beckham's qualities.

'But he's nothing like you were as a footballer, Dad,' I pointed out, still unconvinced. Compared with my father's dashing wing play, Beckham's attributes looked rather mundane. He never took the ball up to a man and beat him. My dad had what they called 'the Matthews shuffle', after the greatest English winger Sir Stanley Matthews. Indeed, the sports press often dubbed him 'the Scottish Stanley Matthews'. He would dribble the ball up to a defender, sometimes just standing in front of him. Then, as his opponent committed himself to a tackle, he would drop his shoulder and streak past him to the delight of the spectators.

'Well, Beckham may play on the right wing, as I did,' Dad replied, 'but he's not a winger. His game is not to beat the man. He's not a dribbler at all. In the old days we would have called him an inside forward or a half back.'

'In the papers they say it's one of his great weaknesses,' I cut in.

'I've read plenty about Beckham's weaknesses,' was Dad's answer. 'But all footballers have things they can't do. The only complete player that I've ever seen personally was Pelé. Footballers become successful by concentrating on their strengths. Young David can hit long passes with both feet, and with tremendous accuracy. He beats the man with a pass, you could say, not by going to the byline like I did. He's a great striker of the ball. He's on the wing to take advantage of his accurate crosses which are whipped in with such pace that you only need to get your head or a boot to them and it's a goal.'

Thanks to Dad's incisive explanation, I gradually began to understand exactly what David Beckham brought to United's team of stars, and why people were starting to become excited about him.

By the time I had my first face-to-face meeting with David, everyone knew what he was capable of on the football field. His rise to stardom had been meteoric, as Dad had prophesied, but neither of us had foreseen his equally dramatic transformation into a style icon and glamorous pin-up. I had gone to one of my regular haunts on the Cheshire social scene, the exclusive Brasingamen's restaurant and nightclub in Alderley Edge. The Braz, as it is known to its regulars, attracts many celebrities to its doors. It is an old building, set back from the main road that runs from Wilmslow through to Alderley Edge. Through one entrance there is a bar and restaurant, which has become a popular eating place with a relaxing, welcoming decor of terracotta, wood and cream, arranged around a beautiful feature fireplace in the centre of the room. Attached to the restaurant is the nightclub, accessed through a separate door which is usually guarded by three bouncers – Tony, Del, Jo and Dennis – who seem to have been looking after me for years. Karen and Alex Wilson, its managers and family friends of ours, have succeeded in creating a family-like business. They have since left to set up a new chain of bar/restaurants called One-Six-One, the first of which, in the heart of Cheshire's Knutsford Village, opened recently and looks as if it will repeat the Braz's success. The Braz has a dance floor and a bar downstairs; up the stairs on the first floor to the left is a VIP area separated off by a rope, where famous footballers and actors, many from the hugely successful soap opera *Coronation Street*, which is filmed in Manchester, congregate. As my young son Alex and I have settled close to my father in Cheshire, you could call the Braz my local nightspot.

That particular winter's night in 2000, the staff at the Braz began suddenly to clear their first floor of customers. This meant that someone very special was about to arrive, and was to be guaranteed the opportunity of enjoying a quiet drink away from hangers-on and people seeking an autograph. I am a familiar face in the Braz, however, where they know I have grown up in the company of famous people, and that I have many celebrity friends. I wasn't surprised when my small party – myself and my two close friends Lisa and Amanda – was not asked to move downstairs with the rest of the crowd. They know that I can be trusted to respect the privacy of any guest. Naturally, though, the girls and I did look round to see just who it was who came walking up the Braz's staircase to the first floor.

David Beckham, as everyone knows, is stunningly handsome. But his photographs, plastered over every magazine cover, had not prepared me for just how beautiful he is in the flesh. He has the ability, despite often wearing street clothes and dressing in an approximation of hip-hop style, always to look crisp and clean. That night he was casually kitted out for a drink with a few friends. He wore trainers, designer jeans, a tight, white T-shirt which showed off his athlete's broad chest and flat, washboard stomach to perfection. He often wears white: it accentuates his permanent light-golden tan and his piercing blue eyes. His hair was growing out of its most radical crop when he had most of it shaved off, but was still short and spiky. On his wrist was the only obvious display of his wealth, one of his collection of designer watches. Despite the informality of his outfit, he was the best-dressed man in the club by a mile, and even in the bar's low lighting he seemed to shine. It was difficult to take your eyes off him.

David moved easily over to the table reserved for him, surrounded by a small group of men. I instantly recognised one of them. As part of the Manchester United family I have come to know many of the players past and present. Steve Bruce was by then an ex-teammate of David's and had made the move into soccer management. Now he is at the helm of the Premier League club Birmingham City, and under his leadership the club is doing well. When I went to the bar for a round of drinks, Steve took the opportunity to come over and renew acquaintances. He is a very likeable man, and he greeted me in his soft Geordie tones with a smile. I don't think Steve would mind me saying that he is quite a contrast in looks to David. His face shows all the marks you would expect from a career in which he made his name as one of the most accomplished and brave central defenders never to have been capped for England. He also had a rare talent for scoring goals with his head. He broke his nose on his United debut, and that was not the only break it suffered before he hung up his boots.

Steve knows my father quite well, and wanted to know how he was doing. We made polite small talk for a while, and I thought about asking him for an introduction to David, but decided against it – I was afraid of looking like another of those leggy blonde bimbos always in pursuit of famous footballers. But as soon as I got back to my friends I regretted it. David was part of Manchester United, and so was I.

Uncharacteristically for me, because I have seen enough star-chasing in the Braz to last a lifetime and always hate it when pushy people can't leave the celebrities alone, I decided that I would go and speak to the United superstar. I told Lisa and Amanda that this was my intention, and immediately I wished I hadn't confided my plan to them. Like all close girlfriends they are skilled in the art of leg-pulling, and began to rib me mercilessly, claiming that I had an ulterior motive and that I was going to chat him up. 'You don't know just how wrong you are,' I told them. 'But I've made up my mind that I shall introduce myself to him before the night is over.'

I decided that I wouldn't go over to his table when David was surrounded by his friends, even if I did know Steve. The boys had all relaxed, and were joking and laughing, swigging from their bottles of beer. David is not exactly reserved when he goes out, but he does tend to take a back seat while the more extrovert characters take the lead. So I waited for the appropriate moment. Minutes later, he obligingly got up and headed for the rest room. As he strolled back past our table, I smiled and our eyes met. He smiled back, revealing the same shy grin that I had noticed in his television interview five years before, though now it was undeniably sexy rather than just nervous.

'Hi, I'm Gaynor.' I spoke quickly, trying to reassure him that I was not trying to pick him up. 'I just wanted to say how much I admire you as a footballer. I know something about the game because my dad used to wear the same number on his United shirt as you.'

Of course, that last phrase had a magical effect. I had chosen just the right way to stimulate his curiosity. 'Who's your dad?' he asked. Although I resemble my father in some ways, he wouldn't know from my appearance.

'Willie Morgan.'

There was that smile again, only warmer and more prolonged. 'Really? I used to watch him playing when I was a kid because my dad is United through and through and Willie was one of his great heroes. What's your dad up to now?'

David knew that he could relax in my company because he was talking to one of the family – the Manchester United family. His praise for my dad was unstinting and generous, while he was completely modest about his own talent. Despite the adulation that was already being heaped on him, it was clear that he had not let it go to his head. I made a comment about how his football had got better over the years, and then paid him the best compliment I could. 'You are a great player, nearly as good as my dad.'

I have met many footballers over the years, and quite a few of them (particularly the ones with far less talent) would not have reacted like David did. They would have been insulted to hear themselves ranked unfavourably with one of the game's greats. David passed the test with flying colours, and I even think I made him blush. He acknowledged my comparison with a smile and a nod, taking it in the spirit in which it was meant. I think he even rather enjoyed it as an antidote to the excessive adulation he often receives. Seemingly in no hurry to get away, he continued chatting about football and the acquaintances that we shared at United. Then we discovered another thing that we had in common: our sons. He loved talking about Brooklyn (this was before Romeo was born, of course) and his face lit up when he got on to the subject of the youngest Beckham's footballing skills. 'I really hope Brooklyn will follow on from me,' he said fervently.

Naturally, as a proud mum, I had to tell him about my boy Alex and the fact that he had only just been selected to attend a football course at the Cliff training centre in Salford, which was United's main training ground until it was replaced by the state-of-the-art, purpose-built Carrington complex. Becks is, as you might guess, Alex's sporting hero – after his granddad, of course – and my son is proud to continue on the Morgan family tradition by playing at number 7. You can't fake an interest in someone else's child, and David was obviously genuinely interested in swapping family stories. I was touched to realise that he was genuinely flattered and wanted to know more about Alex.

I have watched autograph hunters pester my dad for years, and I swore that I would never join their ranks. However, that evening I found myself breaking my solemn vow, quickly borrowing a piece of paper and handing him my pen, thankful that it actually worked. Without any hesitation he wrote, 'To Alex, love David Beckham', smiling to himself as he added a huge X with a flourish. I knew Alex would be thrilled, and couldn't believe David's kindness. I thanked him profusely and then returned to my girlfriends who were secretly agog that I had monopolised the attention of the man every girl in Manchester (and most of the world) was desperate to meet. After a bit of very gentle joking, they wanted to know what we had talked about. 'Football,' I said. 'And our children.'

'Of course you did,' Lisa replied, and she wasn't being sarcastic. She knows me very well.

As I sipped my drink, I only half listened to my friends' conversation. My mind was on something else. When you first meet someone, it is instantly obvious whether the seeds of attraction are there – sometimes you just look at them and you know that there is an instant connection. In my heart, I felt sure that David had been giving me all the right signs. Certainly he felt comfortable, but that was just because of who I was – he knew I wasn't just some groupie going up to him, and I could talk sensibly about football, his first love. He was at ease, and his guard was down.

But there was more. When he spoke to me he looked straight into my eyes, and there was definitely meaning in that look. And perhaps I reciprocated, I don't know. I was, after all, talking to one of the most handsome men in the world. It would be surprising if something about the way I was with him did not speak of the instant attraction I felt.

It wasn't long before I was ready to go. I knew there would be plenty of people in the club sitting it out to the bitter end, waiting until David had left before they even entertained the idea of moving. That's just not the way I am: I wanted to go home, perhaps to sleep, perhaps to mull over the events of the evening. As I stood up to leave I looked over in David's direction. I don't know what I expected, but it was certainly not more attention from him. Whatever kind of spark I felt between us, I certainly wasn't going to let my heart rule my head. He's a married man, I told myself, with everything in the world. The last thing on his mind is other women. He probably doesn't even remember me from ten minutes ago.

But he did. I looked in his direction only to find his gaze directed towards me. He smiled at me – that shy, winsome, little-boy-lost smile that belies the confidence beneath it. He put his hand up and waved. I felt a thrill that he had made the effort to say goodbye. I waved back, and left.

Lisa and I chatted, as girlfriends will. She is my closest friend, the only person I would share my most secret thoughts with, so I told her that I felt there was a spark between David and me. She told me that she could see from the moment I started talking to him that there was something unspoken between us. You can always tell when two people are getting on, and that was what she had seen when David and I were talking: he was totally focused on me, ignoring everyone else milling around him.

I don't deny that I hoped I would encounter David Beckham again some time soon. At the same time, although I was flattered by his attention, I made an effort not to think too much about it. At the very most, all that had happened was that a man and a woman had met in a club, and had got on well. There was nothing more to it than that, no matter how much my friends gossiped about the evening, and no matter how much of a buzz it was having had the sole attention of one of the world's most glamorous men, if only for a few minutes.

Later I tried to work out what makes him such an attractive figure. David constantly surprises you because of the contrasting aspects of his character and behaviour. He is adored and instantly recognised over most of the world, but he is so modest about his achievements. He is stylish and physically confident, but his sweet shyness is so at odds with the initial impression his athlete's grace and strength convey. I caught Justin Timberlake's MTV awards interview where he was asked the secret of his success. Justin is another star who has a great reputation for being natural and unspoiled, and you could see why. Instead of throwing out some flip comment, he thought a little and, after making the obvious point that you need talent, he added, 'a humble attitude'. He could have been talking about David, who has never lost that humility. I don't believe he ever will. He is shy, and he does convey that shyness; and yet there is a confidence about him. There must be confidence in his make-up for him to be able to kick a ball that way, to do what he does week in, week out – and, believe me, that confidence comes across when you speak to him.

Since he signed for Real Madrid and left for Spain, there has been a glut of TV documentaries examining the Beckham phenomenon. One of them I watched, which was about David Beckham's body parts, found him superb in all departments except one: his voice. I couldn't have disagreed more. If he was a very confident speaker with a ready turn of phrase, I don't think that he would have such a following globally. He would be just another of those very handsome men who is completely aware of his own attractiveness. David's slightly high-pitched, soft Essex tones give him a hesitancy that makes you feel that he is vulnerable, a little lost.

He has, it is obvious, become more and more fluent in front of the media. He handled the controversy over United central defender Rio Ferdinand's missed drugs test, and his subsequent suspension from the England squad before he had been found guilty of any offence, with a quiet determination and dignity. He is also a listener, not one of those celebrities who are busy staring over your head into space or looking for someone more interesting and important to talk to. Some people have tried very hard not to like David Beckham, but have not by and large been very successful. Once you have spoken to him, you can't fail to have a soft spot for him.

There is a widespread belief that David Beckham has everything that he wants, and that he must be very happy. His own autobiography stresses his personal contentment. This is not the overriding impression that I gained of his state of mind. I believe that, despite the wealth, the adulation and his celebrity status, David Beckham is a troubled soul. He has undergone a tremendous change in his lifestyle since his rapid rise from obscurity to the dizzy heights of Premier League superstardom. He has a fleet of fabulous cars, wardrobes full of designer clothes, the near worship which accompanies his tours of the Far East. Yet these accessories of megastar celebrity mean absolutely nothing to him. He is quite obviously a simple lad with simple tastes. What he really wants and needs is the friendship and company of others. He likes to surround himself with people from all walks of life. He values his relationships with friends, teammates and, most of all, members of his own family. Sadly, too few of the many commentators who have set themselves up as self-appointed 'Beckhamologists' have any clue at all about what drives him and what it most central to his happiness. Too few people understand the real David Beckham the way I came to do.

That is why I decided to write this book. I was brought up as the child of a celebrity. In Manchester and Cheshire, to be a Manchester United player is to be a very big star, the man that everyone wants to meet. As the children of Willie Morgan, both my younger brother Scott and myself found ourselves the centre of attention, sometimes flattering, but sometimes frightening. We enjoyed privileges, but we also paid a high price for our position. I have spent most of my adult life so far coming to terms with celebrity, and have become a confidant to stars who are trying to cope with all that being in the spotlight means.

Indeed, I feel so strongly about the way in which big celebrities become targets and are not able to defend themselves that I courted serious controversy myself with my defence of Michael Jackson in 2003. After the ITV television documentary which led to accusations that the singer was guilty of child abuse, I asked Dad to arrange for me to visit Michael's Neverland ranch through the singer Johnny Mathis, a very close family friend. Johnny owns a ranch close to Michael's estate, and they are friends because Michael wrote the song 'Love Never Felt So Good' for him. In the numerous interviews which followed I repeated my belief that Michael is essentially a very intelligent, kind and loving individual. The way he lives may appear strange, but I feel he has retreated into his own special world because of the abuse he received as a boy, the allegations against him and his enormous fame. I said publicly that I would be happy for my son to sleep the night in Michael Jackson's room. Since I have spoken out about this, I have been accused of using my child, who is the most precious thing in the world to me, to prove a point and to salvage Michael's reputation. One expert described it as 'taking your pet mouse to sleep with a python'. But I reject these views. To my mind there would be nothing to worry about at all, as I do not accept that the allegations which are being made about Michael are the truth.

In the same way, I have had enough of the nonsense written by those who profess to know David Beckham, the 'insights' offered by those who want to cash in on his name. But I also feel that because of my upbringing I can appreciate the impact of many of the things that David and his family are going through, and perhaps what lies in wait for them in the future. I have no axe to grind, and have been allowed for a brief time inside the barrier that David has learned to erect around himself. I want to explain how David has been torn by the complexities and pressures of his career and lifestyle which have presented him with choices that he has just not wanted to make. I want the public to appreciate the personal qualities which David Beckham possesses, qualities which I hope will enable him to continue to cope with all that fame throws at him. As I intend to demonstrate in the course of the story of our time together, it takes enormous strength of character and moral fibre to be such a recognisable and sought-after figure and not crumble under the weight of that attention.

What soon became clear to me is that the chief ideal which motivates David Beckham, and which has shaped him and made him what he is, is the old-fashioned, very British virtue of loyalty. But, though David would have liked to be utterly loyal to his family, to his friends and to his club, the various and conflicting demands that these groups place upon him mean that he is often torn emotionally, his loyalties divided. His father Ted, Sir Alex Ferguson and his wife Victoria could not all be kept happy. He has a family of his own, but they never became part of the wider Manchester United family. It is no surprise that loyalty to his wife and sons came first. He is already beginning to face what I know from bitter personal experience will be the most dangerous divided loyalty of his life, one that possibly can never be bridged: the conflicting demands of his duty as a father and his duty to his fans.

The rest of this book will deal in more detail with the key influences and conflicts in his life. Using what I have learned from my father about the nature of a footballer's career, I will show how David's initiation into football and his early playing days were extraordinary and shaped him as a player and a person, and how I believe that his football family could not be reconciled with his personal life. I shall give my perspective on what the consequences of his relationship with Victoria have been, and I shall look at the potential threats to the future happiness of Brooklyn and Romeo as they grow up in 'Bubble Beckham', as David himself calls it, through my own experience of how even the most stable and harmonious families, with wonderful parents like my father and my late mother, can be scarred by fame.

There is no doubt in my mind that David is yearning for the simple life. He has recently spent a reported £2 million to buy himself out of the contract he has had with the sports management company SFX, run by Jon Holmes. He cites as his motivation the desire to concentrate on his football. Observers have been sceptical about whether this is really true, but I can assure you that the only way men with the talent of my father and David can ever really be happy is by expressing their exceptional skills on the football pitch, free from other worries. He has trained himself, with a little help from his friends, to hide behind the uniform of celebrity, and he can play the part of the confident superstar well. However, I am convinced that he desperately wants a different role. Will he have the courage, or indeed the opportunity, to pursue that goal?

Can he ever step off the image-building treadmill to reinvent himself as plain David Beckham, footballer and family man, even if he wants to? These are questions to which I don't know the answer, and I'm not sure that he does either; but I did gain the distinct impression that he was intending to put his life through a process of reassessment, and that there might be some sort of sea change on the cards sometime in the future.

But that is for David to decide. I hope that the rest of this intimate portrait of David's life, and my views about some of those closest to him, will help people understand him better and make them less eager to criticise him and to see him fail.

CHAPTER TWO

BOY WONDERS

O n the surface, David Beckham's early years as a
footballer seemed to hold the promise that the
young man would lead a charmed life in his chosen sport.
The exceptionally talented little boy was courted and fêted
by the most powerful British football manager, Sir Alex
Ferguson. He was singled out for extraordinary special
attention. Manchester United rolled out the football red
carpet all the way to the Beckhams' modest Essex home,
but none of this guaranteed that he would have even a
minor career in football. My father's early experiences
were a world away from David's privileged start, and
vividly illustrate the advantages offered to David at such a
young age. But there are parallels between what the two
'boy wonders' went through to achieve their long-
cherished ambitions. These help to explain why David
was, in some respects, born to be a star player, but was
also equally blessed and cursed by the peculiar

circumstances which began when he was spotted by United's London scout.

'Footballers are born, not made' is one of the most frequently quoted pieces of wisdom to explain why it is that so few boys make the grade as professional players. My father believes that, although it is a cliché, the sentiments expressed in that well-worn phrase are absolutely true. He knows that he was born with his footballing talents, and that no amount of practice as a small boy, or indeed later on in life, could have given him the abilities that a professional needs to rise to the very top. The same is true for David Beckham. Both he and my father are natural athletes. As a boy, David was a cross-country running champion at his school, and was also a very good swimmer. My father was gifted with a natural turn of speed, and is still superbly fit in his fifties. Many footballers have exceptional hand-eye co-ordination and excel at a range of ball games. Dad is a terrific golfer, plays a mean game of snooker, enjoys tennis and, at one time, was a better-than-average rugby player. Other assets such as balance, timing and anticipation cannot be manufactured. Another David Beckham could not be created by any amount of coaching.

However, there are many talented young players who never go beyond playing football as a hobby. To represent your country at the highest level, to play for what I believe is the greatest club in the world, Manchester United, can only be achieved by a very difficult and challenging football apprenticeship, through sacrifice and dedication. Football managers and officials talk about the 'wastage rate' among young players. Behind that bland euphemism lie very real tragedies and heartbreak for those who see their dreams in tatters.

David Beckham's football apprenticeship began as soon as he could walk. His father Ted could be described as the ultimate 'soccer dad'. He was a modestly talented amateur player (who, according to David, would have been a better centre forward if he had ever worked out how the offside rule operated!). A true 'cockney red' – one of United's enormous number of supporters from London – he harboured two ambitions: that his son might be a professional footballer, and that he would play for his beloved Red Devils. It is too easy to see Ted Beckham as a man who was making up for his own shortcomings as a player and living his fantasies out through his son. In Britain especially, there is huge suspicion and contempt for the pushy parent, shouting instructions from the touchline, who never allows the pressure on their offspring to drop. But Ted Beckham seems to have achieved the perfect balance between supporting and encouraging his gifted son as he developed his natural gifts, and pushing him forward so that he made the best of what he had been born with. David has constantly expressed his gratitude to his father for laying the foundations of his success.

Some people have asked why Ted Beckham needed to spend so much time on David's football education. Wouldn't a child with talent be spotted anyway, as part of school football, in the normal course of events? After all, the big clubs have a very sophisticated scouting network, particularly geared to searching out prospective young stars and saving millions of pounds in transfer fees in the future. But to argue in this way is to misunderstand the current situation in Britain. If you were to talk to my father about how he negotiated his way along the rocky road to football stardom, you might think that it was all so much easier for him in the late 1940s and early 1950s. He shares with many Scots the national characteristic of a dry-as-dust sense of humour that feeds on understatement, with a tendency to add the phrase 'It was easy for me!' on to the end of his stories, when it was clearly anything but easy. The story of his own football upbringing demonstrates just why David had to follow a path that separated him off to a certain extent from the 'normal' schoolboy world.

Willie Morgan came into the world just as WWII was drawing to a close. He was born in Glasgow, though he was brought up in the small mining and textile-weaving village of Sauchie in central Clackmannanshire, situated on high ground between Alloa and Tillicoultry. Post-war Scotland was an austere place with few luxuries, and sons were expected to contribute to the family income as soon as they could. The two choices open to a boy from a Catholic family were, as he puts it, 'the pit or the priesthood'. I could never imagine my father as a priest, so I suppose that he was earmarked from the start to follow my grandfather underground, working for sixty hours a week as a miner. However, his destiny was not to cut coal, nor to stay in Sauchie all his life as many of the men from the village did.

Willie did not have a 'soccer dad'. It's not that my grandfather wasn't football crazy, being a passionate Glasgow Celtic supporter; but working for sixty hours a week meant that there was precious little time left to coach his son in the finer points of football. Dad does remember that his father used to take him for a walk 'up the woods' with a tennis ball in his pocket. As they walked along the three-foot-wide path which led through the woods, he'd issue his small son with a challenge. If he could get past him with the ball, he'd reward him with a sweet. This was all the encouragement Dad needed, and he never failed to win the prize. Ted Beckham used to play a similar game with David, but for a much greater financial bonus, offering him fifty pence extra on his pocket money if he could hit the crossbar of the goal from a distance.

The streets were the place where my father had his football education; even when it went dark, the children still played on under the gas street lights. He describes his village as being dominated by football. All the fit young boys spent every spare moment playing. 'There was nothing else to do,' he points out, no toys, no television, no telephones in the village, apart from the public call boxes. And they did not play with a ball, as these were far too expensive, but a tin can or, if they were lucky, a 'casey' – the old leather casing of a discarded football stuffed with newspapers. There was always a football game you could join, sometimes thirty or forty a side, and they used sweaters to mark out the goals. Dad says that he knew for sure that he had exceptional football talent when he began to become 'first pick' for these impromptu teams.

Street football has all but disappeared now. Fears about safety have put paid to it, but also there is far less tolerance for the ear-splitting noise and damage to property that can accompany it. Without cars, and in a different age, this was a relatively safe place for young lads to be, and these mining villages have been described as football nurseries – Sir Matt Busby, for example, was born in nearby Orbiston. In those days, Scottish players were in huge demand as the best in the world, and it was not rare for an English football team to have four or five Scots, and often many more.

David Beckham was born over thirty years later in Leytonstone. He has recalled in detail how he was allowed to go to a nearby local park, Chase Lane, to play football, often with boys twice his age. But more often he would be there with Ted who, when he came home from his job as a heating engineer, would take him to the park for several hours to practise his football skills. By the time David reached the age of seven, Ted Beckham was taking his son training on midweek evenings with the adult amateur team, Kingfisher, for which he played. Ted also ran a summer team, and David went along with him to the summer league matches, practising with his father before and after the game.

David always managed to find a game somewhere, but often with men far older than him, something he credits with toughening him up. He also played football with the cub scouts, and in order for him to qualify for the team the whole of his family had to go to church every Sunday. David was in his school team, turning out for Chase Lane Primary School. This is at a time when children did have 'something else to do' and, even though David loved every minute of it, Ted was careful to make sure that his son's focus remained set on football. And he was prepared to spend a great deal of time with him, something which we are told by childcare experts is becoming a rarity.

David's father and mother did not only sacrifice their time for David's football development; they also made a considerable financial outlay to give him the best possible training and broaden his experience. Sometimes they were helped out by David's Tottenham Hotspur-supporting grandfather. David says that he attended every summer school he could, and, as part of the team which was the main influence on him at this time, Ridgeway Rovers, which he joined when he was seven, he went on tours to Holland and Germany. Aged ten, he went to a Bobby Charlton Soccer School in Manchester, which he found a difficult experience and was somewhat overwhelmed by the event. This setback only fuelled his determination to return the very next year when he won the competition held to find the best player, with the prize of a fortnight's training in Barcelona.

When he was thirteen, he went with the Essex county side to play football in Texas. For all that people have portrayed David as an ordinary Essex boy, football had already given him the opportunity to travel extensively, and have a glimpse of a more glamorous world beyond Chingford.

David Beckham's special football upbringing was to enter a new dimension when he was eleven years old, and professional scouts began to watch Ridgeway Rovers. But it was because of his prominence in school football that he came to the attention of Manchester United. When he was representing the district side, Waltham Forest, United's London scout Malcolm Fidgeon was alerted to his potential. His report on the boy Beckham must have been glowing because Alex Ferguson, the United manager, rang the Beckhams personally, praising David's character and behaviour as much as his football talent, demonstrating his shrewdness by saying what every parent likes to hear: that their child was a credit to them as parents.

My father had none of this special treatment, though football did offer him the chance to see something of the world outside Sauchie. He played for his school, St Mungo's in Alloa, on Saturday mornings when he was twelve, and then he had a second match in the afternoon for Fish Cross Boys' Club under fifteens. A football career was not something that you planned for in those days, and Dad did not, unlike David, have any football mentors to guide him. The nearest he got to it was a teacher at St Mungo's, Jim Butterly, who saw my father play in a school game and was convinced that he had something which marked him out from the rest of the boys. My father kept in touch with his teacher throughout his football career and, for my father's testimonial brochure, Mr Butterly recalled how he had gone to talk to him when he was undoing his bootlaces at the side of the pitch. When he asked Willie what he was going to do when he left school, the reply came immediately. 'I'm going to be a professional footballer.' Mr Butterly did not dismiss this as a childish fantasy, as many other adults might have done, but continued to offer encouragement when he could.

By the time he had progressed to St Mungo's Secondary Division, Dad's ability was becoming difficult to ignore. He was given a trial for the county side, even though he was two years younger than the normal age for selection. My father was, however, due to leave school as soon as he was fifteen to start work at the pits. In those days, boys left school at the end of the term in which they reached their fifteenth birthday. As Dad was born in October, he was due to leave at Christmas. It was then that fate took a hand. For the first time in their history, Clackmannan County, for which Dad also played schoolboy football, had qualified for the third round of the Scottish Schools Cup. This was a major achievement, and a source of great pride and excitement. However, their star player, W. Morgan, was about to become ineligible by leaving school altogether before the next round in January. One day my father was summoned into the headmaster's study, an occurrence which usually meant that a pupil was in some kind of trouble. But the headmaster had an unusual request to make. He asked if my father would ask his own dad if he could stay on at school for another term so that he could represent the county in this crucial game.

Despite the school's prompting, my grandfather felt, because of the family's financial situation, that he could not afford it. He had, however, underestimated the determination of the county, and they turned to an even higher authority. No less a personage than the Catholic priest came round to the house and, faced by the power of the church, my grandfather had to give in and agree that his son would leave at Easter instead. Dad was very disappointed. He hated school and was eager to go, even though, unlike David, he was a capable student with a considerable talent for mathematics. His appearance in the high-profile match turned out to be a catalyst for his football career. After the game, football scouts began to knock at the front door. Dad found himself snowed under with offers to have trials at every major professional club in both England and Scotland, including Blackpool, Chelsea and Burnley, who were the English champions at the time, although Dad had never heard of them. Manchester United made contact; but, even more importantly for my grandfather, Glasgow Celtic wanted this exciting young winger on their books.

As Dad had never left the village, he saw an opportunity to broaden his horizons. He decided that he would go on a tour of England, have trials at several of the clubs who had made approaches, and see the country for nothing. The first stop was Burnley's ground of Turf Moor. He was planning to go on to Manchester United, then to London courtesy of Arsenal and Chelsea before returning home via Blackpool. Then, his free tour over, he would join Celtic as he had always intended and follow in the footsteps of his idols, Charlie Tully, who played on the left wing, and Willie Fernie, the inside left.

While he was at Burnley, my father chipped a bone in his toe. David Beckham is not the only footballer to have sustained an injury which has radically altered his personal destiny. This foot injury effectively ended his travel scheme. Dad was forced to stay at Burnley, heavily bandaged, for eight weeks while the bone mended. The champions of the First Division (the equivalent of the Premier League today) treated him royally. The club was very friendly and my father soon struck up a close relationship with the manager, Harry Potts, and many other members of the staff there. When the period of recuperation was over, the patient had some shattering news for his father back in Scotland. He had decided to sign for Burnley and to make the move over the border into England.

My father was taking a step into the unknown when he left home. His family was making a different kind of sacrifice to that of David Beckham's. The sacrifice that was made back in Sauchie was financial, until my father's wages as a professional footballer – the princely sum of £8 a week – began to come in. Aware of his responsibilities to his family, he always sent half of that money home.

David Beckham received quite amazing attention from Manchester United once his potential had been identified. How well they treated him is probably without precedent. Though his recent autobiography deals with this in great detail, there is still the sense that David himself did not quite recognise how extraordinary it was for one of the greatest clubs in the world to court an eleven-year-old boy in this way, especially one whom some observers considered was too small and slight ever to become a top-class professional footballer. From the moment Alex Ferguson rang David's parents, the boy was brought into the Old Trafford inner circle. He was invited to the self-styled 'Theatre of Dreams' every summer. The invitation was also extended to United's away games whenever the team played in the capital. It is not very easy to become a United mascot, and the club do not (as some others do) use it to raise funds by charging for that honour, preferring to select particularly deserving children. However, David was made mascot for a match against West Ham at the Boleyn Ground, and he and his parents were invited to have a meal with the squad at the team hotel at West Lodge Park. The senior players knew that the spiky-haired little boy they saw every time they were in London, who based his haircut on that sported by the United player Gordon Strachan, must have exceptional talent for the boss to try so hard to bind him to the club.

On David's thirteenth birthday he was presented with a red club tie at a home game against Wimbledon and, over lunch in the grill room where the first team had their pre-match meal, a birthday cake was brought in. There is little wonder that he has said since that he felt that he was joining a family. Kath Phipps, who runs the reception area at Manchester United, has become something of a legend herself because of her warm affection for the players and their families, and she took the young Beckham under her wing. In fact, it was part of Alex Ferguson's genius to arrange a whole series of substitute parents for the small, shy visitor from the south. Joe Brown, the youth development officer at Old Trafford, and his wife Connie took him around the club, introducing him to the players. Nobby Stiles, a United legend who had lifted the European Cup in 1968, coached David when he came to Manchester to train in the summer holidays.

It is hardly surprising that, when David had the choice of which club to join at the age of thirteen, he turned his back on Tottenham Hotspur, at that time managed by the charismatic Terry Venables, and with whom he had been training, and signed for United. Alex Ferguson's care and attention to detail, leaving nothing to chance, had paid off handsomely. He showed his understanding of psychology again when David was met by his hero Bryan Robson and brought to the manager's office to sign his name on the contract. David had some time before given Alex Ferguson a pen as a gift, and as Fergie accepted the present he told the young boy, 'I'll sign you for Manchester United using that pen.' As he promised, the pen appeared on the desk. To keep your word over something which might have seemed trivial to other people is an Alex Ferguson trait. It meant everything to the thirteen-year-old boy. With one gesture, Sir Alex was telling him, 'You matter here. And you can have absolute trust that we will look after your interests and value your talents.' By contrast, despite Terry Venables's own brand of personal charm, the young Beckham was left with the impression that he didn't really know who he was.

The period after signing schoolboy forms is a crucial one for a budding football star. David was lucky that United gave him the option of staying in London, living at home and finishing his education; he finally moved to Manchester when he was fifteen-and-a-half. YTS trainees, apprentices as they were called in my father's day, come under very close scrutiny. Every aspect of their character and behaviour is closely monitored. They are under constant observation to determine if their footballing talents will go on developing. The chief concern about David was his slight frame and height. Was he going to be tough enough to withstand the rigours of a man's game like football. Would he be easily forced off the ball and harried out of matches by bigger defenders?

My dad was roughly the same size as David at that time – five foot eight or nine inches, weighing a very light nine stones – but tricksy wingers like him were expected to be wiry, the emphasis being on speed and mobility. Street football had hardened my father so that he was able to withstand anything. Jimmy Adamson, the great Burnley star who was coming to the end of his career when Dad arrived, remembers 'trying every old pro's trick in the book – kicking, threatening, intimidating' to knock Dad out of his stride in a practice game. Dad responded by running rings round him, coming back for more every time. David too was always able to stand up for himself. He was heavily criticised for retaliating when less talented opponents tried to rough him up, but this is a side to his play that he has needed in order to make it in the top ranks and not be discarded as being too lightweight.

Playing against older men in Ted's amateur team made him prepared and able to withstand these knocks.

Manchester United's youth policy is interesting in that relatively small players are not quickly discounted. It is not unusual to see the under-nineteen and youth teams beaten by opponents who all look far older and bigger than the United youngsters, but this does not necessarily matter to the coaches. You will hear them in post-match interviews on MUTV, the club's dedicated channel, expressing the view that the results do not matter as much as how individuals played. A stronger and taller young player may have already peaked and gained an advantage over more skilful opponents because of his size. United looks for potential, and they had seen plenty of this in David. It was now up to him to negotiate the many pitfalls of his prolonged period of apprenticeship.

Young men living away from home are not allowed by clubs to make their own arrangements for accommodation. This has not changed since my father's time. He lived in digs when he went to Burnley, and David did the same at United. Not that the young Beckham gave his landlord and landlady as many problems as my father seems to have caused. In the 1950s, Dad arrived in Burnley sporting the clothes and style of the then-current rebellious youth movement. He was a teddy boy, with drainpipe trousers and narrow, pointy-toed winkle-pickers, a look associated with rock and roll, but also with young males who were troublemakers. Photographs of Dad from this time show him with a flamboyant quiff, where the fringe was rolled up into a sausage shape and combed back with Brylcreem so that it flopped over the forehead. However, although Dad loved the look of the 'teds' and the excitement of the pounding beat of the music, he was not badly behaved. He does admit to getting into a few scrapes, and one in particular demonstrates how much things have moved on since he began in professional football.

David's biggest problem during his apprenticeship was getting out of bed in time for training. Dad's problem was getting back to his digs before curfew having, as he put it, 'discovered girls'. The club was very strict about the 10.30pm deadline, and there was no sympathy for offenders who broke it. One night Dad was back late, and his punishment was swift: Burnley ordered him back home to Sauchie. It was an eight-hour journey, involving four different trains and a bus ride – more than long enough for Dad to reflect on what he was going to tell his father, and wonder how he would react to the news. To make matters worse, Dad had no indication that Burnley would take him back. As far as he knew it was a permanent break. When the interminable trip was finally over, and he arrived on the family doorstep, my grandfather left Dad in no doubt about his feelings on the matter: he was in absolute disgrace. He was left to stew in Sauchie for a week – without telephones, matters could not be patched up swiftly and easily with a phone call. Then Jimmy Stein, the scout who had recommended him to Burnley, was sent round to bring him back. He very nearly didn't return to the north of England. His father had decided that he should stay in Sauchie where he could keep him under control. But the club convinced him that there was no need to take the matter any further and that the week's exile would have knocked all the nonsense out of him.

David's first digs were in the home of a Scottish couple, but he soon left them. He had his own key, but left it behind by mistake when he nipped out quickly one night to buy some chocolate from a nearby garage. When he came back he had to knock on the door to be let in; the husband answered, but also gave him a clip round the ear. When David complained to his own father, Ted Beckham phoned up to remonstrate with the landlord for laying hands on his son, and David was moved to another set of lodgings. My dad was very amused by this story. Times have certainly changed for young players, and there has been a generational shift in football culture. Ted Beckham's very different response, and also David's own reaction that it was not acceptable for him to receive physical punishment from anyone, is illuminating.

Another relic from football's past is the idea that apprentices should carry out various chores around the ground. Nowadays, at a club as rich as Manchester United, this seems a nonsense. Why should their talented young stars spend their time cleaning the senior players' football boots, washing out the team baths and scrubbing down the changing rooms, to name but a few of the tasks that are allotted to them? But they do. The thinking is that this all helps the young professional keep his feet on the ground, and instils discipline. It also fills up the spare time that trainees sometimes find weighs heavily on their hands.

Dad's duties as an apprentice were more like hard labour than a bit of cleaning. He was expected to arrive early in the morning so that all the boots could be cleaned before the start of training. Until 1961 there was still a wage cap on the amount of money that professionals could receive in their pay packets. No matter how successful a team was, the players did not receive a higher basic wage. This meant that clubs could keep relatively huge numbers on their staff – sixty players or more. Dad joined Burnley in 1961, before the removal of the restraints on pay that had been won in that year had chance to take effect. At Burnley, as at other clubs, there were five teams: the Colts for the junior players, the B team, the A team, the Reserves and, at the top of the pyramid, the first team. So there were mountains of boots. The ground had to be cleaned, the terraces swept clear of rubbish. The pitch had to be put back into shape, carefully cleared of debris, and all the divots of turf that had been kicked out put back to try to keep the surface relatively smooth. (The poor condition of the pitches that Dad regularly played on for most of his career would be looked on with horror by today's top professionals.) He then laid out all the kit for the first team before they arrived for training. His reward would be that the apprentices could then go training with the older players, and might get to play in knockabout five-a-side games against them in the car park.

David, with his usual good nature, does not seem to have resented his few tasks at all, unlike some of his colleagues in the youth team. At Christmas, he profited from the generous bonuses that the senior players like Bryan Robson dished out to their boot cleaners. Not only that, but David himself is a meticulously tidy person who must be one of the only apprentices in football history who kept his room and his clothes carefully arranged and spotlessly clean. He never seems to have thought that time spent putting things in order, whether it be his own possessions or those of other players, is time wasted. Beckham acknowledges his debt to his parents for giving him a sense of perspective and not allowing him to become too self-important and swept away by the very special treatment he had been afforded so far.

It is at this point that David's football career seems to have stalled a little, probably for the only time in his life, and an element of doubt began to creep into his thinking. My dad and other top professionals will always tell you that it is no good a player having great ability if he does not also have an ardent self-belief. Dad has said to me many times, 'What I had, I was born with. I did the best with it. And I never lost confidence in my own talents.' There are some very low points in a footballer's professional life, and some players without mental toughness buckle under the strain. When things are not going right, the professional has to endure and rise above his problems, whether these are injuries, temporary loss of form or the manager's displeasure. My dad says that he was supremely self-confident as a young player, even arrogant. As far as he was concerned, he was the best and his talent would allow him to rise to the top at Burnley, even though there were four players in the four teams above the Colts whom he would have to better before he could make it into the first team. Without that belief it would have been a very daunting prospect.

My father was right to be so confident. He broke into the first team at seventeen, and this was exceptional. Players usually had to wait until the age of twenty-five or twenty-six when they had proved themselves ready to be given their chance by going through the system. Bob Lord, the Burnley chairman, had no idea what to do with this precocious young star. In the Burnley first team that year, the right wing was occupied by John Connelly, an England international and ex-Manchester United player. In the end, Burnley's solution was to move Connelly over to the left so that Morgan's electrifying pace and ball skills could be accommodated. Dad pulled on the number 7 shirt which he was to make his own for the first time against Sheffield Wednesday on 23 April 1963. By the next season he was a Burnley regular.

David had no such rapid rise to prominence, even though Alex Ferguson was, in the grand tradition of his predecessor Sir Matt Busby, to give youth its chance. The youth side that David played for at United has become part of football folklore. Not since 1964, when George Best was one of their number, had the United youngsters got through to the finals of the FA Youth Cup. The team that David played in has become known as 'the class of '92', because so many of its members went on to become top professionals, either for United or for other clubs. In the photograph of the victorious 1992 side, David sits on the front row next to Manchester-born Robbie Savage, who is now the controversial midfield 'enforcer' in Steve Bruce's Birmingham. David looks like a small boy, with skinny arms and hair parted down the middle with the fringe gelled back on either side. He doesn't, however, look as young as the baby-faced Paul Scholes, who grins out from underneath a pudding-basin haircut, which looks as if his mother has taken the scissors to his hair. Gary Neville (unsmiling) and a fresh-faced Nicky Butt on the back row were both to become United regulars. Ryan Giggs, who captained the side in its second-leg victory over Crystal Palace in front of 32,000 at Old Trafford (the final score was 6–3 on aggregate to the United lads), was a year older. The following year the youth team reached the final for a second time, but was beaten by Leeds United. Hardly any of that Leeds team has emerged as a star like the Old Trafford boys, an illustration perhaps of the different qualities which United look for, but also of the apprentice's uncertain future.

David's first appearance for the senior side was in the last twenty minutes of a League Cup tie against Brighton and Hove Albion on 22 September 1992, where the seventeen year old came on in place of the Ukranian winger Andrei Kanchelskis. David's excitement was so great that he jumped up and cracked his head on the plastic roof of the dugout. He did well in this debut, but it was not to be the open door to the first-team ranks for which he had hoped. A whole season was to pass in 1993–4 during which David was overlooked by Alex Ferguson. Meanwhile his friends and youth teammates were given frequent opportunities to show their capabilities in the Premiership.

The class of '92 was still successful in the lesser competitions, winning the A League and the Central League (for the first time in twenty years). In the 1995–6 season he was offered more chances. Against the Turkish side Galatasaray he made his Champions League debut, largely because the club was out of the competition by the time they came to play the December fixture. It was during this 4–0 victory that he was able to celebrate his first senior goal. He had also played in some League Cup and FA Cup games. But what eluded him was the all-important breakthrough: a Premier League game. This was the sign that David was looking for to confirm that he had a longer-term future at United. There were no guarantees, and the contrast between the period when he had been a schoolboy VIP as the club wooed him and his parents, and the realities of transforming that into a real success must have been hard to take.

The worst-case scenario was that the United coaching staff had examined him closely, but decided he wasn't what they wanted. He would have to start the lengthy and challenging process of establishing himself elsewhere. There are hundreds of young men who find themselves 'let go', as those in the game call the process of eliminating the unwanted. David's biggest test of nerve and determination so far was about to begin. Alex Ferguson told him that he was being sent out on loan to Preston North End, a nearby Lancashire club which was then in the Third Division and managed by Ferguson's ex-player David Moyes, who has since moved on to take over at Everton.

The announcement came like a hammer blow to David. He interpreted it as a means of easing him out. He turned to another of his substitute fathers, youth-team coach Eric Harrison, who now works for Mark Hughes, the Welsh international team manager. Eric Harrison reassured him and told him that he had to see this loan period as another opportunity. Since David's spell with Preston, which in the end only lasted for a month, United have loaned out somewhere in the region of sixty young players to lower-division sides. But that doesn't mean that it was simply a question of the young Beckham gaining more experience. United would expect very detailed feedback not just on how he was shaping as a player with Preston, but also on his behaviour. It would also have the salutary effect of showing David that there was a football world very different from the privilege and glamour of Manchester United. At Preston players took their own training kit home and washed it. At United there is a laundry and players don't even pick their dirty kit up off the floor. When my dad joined Manchester United the training kit was washed once a week, and by the end of the week it was stiff with mud.

A poor response to a loan could make or break a career. David had the right attitude, being prepared to fit in and do his bit, and Preston apparently wanted him to make the move permanent. Exactly how long it was intended that David Beckham should stay there, only Alex Ferguson knows. There were rumours that Beckham was considered lacking in physical presence, was not 'hard' enough, and Preston was his last chance to prove the doubters wrong. An injury crisis at United ended the loan prematurely after a month, but not before the Preston manager had seen that United were wrong about his courage. David got his longed-for Premier League debut in a 0–0 draw against Leeds United on 2 April 1995, nearly three years after that appearance against Brighton in the League Cup. He was, however, still on the fringes. He had no way of knowing whether he would be back out on loan again once the injury crisis had cleared. By this time he was approaching his twentieth birthday, and was still a young player waiting for things to take off. In contrast, when my father was the same age he had established his first-team place and was attracting the attention of fans and other managers alike for his dazzling play. Manchester United had embarked upon what was to become an unprecedented period of success, after twenty-six years without a League championship.

There would be no way of anticipating the seismic shift which was about to happen in the Manchester United dressing room, and which led to a transformation in David Beckham's fortunes. Despite appearances to the contrary, David's apprenticeship was over. He had survived the most crucial period of a professional footballer's brief playing life. The class of '92 was about to show that it had learned its lessons very well indeed.

CHAPTER THREE

MANAGING TO SUCCEED

David Beckham's relationship with Alex Ferguson is often described as a father–son bond that turned sour, an unequal partnership which could not endure once David grew up, found a girlfriend and then a family of his own. The deteriorating situation between the two of them is always cast in terms of a conflict. People want to lay the blame squarely for what transpired on one of the two men. For Beckham's legion of supporters, Sir Alex is the old-fashioned football man, chauvinist and irascible, increasingly angered by the excesses of the Beckham publicity machine or the interference of his wife in matters which he believed did not concern her. In this version of events, David has been betrayed by his substitute father and forced to leave his home country and the club to which he had given his heart and soul.

Beckham detractors shake their heads over the madness of his increasingly excessive celebrity lifestyle which was distracting him from his football, and opine that he is dominated by his pushy wife, whose desire to relaunch her stuttering post-Spice Girls musical career overrides what is best for his footballing future.

My own father famously fell out with his manager Tommy Docherty in a dispute which ended up in the courts. He was also privileged to play under the man whom many people deem to be the greatest British manager of all time, Sir Matt Busby. From my understanding of my father's experiences under both men, I believe that trying to apportion blame in this way merely serves to distort what happened, and clouds the reasons behind David's departure for Real Madrid. David has always been generous in his praise for the support that Alex Ferguson gave him at some of the most testing times of his career; and rightly so, because without Alex's belief in the aptitude of his young star there would have been no Beckham-mania in the first place. But David is perhaps less able to see that he may have had his own part to play in creating the tensions which exploded in such spectacular fashion in 2003.

I have met the two greatest-ever Manchester United managers personally: one I respect, the other I loved like my own grandfather. Even now my eyes fill with tears when I recall the day I paid my last respects to Matt Busby at his funeral in Chorlton-cum-Hardy.

Dad had spent New Year's Day that year with Matt while he was recuperating from a small operation on his leg. They had talked about going to Tenerife for a brief holiday, and arranged to have a get-together at Dad's house. Matt was taken back into hospital after that, and his condition worsened suddenly until he died in his sleep at the Alexandra Hospital on 20 January 1994 at the age of 84. When the news broke, people flocked to Old Trafford and covered the forecourt with tributes in red and white. This was a spontaneous display of love for the United manager which was to bring people together from all over the country. The following Saturday there was a minute's silence at football grounds all over the country. The United players stood in a circle with their heads bowed and arms interlinked. A single piper played a plaintive lament, which echoed round the silent stadium.

My father was in the USA on important business when Sir Matt passed away. His immediate reaction when he heard the news was to try and jump on a plane, but Matt's son and daughter, Sheena and Sandy, told him to stay where he was. Even now he regrets bitterly that he let his head rule his heart and took their advice. So it was that my mother and I represented the Morgan family at this sad event which saw the whole of Manchester – and much of the country – in mourning. On that wild and wet Thursday, Mum and I rode on the coach which carried the ex-players and their wives and families to the Church of Our Lady and St John which Matt had attended for forty years. Hundreds of thousands of people had gathered in Manchester to mourn his passing. Huge crowds lined the roads as the cortege drove past; red, black and white scarves and flowers were everywhere. I looked out of the window, stunned to see just how many people were lining the route taken by the hearse.

On the coach itself, the atmosphere was very sombre, the grief palpable. Everyone was genuinely devastated, lost in their own memories of Matt. After the Mass at the church, Mum and I were honoured to be part of the inner circle of friends who were allowed to go to the graveside with the family. Pat Crerand and his wife Noreen, Denis Law and his wife Diana, and George Best walked with the family to hear the priest say the final words as the coffin was lowered slowly. We then all took a handful of soil and scattered it down on to the coffin lid, saying a prayer while we paid our last respects and bade farewell to a man who had meant so much to all of us. After the funeral we went back to Old Trafford for some food where we spoke to George Best, whom I hadn't seen for years, and Pat Crerand, to whom we are still very close and who lives locally.

All the ex-players and their families who had known Sir Matt were devastated. Many were overcome with grief at losing the man who had guided them through their United careers and had had such a huge personal impact on their lives. My father was desperately upset for a very long time afterwards. To him, as for others, Matt was a great man. There is no secret to explain why Matt Busby was such a successful football manager: he knew how to inspire love in his players. Dad tells me that there is no other way to express what they thought about Matt. From that love came an enormous respect. Footballers are noted for constant swearing, but no one ever uttered a word of bad language in front of 'the boss', which was, according to my dad, quite an achievement. Matt Busby never needed to lay down any written rules. This doesn't mean that there was any lack of discipline. Far from it: the rules were unwritten and unspoken, and far more powerful for being so.

Busby's managerial style was unassuming. Quietly spoken, choosing his words carefully, he rarely raised his voice. He never spent much time in tactical preparation. Dad says that United never had any tactics or worried about other teams. Occasionally Matt would point out a very good opposition player and tell you to watch him, but that was it. He motivated his men by his belief that Manchester United was the best team and, as Dad says, 'He could pass that belief on to you so that you knew you were playing at the club because you were the best. When you ran out to play on a Saturday, you could beat anyone as you were better than everyone else.' This may sound far too simple as an explanation for the trophies that Matt brought to Old Trafford, but it is the truth. It takes a very special character to be able to instil such confidence into his players.

The Morgan and Busby families became very close because of the friendship that grew up between Matt and my father. They were both from small Scots mining villages and shared a love of golf. As children, my brother Scott and I spent time with the Busby family. Matt was never worried about becoming friends with his players; unlike Alex Ferguson he did not see this as a situation which might prevent him from imposing proper discipline. Players constantly sought his guidance and advice. You could always go and talk to him, take him your problems, but you also knew that he would do what he thought was right for Manchester United, and was not a soft touch.

Alex Ferguson is a very different character from Sir Matt. His players and the millions of Manchester United supporters certainly respect him and are very grateful for all that he has done to make Manchester United the dominant force in English football since 1993, and also for making the club a prime force in Europe again. The alleged feud between Sir Alex and the so-called 'Coolmore Mafia' – the Irish millionaires J. P. McManus and John Magnier who jointly own nearly thirty per cent of United's shares – over Ferguson's part-ownership of the racehorse Rock of Gibraltar brought loud demonstrations in support of the 'Wizard of Old Trafford'. But I think Alex would agree that, whereas the fans and players loved Matt Busby, Fergie will only ever earn their undying respect and gratitude.

I met Alex at a couple of social occasions, introduced to him as Willie Morgan's daughter. Once I was singing with my group 90% Angels in Manchester Town Hall at a charity dinner for the Tommy's Birth of Hope appeal. The event was organised by Sarah, Duchess of York, who was the chief patron of the appeal. Alex supports the charity which funds research and an education and information programme aimed at understanding and preventing premature birth, miscarriage and stillbirth. He came up to us before the performance and offered us some morale-boosting words of encouragement, and even danced during the set, along with the Duchess who delayed her departure so that she could hear us sing.

My most recent meeting with Sir Alex was on a Sunday evening, 21 March 2004 at the Lowry in Manchester where Howard Keel took to the stage for a one-off show at the venue's intimate Quays Theatre to raise funds for The Riley Archive, set up by the world-famous artist Harold Riley, a very close family friend. I had been invited by Harold along with Dad and my son Alex and during Howard's performance we were sat directly behind Alex and his wife. Before the show started Alex was sharing a private joke with Dad, but quickly it became one that he shared with the rest of us as Dad was in fits of laughter at the story Alex had told him. I asked Alex to share with us all what he had told Dad, so he turned around and related the story again. It was about a priest that he knows who would only do christenings in his church with a Manchester United Scarf wrapped around his neck. He had done this for a long time and nobody had ever complained, until one day the father of a child who was to be christened one Sunday afternoon happened to be a Liverpool supporter and was horrified to see the United scarf worn by the priest. He asked the priest to remove the scarf, to which the reply came, 'There is no way this scarf is coming off. If you're not happy, then leave my church.' And that is exactly what the family did!

Alex has considerable personal charm, and is very different from the brusque and somewhat aggressive individual he appears to be in some football interviews. He has a dazzling smile and the knack of remembering the names and faces of people he has barely met. He also has an excellent sense of humour and loves to joke and laugh. My dad was in the same Scotland squad as him at one point, and considers Alex to be a very straightforward man, a judgement which is very important for under-standing what happened between him and David.

Obviously Alex has a very different managerial style from Matt. One of the words used most frequently to describe Matt is 'dignified', but Alex is not in this mould. He still commands the players' respect, though this is won partly through the fact that the players would rather not find themselves on the wrong side of Alex's fiery Glaswegian temper. Players talk about 'getting the hairdryer treatment' from Alex, a very graphic description of his habit of getting up close and letting rip with a barrage of expletives when he is unhappy with them. There are stories about flying teacups at half time. Jaap Stam, the Dutch international centre half who was sensationally transferred to the Italian club Lazio in circumstances and for reasons which are still disputed, controversially revealed in his autobiography that Alex kicked a table at him when he was angry, narrowly missing him.

Of course, sometimes the hairdryer treatment can be taken with a pinch of salt. The sacked United security organiser Ned Kelly describes, in his book about his time at Old Trafford, how Alex came out of the dressing room at half time after a tirade which could be heard from outside the closed door, and winked conspiratorially at him. But Alex's hairdryer is not his only managerial method. There is plenty of evidence from David himself that Alex devotes considerable time to the welfare and happiness of his players. Eric Cantona could count on Alex's very public support in the furore which followed his leap over the barriers at Selhurst Park when he was sent off in the match against Crystal Palace. David was similarly given his manager's instant and total backing when he was sent off against Argentina in the 1998 World Cup.

With the benefit of hindsight, most commentators state that, once David had fallen for Victoria Adams, a rift between him and his manager was inevitable. Victoria has been dubbed 'the Yoko Ono of Manchester United', and she is afforded the same responsibility for breaking up one of football's most successful partnerships as Yoko is for encouraging John Lennon to leave the Beatles. Victoria and David's relationship will be looked at in greater detail in later chapters, but it is significant that David, in an early interview, when he was asked about his manager's attitude towards him dating a world-famous star, pointed out that as far as Alex was concerned the players' private lives were their own business. This is a comment that has often been overlooked. David's private life was his own concern, within certain limits. The manager's business was to make sure that David was ready to give his best possible performances on the pitch. When Ryan Giggs was seeing the television presenter Dani Behr, who was based in London, Alex let his disapproval be known, but was careful to stress that it was Giggs's driving, rather than his choice of girlfriend, of which he disapproved. Given that Ryan later had to change his car because his preferred low-slung sports models were straining his hamstrings, an injury to which he was prone, Alex was proved right.

There were aspects of David's life that became increasingly difficult for Ferguson to ignore, and about which David was not entirely open. In my opinion, David refused to admit to himself that his behaviour came close to flouting the club rules – if not in the letter of the law, then at least in the spirit. Manchester United was not paying him tens of thousands of pounds a week to be on the verge of frequently breaching its disciplinary regulations.

At the start of the 1995 season, Alex Ferguson took the gamble of giving some of his promising young players a more permanent place in the first team, and David Beckham was one of these. Ferguson's hand had been forced by three high-profile departures from the club: Andrei Kanchelskis went to Everton, Mark Hughes joined Chelsea, and Paul Ince was sold to Inter Milan.

Kanchelskis and Hughes had wanted transfers. Ince was the only real shock, but his overbearing and overconfident attitude had supposedly lost him the manager's respect, and Ferguson would no longer guarantee him first-team football.

The team which faced Aston Villa away at Villa Park in the opening game of the season also contained Nicky Butt, Paul Scholes, Gary Neville and Phil Neville. They had all been on the fringes of the first team, but it was the fact that they all appeared together which led to criticism of Ferguson's managerial acumen when United lost 3–1. David scored the only United goal after coming on as a substitute in the second half. Eric Cantona was serving the last few months of the year-long suspension imposed upon him by the FA, but was back by October; his return provided the experience and flair that led the youngest Manchester United team since the Busby Babes to the double of the Premiership title and the FA Cup. David had at last established himself as a first-team regular.

It was during this crucial season that he bought his first house, a three-storey, brand-new build in Worsley, North Manchester. Worsley had a number of new housing developments at that time, and was becoming known as a sought-after area. The house was recommended to him by Ryan Giggs who had moved into a similar home nearby. More to the point, it was only ten minutes' drive to the training ground at the Cliff.

There are certain rules by which footballers have to abide. You are expected to arrive on time for training, and there are a series of fines for those who turn up late. It may seem incredible that professional footballers have to be fined what are often quite large sums of money in order to get into the training ground at ten o'clock. Many people do find punctuality difficult, though, and, without the insistence of absolute conformity to the early start, some players would arrive a few minutes later each week. For forty-eight hours before a match footballers are supposed to spend their time quietly at home, not expending energy that they will need for peak performance. The curfew is sometimes broken by even the most punctilious of professionals, but Alex, just like Matt Busby before him, will usually get to hear if players are out on the town when they shouldn't be. David claims he always took the curfew seriously and only broke it once, in May 1997 before the last match of the season against Newcastle, when United won the title by virtue of their nearest rivals Liverpool losing to Wimbledon. He, Gary Neville and Ben Thornley hit Manchester and celebrated winning the Premier League title twice in a row by having a few beers too many.

After my dad left Manchester United and rejoined Burnley, he had no intention of uprooting his family from their home in Cheshire. Burnley was an eighty-mile round trip, so he was careful to ensure that the club understood he would be commuting that distance and that it was acceptable that he didn't move closer to the ground. Managers generally expect players to be based close to a club, even if it means uprooting the family, disrupting the children's education, and their wives having to live somewhere where they may not have any family or friends to help them settle in. Dad lived near enough to make a move unnecessary, but he did make sure that there could be no possible misunderstanding and that he had the club's blessing.

David bent the rules after he met Victoria. Despite trying to make his home in Cheshire, she spent a large amount of time in London and he was regularly driving a round trip of 400 miles. As an ex-player, my father cannot believe that David was doing this amount of travelling without his manager's permission, but it seems that Alex did not find out from David that his living arrangements were, at times, split between Manchester and London. Ferguson insisted that David must live close to Old Trafford and the training ground; when he learned that he was actually commuting from London, his anger exploded. Things finally boiled over, according to Ned Kelly, on a trip abroad. In a corner of the VIP lounge of the airport, Ferguson ordered Kelly to tell him what he knew about David's living arrangements. Kelly had no wish to tell tales, but he knew that Fergie was only seeking confirmation of what he had seen in the tabloids every day where his star was pictured attending high-profile celebrity functions or on outings with his family. Kelly admitted David was indeed living in London. Alex's response was characteristically blunt: Beckham was making a fool of his manager and the club.

David's defence against any criticism of his travelling at this time is that it never interfered with his fitness or his displays on the pitch. However, when he played so many games for United, like any other United player he inevitably put in some lacklustre performances. A player is not the judge of his own form: that is the job of his manager, and it would be natural for Fergie to attribute his weaker performances to his peripatetic lifestyle.

There are signs that David did sit down with Alex and try to arrive at a compromise. It is claimed that he made an effort to live nearer United for a time, and to those of us who lived in Cheshire this appears to be the truth, even though residing in the North sometimes meant living without Victoria, and latterly without Brooklyn. It is obviously difficult to piece together David's changing living arrangements but, from the times that he was seen most around Alderley Edge and Manchester by the residents, it seems to have approximated to the following pattern: Victoria was an occasional visitor to Cheshire during their courtship, while David travelled to London and then to Ireland while the Spice Girls were living there for a year for tax reasons. He also travelled abroad to meet up with Victoria while she was on tour with the Spice Girls, once flying to Texas to spend an hour with her in the airport.

During Victoria's first pregnancy, in the second half of 1998 and the first few months of 1999, she was either touring or living with her parents near London while the Beckhams' new penthouse apartment in Alderley Edge was being altered to their requirements. Victoria admits to having been very upset by stories which appeared in the tabloids of David's relationships with several women, including a lap dancer. Hysterical scenes followed, one of which involved David secretly leaving his hotel where he was staying with the team the night before an away match and being driven to see her – a clear breach of club rules. David joined up with the England squad as more allegations about his love life were printed. In Victoria's own words, 'David felt like killing himself,' desperately trying to reassure her that these were all lies. They dashed off abroad twice, flying off after games, during which time both Beckhams were 'wrecked' with the strain.

Once Brooklyn was born, the Beckhams appear to have tried to settle down in Cheshire. Alex Ferguson was content. He has always believed that the arrival of a baby settles a footballer down and roots him in an area. Unfortunately it seems that Victoria was, like many new mothers, thrown into turmoil by Brooklyn's birth, and hated being in Cheshire isolated from her family. Once their son was a few months old, the experiment was over and Victoria never again tried to base herself in the North to the same extent. David got back in his car and, if we are to believe the stories, Mrs Beckham came up with a variety of inventive strategies to solve the problem of David's commuting, including using a helicopter and a converted camper van – both of which, unsurprisingly, the club rejected.

It was also in the summer of 1999 that the Beckhams took the highly significant decision to create their dream home. The refashioning of the property they bought in Sawbridgeworth, Hertfordshire into the mansion dubbed 'Beckingham Palace' was a clear sign that the long-term future of the Beckham family was not in the North. Alex Ferguson was certainly perturbed by the Beckhams' plans. David says that he tried to reassure his manager that he would not be commuting to training from Essex, telling him that he had bought a house near London so that he could move back to the place of his birth when he quit the game. He found the manager's reluctance to believe him extraordinary, but it seems likely that Ferguson knew better than David what this signified.

Alex Ferguson had given him several warnings that he couldn't expect special treatment, and it is probably no coincidence that these followed his fairy-tale wedding in

1999. Ferguson had refused to allow the newlyweds extra time for their honeymoon. If David had asked him face to face, who knows what the answer may have been; but he sent his agent Tony Stephens to ask the then club chairman Martin Edwards. David later remarked, rather ingenuously, that Ferguson had wrongly got the impression that he was being bypassed – in all probability exactly what Beckham was trying to do. In August, David was fined for breaking the club curfew by being seen out with Victoria at a London Fashion Week party, an appearance which was splashed all over the press. There were also reports that David had been rebuffed when he asked if he could join the team at Heathrow for the World Club Championship trip to Tokyo; he was forced to travel to Manchester from London to start the journey with the rest of the team.

It is against the background of Ferguson's apparent disappointment that fatherhood and marriage had not led to a material change in the Beckhams' living arrangements that his disciplining of David must be understood. The manager could not accede to David's requests without also allowing other members of the squad the same leeway. Moreover, each of these requests was further proof that London, and not Cheshire, was his base. After spending a few days in London, the eleven-month-old Brooklyn fell ill with gastro-enteritis and David, as everyone was to learn when the story hit the papers, stayed with him when he should have reported for training in Manchester. He was disciplined by being left out of the team for the match against Leeds United. My father felt that Alex Ferguson's response was very wrong. Managers would normally bend over backwards to accommodate a player with a sick child. The rest of the world felt the same: David was only being a caring father, a sensitive new man, and Fergie's attitude was outmoded and chauvinist. Alex had chosen the wrong situation over which to show his displeasure with David. It was out of character too: Alex is a family man, and, when David had phoned him to announce Brooklyn's birth, he was happy to tell him not to return to Manchester to train but to stay with his wife and newborn son.

Things probably wouldn't have been so bad if David had made it clear that his sick son was not in Cheshire, and if his wife had not gone out shopping in London – where she was caught on camera by the paparazzi – when Brooklyn had recovered. Parents know that the child with a raging temperature who can only lie on the sofa in the morning can be running around in the garden as if there had been nothing wrong by the afternoon. Still, taken in the context of the ongoing discussions and disquiet which had been going on behind the scenes, and the pictures in the papers, Alex's actions can't necessarily be condoned, but they can be better understood.

For most of the 2000–01 season, during which I met and became friendly with David, he was trying again to show that he did live in Cheshire, which meant he was without Victoria for much of this time. He was very often seen out in the Manchester and Cheshire clubs with his friends. When Victoria fell pregnant for the second time, the couple bought a barn conversion in Nether Alderley which had perfect facilities for the two boys. But this did not stop the shuttling between Hertfordshire and Cheshire. And maybe it was all too late. My dad believes that, once you have lost a manager's faith, then that is the beginning of the end for you at a club. When David was left out against Leeds in February 2000, Dad observed in a matter-of-fact tone, 'His days are numbered at Old Trafford.' Managers normally do their disciplining very quietly. If he had a problem with you, Sir Matt would just invite you into his office for a private chat, and no one else would know about it. But when a dispute gets into the newspapers, Dad says you know then that, unless you yourself have released the details, the manager is using his contacts in the papers to get rid of you. He may or may not have been right; it is difficult to know how stories get out. David was spotted storming away from the training ground when he found out that he was not even going to be on the bench for the match at Elland Road, and every day there are several reporters on Beckham-watch.

David did try to make amends, and the two men later had a meeting, out of the public eye, to clear the air. Steve McClaren, then Ferguson's second in command and now manager of Middlesbrough, attended, as did Gary Neville, David's best friend at the club, and who was also the Professional Footballers' Association representative at Manchester United. Ferguson ended the meeting with the words, 'Let's forget this now. Let's get on with things.'

The right noises were also made by both sides in the press. 'The players know I don't hold grudges,' said Sir Alex. 'I haven't got the time to hold a grudge. I just want to get on with the game. That applies to all the players, and David is no different from anyone else. I have had a chat with David. All we can say about him now is that the matter is cleared. It's over. It was finished on the day it began. I hope David is now saying the same positive things about the situation.' This is exactly what David was doing, echoing his manager's words that the Scot did not hold grudges. What happened the same afternoon, however, shows that it would take more than that to repair the damage done to a relationship which had been built up for many years.

After training, David had gone shopping in the Trafford Centre, the magnificent shopping mall outside Manchester which is a magnet for all kinds of celebrities. When he was leaving to get back in his car, there was a call on his mobile from his manager. 'Where the hell are you?' was Ferguson's brusque greeting. Fergie at first refused to believe David's assurances that he was just driving out of the Trafford Centre: he had just received a message from a friend that he had seen Beckham at Barcelona Airport. He had checked with Gary Neville five minutes beforehand to see if he knew where David actually was. Alex Ferguson was only doing what he considered was best for Manchester United – but it proved once more that the trust had gone.

Dad's own experience of how a manager can work behind a player's back to get rid of him came under Tommy Docherty. Dad had been instrumental in Docherty getting the job at Old Trafford following the sudden sacking of Frank O'Farrell at the end of 1972. Knowing that Dad had worked under Docherty when he was the Scottish national team manager, Sir Matt asked his opinion of the forthright and often controversial manager. From what he had seen, he told Matt that he thought he would be a tremendous appointment for United, and he supplied him with Tommy's phone number.

At first, Dad's relationship with Docherty was excellent. He made my father captain, and they mixed in the same circle of friends. However, Dad began to feel increasingly uneasy at the manager's treatment of certain players. Docherty seemed to believe that he had been appointed to oversee a clear-out of the team. At first Dad found it very hard to believe, and made excuses for Docherty. He had just committed his long-term future to United, having signed a new six-year contract; but he was only a few months into this when he became the target of Tommy's wrath. Jim McCalliog had been subjected to Docherty's displeasure and, as club captain, Dad went to see the manager on Jim's behalf. When he informed Jim of his intervention, he looked worried and told my father that he had probably bought his own ticket out of United.

He was right, and Dad was in good company: Jim, Denis Law, Pat Crerand, George Graham and Jim Holton all found themselves pushed out of United. Denis even found out he was on the transfer list by hearing it reported on the television. 'Tommy hadn't the courage to tell you to your face what his intentions were,' Dad said of his managerial methods. 'He couldn't tell a player, "Look, I'm rebuilding the team," or whatever his plans were. He just dropped you from the side, questioned your professionalism and fitness, and ultimately put you up for sale.'

Docherty even ended up pursuing my father in the courts. After he had left United, Dad had appeared on Granada TV and was asked the question who was the best manager he had ever played for. It wasn't a very difficult one for Dad to answer: he said that Sir Matt Busby was the best manager, and Tommy Docherty was the worst. Docherty sued him and the television company for libel. The case collapsed on the third day of the high-court action when Docherty withdrew all proceedings against my father and Granada. 'The Doc' had admitted under cross-examination that he had lied about the transfer of Denis Law to Manchester City. The result was that he had to pay costs of £30,000 and face a further investigation for perjury.

Despite the fact that my father was only two years away from what could be a lucrative testimonial, he knew that, once there had been a breakdown in the trust between him and the manager, they could never have the same understanding and confidence in each other, even if they had patched up their differences. He believes it would have been impossible to do this with a man like Docherty.

Whether the row over David missing training was actually the start of his eventual exit from Manchester United, we shall never know, but my dad's experiences with Docherty taught him that, when the bond of trust is broken between player and manager, the relationship will founder. When Dad foretold the beginning of the end for David and Manchester United, I disagreed with him; as always, he was proved right.

CHAPTER FOUR

ONE OF THE LADS

For David Beckham, the most enduring aspect of the Manchester United family has been the friends that he has made in the dressing room. From the time that he first came north to Manchester in 1991, he became reliant upon the close support and loyalty of the other trainees and squad members alongside whom he has effectively grown up. For most professional players, the friends you make in this way are, outside of your family, the most important in your life. There is also a very strong unwritten code which means that what happens on the training ground, in the dressing room, on tour and in the players' lounge remains a private matter, and any disputes are dealt with in-house.

Since football underwent a revival of popularity in the early 1990s, the footballer's autobiography has become required reading; in the case of Manchester United, so has the manager's own life story. Most footballers' life stories are still criticised for hiding more than they reveal; there have been occasions when Alex Ferguson has been accused of saying more than he should about matters which normally would not be aired in public in his highly successful two manager's diaries and his blockbuster autobiography *Managing My Life*.

The only possible criticism of David Beckham from a teammate which reached the public ear is a much-quoted paragraph from Roy Keane's bestselling but highly controversial autobiography. He was talking about the season following United's historic treble in 1999, with obvious frustration at their failure to add to their silverware when they were surprisingly knocked out of the Champions League at the semi-final stage by Bayer Leverkusen, and conceded the Premiership to Arsenal. This he put down to complacency among the squad. Some of the squad, said Keane, had lost the hunger that had driven them to achieve so much. Over-complacent, they were obsessed with the material trappings of wealth: Rolexes, cars and mansions. Given David's well-known penchant for fabulously expensive designer watches, his fleet of cars and the 'palace' in Hertfordshire, this bitter denunciation could easily be understood as a direct swipe at Beckham.

The truth is, David has been very lucky in the calibre of his footballing friends. Unlike many professionals, he has had the special privilege of playing alongside teammates he has grown up with, and there is perhaps a deeper bond between these men than usual. Roy Keane recognised how this set them apart from most of the teams in the Premiership. The 'Six Amigos', as Keane called them, had formed an unbreakable bond to the exclusion of other players. As Mancunians – or in Becks's case having lived in the city from the age of twelve – they invested United with a solid, locally born core, so different from clubs such as Arsenal, Chelsea or Leeds with their many foreign-born stars. This regional identification created a spirit which had been at the heart of United's success. Whoever signed for United had to lock into this Manc attitude, no matter what their nationality or price.

How the close friendship and understanding between the 'Six Amigos' translated itself on to the pitch can best be illustrated by what is probably one of the defining matches from the 1995–6 season, the FA Cup semi-final against Chelsea at Villa Park on Sunday, 31 March. Perhaps it would be better to say the 'Five Amigos', because Paul Scholes was relegated to the bench for that game. Chelsea, under manager Glenn Hoddle, were considered the underdogs, even though United were in transition, in danger of being outstripped for the Premiership by Kevin Keegan's Newcastle United. Newcastle at that stage had a four-point advantage, though United had steadily reeled in the north-eastern team with a fantastic series of narrow victories, courtesy of Eric Cantona's goals. Their progress in the cup was by no means assured. Two of United's established defensive partnership were injured – centre half Gary Pallister and full back Denis Irwin. To make matters far worse, Steve Bruce was declared unfit to play. David, who had travelled as one of the substitutes, found out that he was to be playing on the right wing an hour and a half before kick-off.

Chelsea's highly experienced team – which included the charismatic Dutch international Ruud Gullit and, by a strange twist of fate, Mark Hughes who had left Old

Trafford that summer – must have felt they had a real chance of derailing United's season when they saw the team sheet. The United defence consisted of the untried line-up of Lee Sharpe, playing out of position at left back, Gary Neville at centre half, David May partnering him in the centre of defence, with Phil Neville on the right. Though Eric Cantona and Roy Keane provided experience in the midfield, Ryan Giggs played in front of Sharpe on the left wing and Nicky Butt played alongside Keane. The lone striker was Andy Cole, who had gone five games without a goal. When the teams came out on to the bare, waterlogged pitch, which began to cut up badly within a few minutes of kick-off, apart from the towering figure of Peter Schmeichel in goal, and the sturdy Keane and Cantona, the United players looked like boys taking on grown men. Skinny legged and light in body, United seemed a side that would easily be overpowered by Chelsea in the cut and thrust of an English cup semi-final.

The first opening minutes showed that United's young men would not be overwhelmed. David announced his intentions as early as the fourth minute when he met a cross from the left from Giggs with a shot which rebounded off the inside of the Chelsea post. For the first twenty-five minutes the match was United's, the former youth-team members using their knowledge of each other's play, and the cohesion that they had been developing since 1992, to play effectively in what was an untested formation.

What became clear from the start was how the amigos looked after each other, constantly there as back-up and support. David was tireless. One minute he was back in defence, helping Phil Neville to close down the right side, then he was sprinting along the wing on the counter-attack. His carefully weighted long shots created mayhem in the Chelsea defence, finding Andy Cole who flicked a fantastically inventive overhead pass on the swivel for Giggs, who headed the ball straight at the goalkeeper. The young men of United played without fear, four or five breaking forward with lightning speed at any one time. This is not to say that the makeshift defence was secure. It was sometimes disorganised, and Gullit lurked on the shoulder of the last man, hoping to spring the Manchester United offside trap. The muscular style of Mark Hughes was deployed unsentimentally against his former teammates. Chelsea began to assert their greater physical strength, and took the lead after thirty-five minutes through a combination of United's inexperience and the wiliness of the two Chelsea forwards. David, covering for Phil Neville, seemed to have controlled the ball just outside the United box, when Mark Hughes steamrollered through him and left him lying on the floor. Phil Neville failed to cut out the cross, and Gullit lost Gary Neville, who was supposed to be marking him, heading home from six yards out to put Chelsea in the lead.

Jimmy Hill, one of the two BBC pundits along with Alan Hansen, will forever be remembered for his comment that United would be trophyless that season: 'You can't win anything with kids.' Nevertheless, he was clear when the half-time whistle went that David had been fouled. His youth-team compatriots had all protested on his behalf to referee Stephen Lodge, but to no avail. Commentators John Motson and Trevor Brooking predicted an 'upset on the cards' as the second half began.

None of them reckoned on the spirit of these young

players. Inspired by Eric Cantona, who began to pull the strings in midfield as the tireless Keane and Butt chased and harried and won the ball at every opportunity, they started with a bang. Schmeichel bowled the ball out to Giggs at every opportunity who, even in the heavy conditions, outstripped the Chelsea defence each time. Tellingly, it was the right-hand combination – as Alan Hansen later described it – of Phil Neville, Butt and Beckham constantly playing the ball off each other and switching the play that was causing the most problems. Eventually, after a move that was made up of about twenty passes, Phil Neville broke on the overlap and tricked his way around Chelsea's Andy Myers, playing in a measured cross for Eric Cantona in the Chelsea penalty area. In the fifty-sixth minute, he headed the ball goalwards, and at the last moment Andy Cole poked out a leg to make sure that it crossed the line.

What was to be the United winner came only three minutes later, courtesy of a mistake by Chelsea's Craig Burley whose high-looping back pass came to the feet of David Beckham. His quick wits and fitness allowed him to intercept it with a burst of speed. With considerable élan and assurance, he outstripped the chasing defenders, having the confidence to run with the ball until he was in the perfect position to hit a shot diagonally across the goal to beat Mark Crossley at the far post.

Now it was time for United to hang on for the rest of the game. Chelsea pushed forward for the equaliser, and Gullit particularly always looked as if he could score. Schmeichel spread himself in front of the dreadlocked Gullit when he was through to the goal to block one shot magnificently. Eric Cantona, helping out the younger men, was back on the line to head out the follow-up from Spencer. Then Dennis Wise, the player whom Ferguson famously said could start an argument in an empty room, fouled Beckham, and Phil Neville and Butt rushed to protect him, once again showing their solidarity. David hit what was to become one of his trademark long-range shots from twenty-five yards out, and it sailed narrowly over the crossbar.

There were only seven minutes left of normal time when the United supporters broke into their first rendition of 'Wemberlee, we're the famous Man United and we're going to Wemberlee'. Cantona was by this time imperious in the centre of the United play. The Chelsea team was looking ragged, while the young United lads were still playing crisp passes and running as if they had only just started the game. In extra time, Gary Neville made a superb tackle to deny Gullit, and United were through to the final.

Des Lynam remarked that Ferguson looked absolutely delighted as he patted his young stars on the back. He must have worried that this test would be too much for them. Jimmy Hill gave his verdict on the reasons for the victory. 'It shows the ethos of the club in training up their young players with good habits, and on a day like this those habits come to fruition.'

David had the ordeal of the post-match interview to face. Motson's first question was whether, as Alan Hansen claimed, he had mis-hit the shot that won the game. He blushed, but, though he was modest and self-deprecating, he defended his goal. 'It did get a bobble, but I think I hit it well enough.' He stayed long enough to praise the genius of the Man of the Match, Eric Cantona, then disappeared with relief. The kids had come of age, playing for each other with a fierce loyalty and a telepathic understanding.

David seems to have the gift of bonding easily with those players he has met during his career, and he gives and inspires tremendous loyalty among them. The two closest colleagues he has retained from his early days, Dave Gardner and Gary Neville, followed very different paths in their careers, and are highly dissimilar characters. Dave Gardner, with his closely shaven head, is much more of a 'Manc lad' with a shrewd eye for business. He never went on to make it as a professional player, but maintained a successful working partnership with Beckham through his work for SFX, the sports management company run by Jon Holmes. David was often out with Dave Gardner in the Braz and elsewhere, and was best man at his wedding to the heiress and actress Davinia Taylor.

Gary Neville was David Beckham's best man, and David has retained a very close bond with Gary despite moving to Madrid, partly as they are both members of the England squad. Their continuing friendship was celebrated, albeit in a very tongue-in-cheek fashion, by a Vodafone advertisement. David, tanned and relaxed and dressed in the height of designer fashion, is being shown round prospective new homes in Madrid. He uses the camera in his mobile phone to capture images of the dazzling sun, the swimming pool, the bright blue sky. The scene then cuts to the recipients of his picture messaging – Gary and his younger brother Phil, sheltering from a downpour in a tent, sitting miserably with mugs of tea on camping chairs in their waterproofs. Gary shows Phil the picture, then glumly shakes his head. The advert cleverly exploited the very different images and characters of the friends. Not everyone enjoyed the joke. There were complaints in Manchester that the northern city was once more being stereotyped as rainswept and provincial compared with the European sophistication of the Spanish capital.

David's mother and father became friendly with the Neville parents, who also went to every match to see their two sons play. Gary's father has the distinction of having the same name for his Christian name and surname: Neville Neville. David says that Gary has a very dry sense of humour and is able to enjoy himself, but when I met them Gary didn't show much evidence of either. He can appear very serious, cold and unsmiling, and I think that he has a very strong sense of responsibility towards David, perhaps even seeing himself as something of a minder. David himself confirmed this in his description of Gary's attitude when they went out together when they were youth-team players. Their group usually numbered four: Ben Thornley, Dave Gardner, Gary and David. Although Dave Gardner would always know the best places to go to in Manchester, without Gary's approval they would leave straight away. In fact, David says that Gary was 'one of the most paranoid people ever'. All it would take for Gary to order them out of a club or a bar was a funny look from one of the other customers, or maybe even just an atmosphere. When I had my longest and most intimate encounter with David at the Reform Club during the Manchester United Christmas party in 2000, it was Gary who dragged him away to go and talk elsewhere, as if David might be in danger of setting tongues wagging by being in my company for too long.

On the pitch, Gary can be a fiery character, a committed player who wears his heart on his sleeve – especially when United face their traditional rivals Liverpool. His song, 'Gary Neville is a Red, he hates Scousers', is frequently aired in these games. He gained no little notoriety for his habit of celebrating a United goal by planting a kiss on the lips of the scorer. Gary is also not afraid to shoulder responsibility. He is obviously an intelligent man prepared to take a major part in discussions about the rights of players. He was dubbed 'Red Neville' in the winter of 2003 for his leading role in the protests which followed the Manchester United defender Rio Ferdinand's suspension from the England squad. There were plenty of newspaper columnists who called on him to 'shut his big mouth', as one charmingly put it. These are the same columnists, of course, who delight in decrying how stupid British professional footballers are, and how they only care about drinking, women and cars. When someone like Gary, who has been willing to take on the job of the Professional Footballers' Association representative for Manchester United and England, speaks out on what he considers to be a point of principle and shows an undeniably intelligent side to their nature, they still stick the knife in.

Gary took over as PFA rep at United after Brian McClair, the United striker and midfield man, left to join Motherwell at the end of a distinguished United career. It is not a job that many players would feel capable of doing, but is very necessary. McClair, a clever and shrewd Scot who now coaches the United under-nineteen side, had also run the players' pool, a fund into which players put all their money for interviews during cup runs so that all members of the team could benefit equally, and Gary also managed this. He has also been given the credit for being the team's party organiser, especially for the now legendary Manchester United players' Christmas party, one of the biggest and hottest nights out on the exclusive Manchester party circuit.

During the controversy that blew up around 'Riogate', David and Gary stood side by side, both fiercely loyal, but also statesmanlike and articulate in their defence of their fellow United and England player. Gary put himself in the firing line in interviews and David, as team captain, to the surprise of many who had subscribed to the 'pretty but dim' estimate of his intelligence, displayed his growing confidence and maturity as a public speaker. His calm, studied responses to the frequently very hostile questioning he faced revealed a new dimension to his character, and showed how he had blossomed since he was handed the captain's armband by Sven-Goran Eriksson.

Gary has been beside David at some of the most emotional moments of his life. The story of how David decided that he was going to marry 'the one with the legs' in the Spice Girl video for 'Say You'll Be There' is well known. The recipient of David's confidence, watching the television lying on his bed in a hotel room in Tbilisi before the World Cup qualifier against Georgia in November 1996, was Gary. After David had been sent off against Argentina in 1998, Gary sat next to him on the team bus and helped him pull himself together, telling him he had nothing to be ashamed of and hadn't done anything wrong. He helped David begin the process of weathering the media storm which was to follow. When David learned that Victoria was pregnant with their first child, Gary was the first to hear the news, and used it to put things into their proper perspective with the comment, 'It was a football match. This is a new life.' As best man at David's wedding, Gary brought the house down at the reception when he stood up to make his speech wearing a sarong.

Ben Thornley, the other member of David's little group, was tipped by many observers as a big star of the future. A handsome, dark-haired forward and midfielder, he was born in the Lancashire town of Bury, as were Gary and Phil Neville. He made an appearance as a substitute against West Ham in 1993, a season before David made his debut. Ben, however, was very unlucky, suffering a knee injury which Alex Ferguson described starkly as 'horrendous'. He came back from that to play in a Coca Cola Cup tie against Swindon Town in 1996, alongside the two Nevilles, Chris Caspar and Paul Scholes, who replaced established first teamers for the night. Thornley did well in that match, but he did not get many more chances to establish himself, and left United in 1998 to go to Huddersfield. Ben's room in his parents' house in Bury provided somewhere for the lads to sleep after their nights out in Manchester, though it was hardly the most comfortable place to be put up for the night, as David and his friends shivered on the floor in the freezing-cold room. The Thornleys are a good-looking family, and Gary became engaged to Ben's sister Hannah, a very beautiful and spirited girl with a lively wit – he often had to put up with teasing about the apparent differences in their character. Hannah later made the papers by breaking off her engagement to Gary for a local boy, saying that she was looking for a partner with a more extrovert personality who enjoyed going out. 'Money,' she said, 'is not everything.'

Paul Scholes, Nicky Butt and Ryan Giggs were three Manchester schoolboys who regarded David as a 'right flash cockney' when he first came to United. Paul Scholes is the last person you would see out on the Manchester and Cheshire social scene, much preferring the quiet life away from the spotlight and the celebrity circuit. Nicky, born in the tough Manchester suburb of Gorton, was sometimes seen in the Braz, and had to face a police investigation into allegations that he had hit a woman during an argument in the club one night. But he was more likely to be out with Giggsy, in whom he found a kindred spirit as a fellow joker, than David.

Ryan Giggs, the flying winger, was a year older than the rest of the youth team, and a figure that the younger lads looked up to, having already broken into the first-team squad. The early attention that Ryan received on and off the pitch has receded in popular memory, as David's media profile has eclipsed everything else. However, Ryan's spectacular early form, which led to him being saddled with the label 'the new George Best' – usually the kiss of death to a burgeoning talent – meant that he was the face used to promote merchandise, especially to the younger fans. He became a teen pin-up, and commentators worried whether the hype would go to his head. In March 1995, one pundit in the football magazine *When Saturday Comes* expressed disapproval over the piles of Ryan Giggs duvets, towels, calendars and posters in the club shop, and asked whether he would be allowed the freedom to develop his skills away from the demands of United's commercial department. 'What can save him?'

the article asked, before adding prophetically, 'Maybe another winsome seventeen year old from "Fergie's Fledglings" might emerge.' But the commentators of the time needn't have been concerned. Roy Keane summed up Giggs as a wolf in sheep's clothing. Beneath his innocent exterior lurked a Salford lad with a mischievous sense of humour, whose angelic looks had allowed him to get away with a multitude of sins over the years.

Ryan, who came to live in Swinton when he was eight years old (his father Danny was a dazzling rugby league player for the club based there), has always hung around with his circle of very close friends from his schooldays. He drank with them in the Barton Arms in Worsley, and David was adopted by Ryan as an honorary member of the 'Worsley Crew' when he became his near neighbour with the purchase of his first house. Giggsy was the first person David phoned when he surprised an intruder in his back garden, and he rushed to the scene with a baseball bat. Perhaps it is fortunate that by then the man had disappeared.

Ryan's eye for a pretty woman and his determination to enjoy himself were well known in Manchester. One of the never-to-be-confirmed stories that circulates as an alternative to the very romantic versions given by David and Victoria of how she selected him as her preferred footballer from a picture in a magazine is that Victoria had a crush on Ryan Giggs and was really looking to snare him when she came to Old Trafford. Whether this is merely mischief or not, Ryan's affair with the girlfriend of Dave Gardner, Stacey Cooke, who is now his fiancée and the mother of his daughter Liberty, as well as his ditching of Dave's sister Emma, appear to have caused a big rift among the friends; it was allegedly threatening the team's cohesion at one point.

What of David's other teammates at old Trafford? It was perhaps no surprise that David became good friends with the Manchester United striker Teddy Sheringham. Teddy was something of a surprise signing by Alex Ferguson because he was already in his thirties when he came to United. A Londoner who previously played for Tottenham Hotspur, he suffered from the ingrained northern prejudice with which the Manchester crowd greets every player born south of Birmingham. There have not been very many southerners who have played for United's first team in the whole of the club's history: there have been less than fifty, and David had every justification in believing that the United scouts would never find him so far south. Teddy and David were thus quite unusual figures in that respect. Stories soon circulated that Teddy was another flash cockney – a very flexible northern expression which covers everyone born south of Watford – especially when he was seen driving up and down Deansgate, one of the exclusive shopping areas in Manchester city centre, in an open-top car.

That image did the softly spoken, very humble man who I first got to know at a function to raise money for a children's charity a huge disservice. Not long after this brief first meeting, I was organising a large function at the beautiful, world-famous Mere Golf and Country Club in Cheshire. This was my opening foray into running large celebrity charity events, and because Teddy had been so approachable and kind, without a trace of arrogance in his manner despite his success and status as an international footballer, I had no hesitation in approaching him to ask if he would be prepared to attend the event with his then girlfriend, Nicola Smith. When I called him he couldn't have been more helpful, and said that he would love to come.

The event was on behalf of The Children's Adventure Farm, with around 500 guests. The function room was beautifully laid out: round tables were draped with long silk tablecloths and there were stunning arrangements of fresh flowers on each table, carefully selected to complement the room's colour scheme. The evening turned out to be a huge success, and we managed to raise over £50,000 for the charity. Teddy was charming in his quiet way, but Nicola was initially rather reserved towards me. She had become a minor celebrity in her own right because of her sister Mandy's infamous marriage to the Rolling Stones' bassist Bill Wyman. Their relationship caused a storm because of the age gap between the two: the very beautiful Mandy was only sixteen, and they had been dating since she was thirteen years old. Nicola was blonde like her sister, but, whereas Mandy had very classic but ultra-feminine, almost fragile features, Nicola had none of this softness.

I think now that Nicola viewed me with suspicion at first as I had called Teddy to invite him to my event. I learned later that she could be very ruthless towards women whom she thought might be potential rivals for Teddy's affections. But she slowly warmed towards me, and we did become quite good friends. Nicola often used to talk about her friendship with Victoria Beckham. She and Teddy often used to go out to dinner in a foursome with the Beckhams, and I think Nicola hoped that she and Teddy might emulate their relationship in some way.

Teddy shares David's attitude that nothing was too much trouble if it would raise money for charity or delight a fan. I wasn't afraid to take advantage of his good nature. I called him once to ask if I could pop round with some football shirts and other merchandise so that he could sign them for a charity auction that I had organised. 'Sure,' he replied, just as I had thought he would. 'I'm in now, come round if you want.' I jumped into my car and drove to his flat in Bowdon with a bin bag packed full of items for him to sign. When he opened the door and saw the size of the bag I was holding, his face was a picture. 'Oh, my God,' he exclaimed. 'I thought it was only going to be a few bits and pieces.'

I was very embarrassed but decided to press on. 'Well, just think of all those kids you are going to help!'

But Teddy was already laughing at me. 'I was only kidding. I'll sign as much as you want.' It took him twenty minutes to work through all the items I had brought, and he never stopped smiling and chatting the whole time.

Teddy's attitude, so similar to David's, probably made it easy for the two to become friends. Teddy had something of David's rapport with children as well. When he came to play in the Howard Keel Golf Classic one year at the Mere, he made friends with my son Alex and had a picture taken with him which he later signed. It was also important that Teddy was older and more experienced, and could offer David advice. Teddy had himself been pursued by the paparazzi at times and had graced a few tabloid front pages after being caught in what were deemed to be 'compromising' situations, so he could understand the pressures that a famous footballer came under and how to deal with them.

David also struck up a later friendship with another player who was very similar to him in character, though he was born thousands of miles away from Essex. The handsome young Uruguayan striker Diego Forlan joined United in January 2002 for a fee of £7.5 million. Though he has found it hard to establish himself in Manchester United's first team as a regular player, Diego has become a real crowd favourite because of his fantastic attitude. He does not whine and complain when he is left out of the team, merely expressing the belief that he can show his best form if he is given the chance of being a regular forward. When he does play, he puts his heart and soul into his football, celebrating with unrestrained boyish exuberance when he scores. He is very unspoiled, and has no sense of the status that being a Manchester United player gives him. I even gave him a book once to teach him something of the club's history. *Manchester United: Player by Player* has profiles on Manchester United footballers past and present – including Diego – which I thought he would like.

My acquaintance with Diego began through my close friend Lisa, whom I have known since we met on the junior tennis circuit when I was twelve. She has become almost part of my family as we have grown up together over the years, and we spend a great deal of our time together. Lisa is a tennis coach at the David Lloyd centre in Cheadle, where Diego's brother Pablo, an excellent tennis player himself, became a member to use the indoor facilities. Pablo came over to Manchester with Diego to help him settle down in the area, and he and Lisa soon became mates. Pablo and Diego were both keen to meet new people in the area, and Lisa told them

Above: Devoted dad Willie Morgan with his little girl.

Inset: The Morgan family: my mum, brother Scott, me and Dad.

Morgan Junior on the wing! Demonstrating an early aptitude for sport, although it was tennis that became my chosen game.

bove: Glory days – the team under Matt Busby. Dad is in the front row, third from the left.

low: Dad playing alongside George Best. When he joined the team, Dad famously
ok the Number 7 shirt from George.

A night at George Best's house. *Left to right*, Dad, Jimmy and George Best.

The young David Beckham, a rising star.

Inset: Beckham as a boy, showing his early passion for football.

© Rex Features

Two of the Magnificent Sevens in action.

Above: Dad with one of his best friends, Rod Stewart.

Below: Sir Matt Busby and Bobby Charlton at the opening of Dad's sports shop.

all about me and the link I had with Manchester United. We took the job of showing them the attractions of Cheshire and Manchester very seriously – starting with the Braz, of course.

I remember one occasion when we were invited round to Diego's for dinner. As our car pulled up in the drive we were aghast to hear loud shouting and screaming coming from his garage. It really did sound as though someone was being murdered, and we banged on the door to try to stop whatever was going on in there. The door swung up to reveal Diego and Pablo standing either side of their table-tennis table. They were both very fired up, competitive to the last, and each determined to beat his brother. We joined in for a while, but it was obvious that we were in the way of this fight, so we went into the house to join another friend of Diego's for drinks.

Diego always appears to have his house full of visitors, whether it be his friends or family, and that evening we had just missed David Beckham who had popped in to say hello. Like David, Diego would rather surround himself with close friends and family than go out on the town. He even had a stairlift installed for his sister who had been involved in a horrific car accident and is now in a wheelchair. His obvious compassion and devotion to his family is very touching. Pablo asked me if I knew any 'nice young girls' that I could introduce to Diego, but I was not very helpful as, frankly, I wasn't really confident that I could trust any of the young girls of Diego's age I knew not to take advantage of his unworldliness and good nature. Pablo found it hard to believe that I could not think of one nice girl in the whole of Cheshire!

One night Lisa and I went round to play the Forlans a

CD by our band 90% Angels, and we ended up after a few glasses of wine in the middle of Diego's lounge performing one of the tracks from our album. The song was called 'You Want It, I Got It', and it was not intended to have any ulterior message, even though the dance routine was quite seductive. The singing seemed fine at the time, but when we thought it over the next day we couldn't help feeling rather stupid, even though the boys had voiced their admiration for our performance. Diego had also expressed a keen desire to learn how to salsa. Lisa is a very experienced salsa dancer and she promised to teach him, even taking one of the top instructors in the country over to his house one night to start the process off. I joined in and we had a lot of fun. It's probably pure coincidence, but, soon after Diego started lessons in this sensuous Latin American dancing style, he began scoring in football matches. We used to joke with him and say that those goals were all down to his new salsa moves.

Diego, like David, knows just how important fans are. Pablo coaches some children's classes in football at the David Lloyd centre, and whenever possible Diego goes down there to meet the kids and sign autographs for them all. Like Teddy, he has also been very obliging when it comes to signing things when I am raising money for charity.

Diego has left his mark upon David Beckham in one very significant way. I can't understand why it is that the gossip columnists and style commentators have never picked up on a major similarity between David's and Diego's appearances. Though Diego has had his flowing blond locks trimmed slightly shorter since he came to United, he still has striking long hair very much in the continental style, wearing a black hair band to hold it back from his face while he is on the pitch. After they became friends, David's image began to change: he grew out his spiky, blond-tipped cut, and then appeared wearing a band in his hair very like Diego's. I am almost certain that, consciously or not, he was influenced by Diego's romantic, Latin American look.

The Six Amigos, Teddy Sheringham, Diego Forlan: in his teammates, David had a whole support system to hand. The Manchester United dressing room, despite the whispers of a rift over Giggs's love life, really does seem to have been mostly harmonious for the bulk of David's time at the club. My father, despite being at Manchester United during some of its most turbulent years, insists that dressing-room arguments, apart from 'the normal ones you tend to get in the day-to-day business in football' which were quickly resolved, were very rare. All too aware of the code of silence, he does say, while not naming names, that there were one or two players who weren't popular. These men tended to keep themselves to themselves, and had a low profile. What my father remembers above all was the camaraderie. Some things never change.

CHAPTER FIVE
QUEEN VICTORIA

The staff in the arrivals area at Manchester Airport were buzzing with excitement. David Beckham was waiting there patiently for someone to disembark, and there was no doubt in their minds that it would be Victoria Adams, his glamorous girlfriend. Every day the newspapers carried a story about the world's most famous lovebirds, and they were dominating the gossip magazines. Victoria had been away on a Spice Girls tour, and two lovers were about to be reunited. Everyone knew how devoted the couple were to each other, and expected to see a touching and romantic reunion. But someone as high profile as David could not stand on the concourse without someone rushing up to him to ask for an autograph 'for a friend'. David, of course, was happy to oblige, signing the paper thrust at him and even taking the time to chat about his football briefly and tell his fan that it was 'absolutely great' to be a Manchester United player.

Then the woman David had been patiently waiting for came into view. He jumped up from his seat 'like an excited puppy', as one onlooker put it. Victoria, immaculately groomed, strutted through the door on her very high heels, making a big entrance. Her sulky expression altered not one bit when she spotted the man she supposedly adored.

Even though it was the middle of winter and freezing cold, Victoria was wearing a micro-miniskirt and her trademark collarless leather jacket. One hand pulled her bulging suitcase behind her, the other held her mobile. She was seemingly engrossed in her call. David gave her the biggest, flashing smile in welcome and held out his arms. And how did his princess respond to this open and unaffected display of his love? Spectators were aghast when, still talking on her phone, she marched up to him and, without any acknowledgement, word or gesture, dropped her bag on the floor and strode off towards the exit, mobile glued firmly to her ear. David's face crumpled. He was utterly disappointed and didn't try to conceal the fact from onlookers. Looking crushed, he meekly picked up Victoria's bag and followed, walking obediently behind her and making no further attempt to make contact. She continued her telephone conversation all the way through the doors until they could no longer be seen.

Those who witnessed this scene at Manchester Airport were left with no doubt in their minds as to who was in control of this particular relationship. In Manchester and Cheshire, this has remained the overriding impression of the power balance between the two, and it has done little for Victoria's popularity, despite all her attempts to establish that she and David are equal partners, and he is not merely her obedient lapdog. In 2003 she made an appearance on Michael Parkinson's Saturday-night celebrity-interview show. Her appearance was designed not only to promote her Christmas single, but also to quash some of the rumours which had sprung up about her marriage. David, some noted, was alone in Madrid, living in a hotel, while his wife was thousands of miles away, yet again relaunching her post-Spice Girls musical career in a collaboration with US hip-hop producer and entrepreneur Damon Dash in New York.

Victoria came over very well in the unchallenging interview. She worked hard to impress upon viewers that she was not the controlling, moody ego-maniac who appeared in the tabloid stories. But she seems to be finding out that it is not what you say you are that makes up people's minds, but what you do and how you behave.

I have never met Victoria Beckham in a social or professional capacity. However, I did bump into her once – literally. Indeed, I had the same sort of encounter with David's wife that most inhabitants of Alderley Edge had with her: brief and unimpressive. Like my brother Scott, I inherited some of my father's sporting ability. I won several junior riding championships, but tennis was the sport at which I excelled. I still play regularly now, at the David Lloyd centre in Cheadle where I coached for a while. I do wonder what things would have been like if I had continued with my budding professional tennis career. I had made it as far as the professional circuit, played the qualifying rounds for Wimbledon, and was ranked highly in Great Britain; but the touring and the physical stresses of playing tennis at that level convinced me that I couldn't make it my life.

One afternoon I was going into the David Lloyd centre when I brushed into someone rushing in the opposite direction. She hadn't seen me as she had her head down, looking at the floor. It was one of those everyday accidents, where the automatic response is to apologise profusely to the other person, ask if they are all right and then go on. But the woman I'd just bumped into, hidden beneath a baseball cap pulled low down over her face, was none other than Victoria. She was completely ungracious, glaring at me as if I had knocked into her on purpose, and muttering under her breath. I barely recognised her at first, as her face was bare of make-up, her appearance very ordinary, unlike her usual immaculately groomed self. Her skin was blotchy, and her hair was scraped back and tucked under the cap. My hasty apologies were cut short by her furious scowl. Then she just blanked me and marched off.

It is little wonder that so many people from this area gained the distinct impression that Victoria hated every moment of the time she spent in the north of England. David was careful to contradict this belief in interviews time after time. 'Victoria didn't have a problem with Manchester at all or me playing there. And as for me, I had absolutely no intention of ever leaving United.' But Victoria was less diplomatic, admitting at one point that they had argued when David signed a new contract with Manchester United rather than moving to a club nearer London. David is almost universally considered a nice man. He has been aggressive with some freelance photographers and professional autograph hunters, and can lose his temper when he thinks his family is being threatened, but generally he copes well with what northerners colloquially refer to as 'mither' – being pestered and bothered. He can go and do ordinary, everyday things, behaving in a perfectly pleasant manner to shop assistants, neighbours and the rest. By contrast, Victoria's name was mud in the exclusive Cheshire village where the Beckhams bought the penthouse apartment which was to be their first family home.

At first sight it seems very odd that such a high-profile couple would choose a flat in which to bring up their child. Ensuring that it would be secure from intruders when there were other inhabitants of the house and their visitors around would be far more difficult than with a single-owner home, one might think. Victoria explained the choice as one of expediency. Shortly after their engagement in 1998, the incident occurred at David's house in Worsley that required the intervention of Ryan Giggs plus baseball bat. Neither felt the house was safe to live in after that. Victoria was away on tour and David was having to drive around looking for suitable properties after training. It was while he was coming back from another unsuccessful viewing in Alderley Edge that he noticed two Victorian mansions that were being converted. The flat's secluded position was ideal, set far back from the road at the end of a lane. There was separate, private access via a lift which went up the side. Until then they had not considered a flat at all, but suddenly Victoria saw it as the perfect solution. It wouldn't require extensive building work to render it secure, unlike the other properties they had viewed. However, she soon became unhappy with the flat's security after Brooklyn was born, and moved out to Gary Neville's house in

Bury for a time when a security system was being fitted. The Beckhams wanted security gates installed, but the other residents would not agree. She admits that she felt it would be a waste of money buying a large house when their sojourn in Manchester was only temporary. She did not envisage that David would see out his career at United, but, even if he did, it would present no problem as this would only mean nine more years in the north at most. As Londoners, they would naturally settle down and raise their family in the capital.

David was then twenty-four years old. He could easily play for another ten years – to finish your career at thirty-three is quite early, unless you are unfortunate with injury. Dad hung up his boots when he was thirty-eight, and even then Paddy Crerand said that he had ended his career prematurely. 'I know he is thirty-eight,' argued Pat, 'but he is fit enough and it's a shame that his skills are being wasted.' I am sure that someone as naturally fit as David, whose game does not rely on blistering pace, would expect to play on beyond his early thirties, especially as his appetite for the game is so strong. Victoria's comments seemed to point to her intention to move south when David changed clubs in a few years' time.

Their neighbours in the exclusive set of apartments, where they lived in the light and airy top flat with lovely views of the Cheshire countryside, had a lot to put up with. Some of the trouble that followed the Beckhams' arrival appears to have been the famous couple's fault. The other residents were not happy with the state of the Rottweiler puppies, Snoop and Puffy, on which David and Victoria doted. They were not allowed in the house and so a small concrete holding run was built for them outside.

One resident described how they were there day after day, with insufficient exercise until someone came on behalf of the Beckhams and took them away for good.

As professional middle-class people who would have to have a large income to afford one of these homes, the neighbours were polite and would certainly not hassle the pair unnecessarily, and would rather protect their privacy if they could. In fact, I know from a friend that the man who lived directly beneath them was offered £40,000 by a leading tabloid newspaper to let out his flat to one of their reporters so that he could spy on the Beckhams. He turned it down immediately. But this didn't mean that, after having paid a lot of money to live there, the neighbours were going to allow the Beckhams to dominate the building. Everyone in the six apartments which made up the block was allocated their own parking space, and your ownership of the space was always respected. But Victoria was not happy with the position of the bay allotted to her, as she thought it was too far away from the main entrance. Consequently she regularly parked in the nearest one. The owners of this space, after this had gone on for a while and was obviously not just accidental, put a friendly note on her windscreen asking her not to do it again. They left many such notes: Victoria just ignored them.

Not all of the Beckhams' problems were self-inflicted, though. The man who had refused to sell out the couple to the press got a taste of the perils of celebrity himself when a woman who had been stalking David and stealing his post knocked on his door in the mistaken belief that it was the Beckhams' flat. As he answered, she flung up her arms and shouted, 'David, David.'

'Do I look like David Beckham?' he replied. She had to agree that he didn't, and hastily turned around and disappeared.

Victoria's tantrums have become famous, which is why she has such an ambivalent image in this area of the country. She appeared graceless and rude; more interestingly, she also showed that she was hyper-sensitive about status. The mother of one of my friends owns a dress shop, Gina's, on Sloane Street in London. Victoria went in there and demanded that they close so that she could have a personal shopping session. She was so rude that the owner refused politely. Cue a Victoria tantrum, during which she knocked over another shopper as she turned round and barged her way from the shop.

Our family home was often visited by celebrities – very big international stars as well as people more famous in this country alone. One morning I went downstairs to get ready for school and ran into Rod Stewart who was adjusting his spiky haircut in the hall mirror. Rod stayed for dinner and literally sang for it, serenading us with an a capella version of his huge hit 'Maggie May' at the table. The singer Johnny Mathis is probably a bigger star in the US than in this country now, but people remember him here for his Christmas hit 'When A Child Is Born'. For me, he was just Uncle Johnny who would come to stay for a couple of weeks at a time to relax and play golf. Uncle Johnny was to be very kind to me when I briefly dallied with ideas of a singing career. I have learned that one thing unites the really big celebrities and marks them out: most of them are very pleasant and do not have to indulge in the 'Do you know who I am?' routine. After all, everyone does know who they are, and they don't have to label the rest of the world 'nobodies' in order to feel somebody themselves.

Victoria has said that in England people do not value good businesswomen, whom they see as hard-faced, and that people who don't know her think that she is a 'miserable bitch'. The English, she feels, don't like people who have come from nothing and made it big. She pointed out what Richard Branson said to her in confirmation: 'If you get a Rolls Royce in America, they pat you on the back. If you get one in Britain, they scratch a key down it.' Another way of looking at that, I suppose, is that having money in Britain doesn't automatically gain you respect if you continually remind everyone about it. The tabloid press has not given her an easy ride, but some of the responsibility for the negative things written about her lie firmly at her own door. Victoria was apparently very lonely in the north of England and didn't make any friends of note here. The impression that the people of Cheshire got was that she was hardly ever here to start with, and that she had no intention of settling in the area for any length of time. David was either flying or driving to see her – or, as increasingly seemed to be happening in the winter of 2000, going out on his own with his friends while she was away.

There were other things which were the talk of the town in the little enclave of Cheshire. People used to ask why David was a regular at the David Lloyd centre in Cheadle (I had by this time given up my job there to start my events business) where he went to top up his tan on the sunbed. Surely someone as wealthy as him would have a state-of-the-art one at home which he could use without the inconvenience of going out. Even when he broke his foot, his father Ted drove him to the sports complex. The lucky girls in Beauty Works, the local Alderley Edge beauty salon, also saw a great deal of David at this time. He would spend hours in there being pampered. Of course, every time this happened the news would spread like wildfire around the village. It all began when Victoria was supposedly away most of the time as she was recording her first solo album. The general conclusion was that he hated staying in an empty house and had gone out to be around people, to chat and get some personal contact. He also used to go and sit in Starbucks in Wilmslow every morning before training, presumably for the same reason. He was definitely out at night far more than he had been before – this is the period when I kept bumping into him. There was a real sense that he was very lonely at that point.

I don't want to sound as though I have no sympathy at all for Victoria. Having such a handsome and sought-after husband has been a boon to her since the Spice Girls, and will presumably be so in the future. However, going out with David, even in the exalted ranks of the international megastar circuit, must be well-nigh impossible to enjoy. If there aren't drunken men trying to get into fights with him or being abusive to her, there will be women who shamelessly try it on with David, completely ignoring the fact that his wife is standing next to him.

Again, I can illustrate a little of what she must go through from my own recent experience. My dad is now in his late fifties, but is still very fit, with a full head of hair – and handsome with it. My darling mum died in August 2003 at the Christie Hospital in Manchester from cancer. Dad, my brother Scott and myself had stayed by her bed for the last week of her life, sleeping in her room for the last four nights, and the moment she took her last breath was the worst of my life.

Not long afterwards, I accompanied Dad to a charity dinner, the first time we had been out since Mum passed away. Dad and I were sitting at a table of ten, and a woman who was on her own had started to say that she had bragged to all her work mates that she was coming to this charity event and would be out on a date with Willie Morgan. She meant no harm at all, but I couldn't cope with her complete lack of respect, especially as she did know that Mum had died recently in such tragic circumstances. The hairs stood up on my arms, and I could feel myself getting flushed and angry. How dare she say that about my father who was devastated by his grief? For some reason I got the idea that there might be rumours that this was a genuine romance, as I know full well how false stories can spread and might even reach the papers. An overreaction I know, perhaps one of an over protective daughter, but nevertheless an example of how predatory and insensitive women can be when seeing someone who is their idol.

The Beckhams brought their new baby boy Brooklyn to the flat in Alderley Edge in March 1999, following his birth by caesarean section in the Portland Hospital in London. Anyone who has had a baby knows that this is one of the most stressful times for a new mother, and it is one time in your life that you really do not want to be isolated from your family. Even a dancer like Victoria, with a high level of fitness, would take many weeks to recover from the debilitating effects of the operation.

Lifting a baby, even to feed it, is very painful: the back tends to take the strain, and backache of some severity is very common.

Both David and Victoria have said that Brooklyn was not one of the easiest babies to look after because he had an intolerance to milk and was always being sick, projectile vomiting several times a day. Like many little babies, even without the additional problem of his lactose intolerance, he had dreadful colic and was always crying. Victoria stressed how difficult she had found it in those first few months. Brooklyn slept for a maximum of twenty minutes at a stretch, day or night, before he awoke screaming with pain.

Victoria's mother was a frequent visitor, taking over in the middle of the night so that Victoria could sleep. Victoria had no close acquaintances in Manchester, and every day she spent in the flat, staring at MTV, underlined the stark contrast of her present loneliness with her past life as Posh Spice. The isolation affected her mental state. For three months she says she cried for hours every day, not bothering with her appearance and moping around in a tracksuit.

Victoria, possibly suffering from postnatal depression but probably just experiencing the same process of readjustment gone through by all new mothers, became more and more downcast, alone in the apartment waiting for David to get home from training. Perhaps it is not surprising that she did not continue as a housewife and mother, content to stay behind the scenes in Cheshire while helping David to get on with his career, but threw her efforts back into the Spice Girls and then her own solo career.

Young mothers reading these comments from Victoria about her situation will identify with them, but they might also feel somewhat critical. Many parents cope with similar, and indeed often far greater, problems without the Beckhams' considerable advantages. The couple were extremely wealthy, and lived in a brand-new converted flat with a kitchen that reportedly cost £40,000 from Harrods. Victoria had her own car and was not struggling to push Brooklyn around in a buggy or on public transport. If they had had a nanny to live in, or just some occasional childcare help, things might have been different; but the couple rejected this, preferring to enlist the support of Brooklyn's grandparents, both sets of which lived at the other end of the country. Victoria must have felt that her fame precluded her from joining the mother-and-baby groups which are often the only link isolated mothers have with other women who are in the same boat. It was David who was later to be seen ferrying an older Brooklyn to the Tumbletots baby-activity sessions in Cheshire. It was tough for Victoria, but it seems that she could only be pacified by moving back down south.

It was about this time that attention focused on Victoria's noticeable weight loss. She has been very candid, but also very defensive, about what she terms her 'past' eating disorder, which she says began when she was living with the other Spice Girls. Geri Halliwell, she claims, made her aware of low-fat food and dieting, but Victoria always remained heavier-looking than some of the other girls because of her medical condition of polycystic ovaries. Victoria puts her weight loss after Brooklyn's birth down to the extra efforts of bringing up a baby, and a punishing work schedule outside the home. My own understanding is that there are not many celebrities, male or female, whose success depends on their looks who do not have an eating disorder of some kind.

I would also argue very strongly from my personal experience that eating problems, whether these are caused by anorexia or bulimia, are like alcoholism: you can never say that you have been 'cured' of an unnatural relationship with food. In my opinion, Victoria is still anorexic. Attempts to show that she does eat, for example in the fly-on-the-wall documentary *The Real Beckhams*, fail to convince. She picked at a plate of salad and actually ate very little of it. I feel that I am qualified to express this opinion as I too have suffered from anorexia since an early age. When you are introduced as Willie Morgan's daughter, you feel very strongly that people have a certain expectation of you. They don't put this into words, obviously, but you know that they believe you should be perfect in your appearance. A perfect dress size, perfect hair, perfect nails and make-up. It is a very hard feeling to describe, but you always feel under scrutiny, and have a fear of failing to match up to that image. As a young teenager I began to battle with bulimia. I made myself sick after eating to make sure that I was always a size ten. But when I could not deal with the unpleasant physical side effects of being sick in this way, I 'progressed' to anorexia. Often I didn't eat at all. I could not even see that I had lost any weight. I am five foot nine and a half inches tall, and I weighed six stone when my mum and dad asked me to sit down with them and talk about my eating problem.

I was nonplussed. I was six stone, and if I had a problem it was that I was too fat. Shortly after that my best friend Lisa, who had gone to live in London, returned after eight months away. She burst into tears the first time she saw me. My legs were like sticks with bony, protruding knees. I have to thank my parents for getting me through and encouraging me to eat enough to stabilise my weight. But it has never left me. Like an alcoholic I am an addict, addicted to controlling how heavy I am. My current eating habits are, I freely admit, ridiculous. Although I can control my addiction, I prefer to eat at home where I can choose what I eat. If I go out for dinner I will only eat at certain restaurants where I know I can order a low-calorie option. I have to feel in control of what I put in my stomach.

It is easy when you have been in that situation to see the signs of anorexia, or another eating disorder, in someone else, no matter how much they deny it. Everyone could see Victoria had a problem when she first hit the headlines as 'Skeletal Spice', flaunting her coat-hanger collarbones and prominent ribcage in tight, shoulderless sheath dresses with asymmetrical hems, or in the basque-style tops she favoured for a long time because she felt they pushed up her breasts and gave her a feminine shape. Looking at the photographs of Victoria from this time, the overall effect is distinctly unattractive. Her head has the tell-tale, plastic-dolly look – too big for the frail body underneath. Her arms, which are completely bare, appear stick-like, and her famous long slim legs have lost their shape. The fake tan that she wears serves only to accentuate her wasted appearance.

Victoria is adamant that this was not the result of an eating disorder but a medical problem. She agreed with the general verdict that she lost too much weight, but insisted that she had no idea why this was happening, or how to stop it. Ironically, rather than starving herself, she says that she was eating more than she had done for years. Craving sugar to stop herself fainting, she gorged on tins of fruit.

In search of a solution, she consulted a Chinese doctor (recommended tellingly by Mandy Smith, another 'former' anorexic) who told her that she had a zinc deficiency and candida. Her own doctor though she might be hypoglycaemic. She lay in bed without any energy. Eventually she went home to her parents' house where they tried to get her to eat what they called 'proper food'. I recognise all of these as symptoms of anorexia, sent into overdrive by the various stresses in her life. The compulsive eating – sometimes up to five tins – of tinned fruit, probably in its own juice, which is very low in calories, is particularly common. There are certain foods which you feel you can trust not to make you fat, and you tend to concentrate on these to the exclusion of more nutritious items. She rejected her parents' advice about 'proper food' because she believed it would make her put on weight.

Though Victoria was very angry at the media outcry about her appearance, it may have done her a favour in facing her with evidence of her own problem that she couldn't deny. I remember feeling intense guilt for the way I was behaving, constantly deceiving the people who loved me, and I am sure Victoria did too. It was only the honesty of Princess Diana in talking about her own bulimia that made me feel better about myself. I felt that, if someone as fantastic as her could share my problem, I was not a bad person after all. It is not helpful to ordinary people with eating disorders – or simply problems with their body image – to see celebrities saying that their exaggerated thinness is not the result of out-of-control dieting which is dangerous for their health.

Similarly, Victoria has denied that she has had breast-augmentation surgery. She may prefer not to share such personal details, but to deny it presents an image to the impressionable of an unnatural body shape. Nicola Smith was once having her hair done in Altrincham when her mobile phone rang, and she had a discussion about 'boob jobs' with the caller. She has had one herself, which she is completely open about. When the conversation ended, she told the girl styling her hair that it was Victoria complaining that her boobs were really hurting her 'this time' – suggesting that maybe she has been under the surgeon's knife more than once.

Victoria's nine months of turmoil, as she put it, after Brooklyn's birth and her extreme weight loss, appear only to have ended when her solo musical career temporarily took off. Her collaboration with Dane Bowers on the dance single 'Out of Your Mind' produced, in the eyes of most critics, a very mediocre track, but Victoria threw herself into the single's promotion, even enlisting the services of David at various events: one at Woolworths in Oldham attracted a crowd of 6,000 fans and had to be controlled by mounted police. Stories about David and her mother buying multiple copies of the single were unproven, but were trotted out to sneers from every quarter about her desperation. She also made one of her famous tacky comments about David, saying that he would streak naked around Old Trafford if she reached the top spot with her single. It is part of pop history now that even David's intervention could not earn Victoria the number-one single she had wanted to match the achievements of the other Spice Girls' solo efforts; but the single did reach number two, and was only beaten into second place by Spiller's 'Groovejet', which has since become something of a dance classic.

Whatever the merits or otherwise of Victoria's musical talents, she is also a footballer's wife. The combination of international stardom and being married to a football superstar is very unusual, and reconciling the conflicting demands of her lifestyle had significant effects on David's career at Manchester United ...

CHAPTER SIX

FOOTBALLERS' WIVES AND GIRLFRIENDS

O ne of the cult shows on television, which started its second series in February 2004 with two new characters – a Posh and Becks lookalike couple Conrad and Amber Gates – is *Footballers' Wives*. In the first series, Kyle and Chardonnay (a page-three stunna) exchanged their marriage vows in ridiculously over-the-top style, with considerable debt to the Beckhams' fairy-tale fantasy wedding at Luttrellstown Castle. The programme is unashamedly trashy but glitzy. The wives of the title are sexually rapacious, bitchy, drug-addicted, compulsive spenders with an eye for designer labels. I doubt whether the Beckhams' way of living is anything at all like the show. I know for a fact that life for the 'ordinary' footballer's wife is a world away from what we see on the screen.

Footballers in this country do not usually marry celebrities, especially women with the level of fame that

Victoria had achieved when David first met her. The first footballer to marry a celebrity was Billy Wright, then considered to be one of football's most eligible bachelors. He was England captain and, in the terms of the fifties and early sixties, was a media star. His bride was Joy Beverley of the Beverley Sisters. Modern eyes would find the attention their marriage received quite quaint, but it made news, and the couple tried to keep things secret with a simple ceremony in Poole. However, the location leaked out, and hundreds of people turned up to wish them well. The worst claim Joy had to refute during their marriage was that she didn't like Wolverhampton.

In more recent times, Leslie Ash, the actress known for her appearances in the hit comedy series *Men Behaving Badly*, married the then Leeds United striker Lee Chapman. The singer Louise married Jamie Redknapp who was then playing for Liverpool, but they have had a relatively low-profile relationship, refusing to market themselves as a couple and keeping their careers separate.

Two important reasons why more footballers, as eligible young men who can earn high salaries, do not marry celebrities is that footballers tend to marry young, and they do not always start out as superstars. Another key factor is that the footballer's life, even at the lower levels of the game, involves large amounts of travelling, and he can be away for long stretches of time. The responsibility of running a household, especially when there are children, is of necessity that of the wife. She holds the home together. I remember how my own mother made the house a home and was always there when my brother and myself came home from school. A very beautiful woman, a natural blonde with translucent skin, she received many offers to do modelling and other promotional work. But she decided to take on the role of homemaker and to give up what she could have done with her own career when she married a footballer.

My mother's decision meant that my father gained the stability and loving centre he needed, despite his unusual existence as a professional footballer, away for weeks, even months at a time, training then being at home for odd hours, busy doing his own promotional work. Very few of his contemporaries had wives who worked – he cannot think of any who had a career outside the home. As he puts it, 'Pat brought up the children. She just had to get on with things when I was away. It was part of the lifestyle and there was no choice about it.'

Things started to get worse for footballers' wives in the early seventies, when certain managers began bringing in the practice of the team staying at a hotel before home games. At United during Sir Matt's term as manager, as was customary at other clubs as well, players were forbidden to go out on a Friday night before a home game. They stayed at home with their families, relaxed in their home environment, slept in their own beds and had a normal routine. On the Saturday morning before the game, Dad says that players 'got up, ate breakfast and cut the grass, then went to Old Trafford to play!' Tommy Docherty had the idea, which was based on what was becoming common practice on the Continent, of taking the squad away to a hotel so that he could be sure that they were not jeopardising their fitness in any way. United usually stayed at Mottram Hall in Cheshire, which is near Alderley Edge.

My father was not a fan of this practice. In his opinion

the alien environment of the hotel merely served to disrupt preparations, rather than aid them. Players would sit down to an enormous four- or five-course meal, which they would never have done at home, then couldn't sleep properly in a strange bed, particularly if they roomed with someone who snored. When he was at home, Dad would have an enormous bowl of pasta for his pre-match lunch, or home-made rice pudding with lashings of milk. This was Matt's recommendation. I can remember him now saying, 'You need your carbohydrate, plenty of carbohydrate.' As the English game had a reputation for not understanding the science of sports nutrition, Matt was obviously ahead of his time.

Even when there were away matches in this country, it was unusual to stay overnight, except for the very furthest games. The team travelled by coach on the morning of the match, and came back the same day. My father also points out that it was not unusual for players to go out without their wives after a game to unwind, 'sometimes till the early hours of the morning'. But now away games might easily mean an overnight stay.

My father could not have had the settled home that he enjoyed if my mother had worked. It is hard to imagine how both David and Victoria organise their lives so that they can spend any amount of time together. David cannot have experienced the type of footballer's home life that was expected in my father's day, Victoria being one of the forerunners of a new breed of footballer's wife – a woman whose earnings (at least when they first met) far exceeded her partner's, who disagrees with the notion that her own career should be exclusively running a house for her man and looking after her children. This is, of course, a reflection of the changing position of women in society over the past decades generally, but it does present enormous challenges for the couple themselves, and also for those managers who usually rely on a footballer's wife to settle him down.

In his autobiography, *Managing My Life*, Sir Alex reflected on the price that David had paid for his romance with an internationally famous pop singer. The glamour and excitement would have worn off very quickly, once they were subject to incessant and intrusive media attention. Settling down in Cheshire with Victoria and Brooklyn had, he believed, restored the ordered lifestyle that David's football required. As we have seen, these fervent hopes were to be unfounded.

The other aspect of Victoria's time as a footballer's wife at Old Trafford was her role on match day. Her instantly recognisable face, regrettably, laid her open to becoming the subject of some vile abuse from the terraces, usually from United's own fans. There is a school of thought among those who reckon themselves the hardcore of football supporters that anything goes as far as verbal abuse at a football match is concerned. Racist abuse, though it has not disappeared altogether, is a rarity, and it would be wrong to say that the hardcore fan would consider it right. But sexist abuse seems to have taken its place. The obscene and puerile chant that Victoria had to endure was never funny, but it was a 'joke' of which some never seemed to tire. The justification for this was the sensational comments that Victoria has a tendency to make about David. These supposedly off-the-cuff remarks, which Victoria claims are just evidence of her wicked sense of humour, are seen by many commentators as strategically planned, made to extract maximum publicity value from interviews. The most famous of these is the 'thong' remark. Following Geri's departure from the Spice Girls, the four remaining members gave an interview to the teen pop bible *Smash Hits*. In June 1998, David had been ridiculed for wearing a Gaultier sarong while he was on a break with his fiancée at Elton John's mansion in the South of France. When asked a question about this, Victoria replied, 'It's nothing out of the ordinary, David wears my knickers as well. He's getting in touch with his feminine side.' She told the same story on Channel 4's *Big Breakfast*, creating a media storm.

For some United fans, if they strongly suspected that wearing the sarong must have been Victoria's idea, they had no doubt that responsibility for the knicker story lay firmly at her door. In their minds it served to invite ridicule for David, and his energies had to be directed to denying and dealing with the resulting furore rather than to matters on the pitch where his focus should lie. Part of the abuse, however, just stemmed from the fact that, unlike most other footballers' wives and girlfriends, whom most fans would never recognise, they knew Victoria instantly. Such was the level of the aggression that she felt was directed towards her at football matches, whether it be United or England games, that she seemed to believe that her safety and that of her family, and even her life, was in jeopardy from enraged football supporters.

To someone who is unused to the often appalling behaviour of some people in football crowds (and Victoria had no interest in football before she met David, and doesn't particularly enjoy it now), or even just the general mayhem that results from the concentration of sometimes more than 67,000 people in one small space and the logistics of getting them all in and out again, I expect that Old Trafford can seem a very daunting and occasionally frightening place. I wonder what Victoria would have thought of the late sixties and seventies football scene when my father was playing, when the Stretford and Scoreboard ends were jammed full of standing fans, roaring the team on, and when hooliganism was rife. Then you really did take your life in your own hands attending a football match, though in the seats reserved for players' families we were cocooned to a certain extent from the rough and tumble.

In the depths of her depression following Brooklyn's arrival, Victoria began to dread her time alone with the baby in the Alderley Edge flat while David was at training. She became convinced that she and her new son were easy targets for the Manchester United fans who loathed her and might be plotting to do her harm. I know from my own experience that the threat of kidnap and harm to a celebrity's family is always there, and I have much to tell about this in a later chapter; but I think I can say that those United fans who hated her were a very small minority indeed. The vast majority merely found her irritating.

However, no one could blame the Beckhams for being concerned about safety. David apparently used to be very agitated before matches unless he could see that Victoria had reached her seat safely and was settled there. Manchester United's security men used to find the Beckhams' demand for extra attention at games and team functions particularly irksome, and Ned Kelly, the man in charge of arrangements, gives the distinct impression that he considered their fears exaggerated. Victoria constantly put her own security first, demanding extra cover. As the Spice Girls' fame had dimmed somewhat, Kelly considered this level of protection unnecessary. Victoria was, for example, extremely unhappy at the celebratory party held in London at the Royal Lancaster Hotel following United's 1999 FA Cup victory. The Beckhams had left without asking to be escorted by security, and had been approached by photographers in the hotel reception as they were on the way to their suite upstairs. Victoria wanted the photographers ejected, but Kelly told her that, as it was a public place, they could not be thrown out. He describes how Victoria ranted at him while David stood by with his head bowed until she had finished.

Footballers' wives and their families or their girlfriends usually meet up with their partners after a home match in the players' lounge at Old Trafford. Any illusions about the glitz and glamour of the football social scene are easily punctured by the less-than-luxurious surroundings where post-match celebrations or commiserations take place. Space is at a premium in the United administrative buildings, flanked as they are by a railway line. The players' lounge is not huge, and its style can best be described as functional. The carpets look as though they have seen a great deal of use. There is a modest bar on one side, and a small room which functions as a crèche leads off it. The lounge can become very crowded when all the various friends and family members of the squad have been accommodated. Some visitors find it intimidating there, particularly if they do not have many acquaintances among the other guests. Alex Ferguson and others have tried to restrict the numbers on many occasions, but found it difficult.

Victoria did not tend to mix with the other wives. There were rumours that they felt she was too good for their company, as she earned her own wage and was not dependent on her husband. The same allegation was made about her attitude to the wives of the England players. Victoria said that she was too busy to attend the opening match of the Euro 2000 tournament as she was rehearsing with the True Steppers and looking after Brooklyn. However, when driving into work that day, listening to Capital Radio, she heard a report of a story in the *Daily Mail* about how her non-attendance was a snub to the other England wives. She then changed her mind and went off to the game, but did not enjoy the day. David had advised her to dress down for the occasion, perhaps not wanting her to upstage the other wives in a micro-mini and heels. As it was, according to Victoria, the other women were all wearing short skirts and she was in her jeans, looking a mess.

Her closest link was probably with Nicola Smith, another London girl. She also struck up a friendship with Sarah Bosnich, then the wife of the Australian international goalkeeper who never saw eye to eye with Ferguson, and whose Old Trafford career was over practically before it had begun. Nicola was to drag Victoria into one of the most notorious stories which spread about her attitude towards the other players' wives and girlfriends. There are several versions of this incident currently circulating; my own account came courtesy of Nicola herself, and was told to me just after it took place. As she had no reason to misrepresent the events of that afternoon, I think I can safely say that it is probably the one which is closest to the truth.

The very mention of Dwight Yorke's girlfriend at that time, the glamour model Jordan, caused Nicola Smith to lose her temper. She hated her with a vengeance. The reason was very simple. Nicola's relationship with Teddy was very much an on–off affair and the pair had parted a few times. In the interim during one of these separations, Teddy had briefly dated Jordan. This was enough to put her firmly into Nicola's bad books. In her mind, Jordan was competition. Recently, Jordan's reputation and standing with the British public have been considerably rehabilitated by her appearance as one of the contestants in the Australian jungle in *I'm a Celebrity, Get Me Out of Here!*, the ITV reality show with a twist. I gained a very favourable impression of her long before then when I met her in the Braz one night with her new boyfriend Scott.

Many unflattering things have been written about her breast enlargements, but when you see her in the flesh she is stunning. She has a beautiful face and a fabulous figure, surprisingly petite and slight. Most of all she has a tremendous presence which draws attention wherever she goes. She oozes confidence and sex appeal. Jordan was wearing a denim miniskirt, a low-cut T-shirt and high boots. She was heavily made up, but was able to carry it off, looking dramatic rather than tarty. Her hair was worn down, long and flowing, and every male in the place was staring at her. Scott was angry at the attention that men were giving her, but she dealt with it really calmly, trying to talk him out of it. She looked at me and rolled her eyes in that classic 'here we go again' way. I smiled back in sympathy and she moved away from her agitated boyfriend and walked towards me.

'Men!' she announced, not having to say anything else to make her feelings clear.

'Yep,' I replied. 'They're all the same.' This made her laugh, despite Scott's continuing outburst.

'He's giving me a really hard time,' she sighed.

'Just ignore it and try to enjoy yourself,' I advised. Then I took the smile off her face by adding, 'We have a mutual friend, Nicola Smith.' Her expression changed to one of panic, before I quickly said, 'Look, I'm only kidding. I know she has given you a hard time at United.'

Jordan breathed a sigh of relief and her face softened. 'We just don't get on.'

'Ditto,' I sympathised. 'She is very selfish. Anyway, we must meet up next time you're in the area and have a proper chat.'

'Yeah, let's do that.' She smiled, and then was gone, with a crowd of adoring men following her every step.

The problems that Nicola had given Jordan at Old Trafford demonstrated that Nicola had a very spiteful side to her nature. She was quite proud of what she had done when she told me the story at a meeting of my band 90% Angels at Teddy Sheringham's Bowdon flat. 90% Angels was an idea that was dreamed up by myself and a few friends over lunch one Sunday. We were discussing all-girl singing groups, and were of the opinion that we could do things far better than most of them. For a time we couldn't think of a name, until I remembered the gold necklace that my parents had bought me in the States one year which bore the motto '90% Angel'. It was adopted unanimously. Later we added an extra 's'.

Nicola had offered to take over as our manager when our growing workload meant that Mike Tait, who had been representing us, felt that we needed more time than he could devote to us. Nicola was full of what she could do for the band using what she claimed to be her widespread showbiz contacts, one of whom was Victoria. She was always saying that she could arrange a meeting with Posh and bring her over to hear us sing. As you might expect, this never happened. Eventually, we felt, Nicola let us down badly, and launched her own singing career.

Jordan, according to Nicola, had come into the players' lounge to wait for Dwight to join her after a game in February 2001. The model has herself said that she always found the experience nerve racking, as the whole scene was very cliquey. Dwight took his time getting ready and he was always the last to emerge from the dressing room, so she took a friend with her rather than wait in a corner on her own. They both went to the adjacent ladies' toilets (which are quite cramped, and when I last saw them were decorated with cigarette burns) and when they returned Victoria was there with her parents, Brooklyn and Nicola. The novelty hit by the Baha Men, 'Who Let the Dogs Out', had been in the charts, and as Jordan walked by someone sang the chorus which gives the song its title, and began to bark. Jordan says she heard Nicola and Posh singing. Nicola told me that she alone sang the song to taunt the woman she still considered her rival. It seems from Jordan's account that Victoria found the whole thing very amusing and giggled along with Nicola, which may have led the model to believe that Victoria had actually partnered her in her little insulting ditty.

Naturally, when the story leaked out, the press was

happy to suggest that the main responsibility for this immature scene lay with Victoria, as it was a far bigger story. But Victoria was only too pleased to add fuel to the rumours that she had instigated the scene by later calling Jordan 'vile' in a television interview, despite her generous offer to settle their 'feud'. Jordan did get the better of their exchanges I think, when she replied to Victoria's uncalled-for remark with rather more style. 'I really don't know what's she's got against me – I've done nothing wrong. She's got a great-looking husband, a little boy and all the money in the world. She hasn't got the looks – but you can't have everything. At least I'm not too posh to push!' The latter comment was a reference to Victoria's caesarean delivery; Jordan's son with Dwight Yorke, Harvey, was born naturally. In February 2004, a series of photographs appeared in a tabloid newspaper, purportedly showing Victoria, looking bored while she watched David in a Real Madrid game, receiving a text to say that Jordan had been voted out of the jungle on the reality show. Her mood improved considerably when she passed the news on to her mother and a family friend sitting nearby.

Nicola was also supposed to have tried to have Jordan barred from the players' lounge altogether at one point, but her constant jealous guarding of her boyfriend from other women did not have the outcome she so fervently desired. Shortly after her engagement to Teddy, the band were with Nicola at the house of our voice coach, Sonia Ramsay, and she commented on how nice her engagement ring was. Nicola's response was extraordinary. She leaned over the desk where Sonia was sitting, slammed her hands down on it and said, 'Let me tell you something, I own him!' No one really knew how to reply to this outburst and we changed the subject. It transpired that Nicola's ownership was not as complete as she seemed to believe. When Teddy left United to return to London to play for his former club Tottenham Hotspur, the couple parted for good.

Victoria upstaged the wife of another player, her husband's close friend Phil Neville, on her wedding day. Phil's bride, Julie Killelea, the daughter of a local millionaire, had briefly dated David before he met Victoria. She then started a relationship with Phil and in December 1999 they were married. The guests were asked to wear the team's colours of red, white and black, and David obliged in a black gangster-style suit with a long coat and hat. Even baby Brooklyn was looking adorably cute in black, his tiny feet shod in mini black-and-white mock football boots and a red and black pull-on hat. Victoria seemingly could not resist the opportunity to demonstrate that David had made the right choice. She arrived wearing a strapless designer creation which did not fit the requested colour scheme by any stretch of the imagination. The tight-fitting sheath dress had a revealing split up to the thigh on one side. The material was made up of a sheer black lacy voile overlay with a floral pattern, backed with a beige lining. The bridal couple had, following the example of the Beckhams, signed an exclusive coverage deal with *OK!* magazine, albeit for the relatively modest sum of £100,000. It was a discourteous gesture by Victoria to upstage the bride in this manner, and unnecessary, as the Beckhams would have commanded much media space anyway without her rather childish attention-seeking.

Victoria has also been viewed as one of the new breed of footballers' wives because she is accused of interfering in David's football career, often to detrimental effect. She has not been afraid to make her feelings about Alex Ferguson known to the public and the tension, if not enmity, between the two of them was common knowledge. In 1999 she accused Manchester United of underpaying her husband, given that Roy Keane was earning £50,000, twice as much a week as David. It is rare for a wife to be prepared to interfere in this manner, especially when the manager is as formidable as Alex Ferguson, although they have on occasion made their presence felt in other ways. Shelley Webb, wife of 1990s United midfielder Neil Webb and now divorced from him with her own media career, famously crossed swords with Alex over the facilities for the United families. It is customary for the children to be brought along to see some home games, but keeping very small children entertained for what is effectively two hours can be very difficult. Shelley campaigned for a crèche where the children could be safe and kept entertained by a video and toys. Fergie considered this unnecessary and was irritated when Shelley refused to give up her crusade. Though the room allocated is hardly enormous, the existence of the Old Trafford crèche is testament to her energy and spirit.

On the other hand, a footballer's wife must be loyal to her husband: she also has to suffer with him when his relationship with the club is in difficulties, or he has an injury and cannot play. My father is quite categorical in his opinions about Victoria's supposed interference in matters that do not concern her. 'Of course she should. It's her business to be supportive of her husband and to back him in any way that she can.' As an ex-player he interprets her remarks to the press about David's future at Manchester United and in football generally very differently from others who do not have his insight. He surprised me greatly with his next comment. 'She's only doing what your mother did for me.'

I was very surprised. As far as I knew, Mum had always shunned the spotlight and refused to do even family photo shoots and interviews about life with Dad, let alone talk to the press about weightier matters. My father explained further. 'You see, footballers have it in their contracts that they cannot talk to the press about disputes they are having with the club in any form. It was the same for me. I could not go to the press about my dispute with the United manager Tommy Docherty without committing a serious disciplinary offence. So your mum had to do it for me so that I could put my side of things across. I've got a newspaper clipping about it somewhere. I'll dig it out for you.'

The half-column article is from the *Daily Mail*, dated 25 April 1975. Its headline announced: MORGAN'S WIFE HITS OUT AT THE DOC. 'Soccer wife Pat Morgan said last night that her husband Willie's career at Manchester United was being threatened by the actions of manager Tommy Docherty. "I'm just about sick of it," she said. Docherty is reporting the Scottish World Cup star to the board for allegedly refusing to go on United's summer tour. Morgan was unavailable at Corby where he played in a testimonial last night for former United forward Alex Dawson. But Pat said angrily: "It's just not true that Willie refused to tour. The whole thing is beginning to get on my nerves. It must be a mystery to the fans. I'll probably get myself into trouble now but I don't mind. Why should my husband have to sit back and hear so many things said against him?'"

David Barnes, the reporter who covered the story, was very sympathetic to my father's case. He finished the piece with a criticism of Docherty's policy. 'United are to tour North America, Hong Kong, Australia and New Zealand for a month this summer. It would have made sense, I believe, to insist that Morgan stayed behind. After a strenuous season doing his utmost to try to save a doomed United, he was involved in Scotland's World Cup effort last summer. This would have been the ideal chance for him to recharge physically and mentally for a fresh challenge in the First Division. Instead United are likely to sell, for about £70,000, a player with the class and experience they may need next season.' United had been relegated to the Second Division (the equivalent now of the First Division) in 1974, but regained their place in the highest league at the end of the 1975 season.

Being part of a United squad which has been hugely successful, at one of the greatest times in the club's footballing history, David has had relatively few disappointments to endure: he has been knocked out of the World Cup twice with England, and United only won the European Champions League once in his time at the club, and did not win the Premiership or the FA Cup every season. But, for most professional footballers, coping with frequent defeat and never experiencing what it is like to win any sort of trophy, let alone the greatest in Europe, is the norm. My dad won two Second Division Championship medals with United and Bolton, and considers this a very disappointing tally. David was also lucky with injuries while he was at Old Trafford. This may seem an incredible comment to make, given that he broke a bone in his foot shortly before the 2002 World Cup in a Champions League match against Deportivo La Coruna, and was not fully fit for the tournament. But he did not have to face the trauma and depression which follows a long-term lay-off after serious injury. He always knew that he would recover in a short time from his metatarsal fracture unlike, for example, Wes Brown, the young United central defender who has twice fought back from cruciate ligament damage in his knees. As Roy Keane, who suffered the same injury in 1997, discovered, the lengthy rehabilitation period can be harrowing. He had to undergo six weeks of special exercises to build his leg muscles up before he could even have the delicate and still-risky surgery. There then followed a slow and painful process by which the leg is kept mobile, then months of lonely work in the gym. He admits that during this period, though he obeyed instructions about his knee recovery to the letter, he began to drink too much at weekends after his week's leg work was concluded. At one point, when he had verbally abused a member of the bar staff at the reserve-team Christmas party, Alex Ferguson disciplined him by banning him from attending any further team celebrations.

All too often it is the footballer's wife who has the responsibility of supporting her husband through his blackest times, whether through injury or defeat, and some can pay a high price. Victoria's first real experience of how defeat affects a footballer came after England exited the World Cup in 2002. She and David went on holiday for a week, and David was morose and taciturn, wrapped up in his own disappointment. He gives Victoria much of the credit for putting matters in perspective for that same season, when David began to notice Ferguson's hostility towards him, and his mental anguish affected his wider circle.

He had support from other sources, of course. Both sets of the Beckhams' parents made public and private interventions in the row between Alex Ferguson and David. Sandra Beckham, alarmed by David's depression at the worsening relations between her son and his manager, took it on herself to raise the matter with Alex, but with little positive result. She had run into him by chance in the corridor and felt that it was an opportunity that she could not afford to turn down if she was to be able to help her son. Following the incident which saw David sustain a cut eye when Alex kicked a boot at him in the dressing room after United's defeat by Arsenal, Victoria, after meeting David in the players' lounge, wanted to go and confront Ferguson immediately, but David stopped her. His father Ted, as matters worsened over the summer of 2003, made several statements that David did not want to leave United. Victoria and her family were as important to the footballer as his own parents, though: when the news about David leaving the club broke, Tony Adams, Victoria's father, phoned a local London radio station to say that David had decided to go while talking it over with his in-laws and Victoria.

A famous footballer's wife, because of the sort of public attention that footballers attract, will have to share him with the public, even long after his career is over. Sometimes that also means very unwelcome attention. Quiet nights out can be interrupted by demands for autographs, but they can also be ruined by drunken or aggressive people who do not care what they say. Perhaps only someone with Victoria's star profile could cope with the media and public attention David has received.

Towards the end of her life, my mother retreated from my father's continuing celebrity lifestyle. The post was full of invitations to charity and other events but, although she had accompanied Dad to these throughout their marriage, she decided that she did not want to do so any more. Her lifestyle became reclusive, and she didn't like leaving her own home. As I grew up I began to understand how difficult it all was. She was always second best in a social situation – you could describe it as 'always having to walk a step behind'. This phrase has a special resonance, as my father chose one of his favourite songs for her funeral, 'Wind Beneath My Wings' – a version sung by one of their closest friends, Howard Keel – because some of the words in the song reflect the way he felt about her. Particularly significant is the verse which pays tribute to how the singer's love had been content to shun the limelight and remain in the background, offering support without complaint, always walking 'a step behind'.

Mother never once stopped my father attending events if he wished. Instead I began to accompany him when I was old enough, looking after him for her. I then saw how people clamoured for his attention and shut out whoever was with him. Once I interrupted a woman who had been monopolising his time and she turned on me. 'Who the hell are you? I'm talking to Willie Morgan. You'll have to wait your turn.' I exploded and put her in her place, but she had made two important points about my life. Who was I? I was Willie Morgan's daughter, as my mother was

Willie Morgan's wife. And she was right: we did both have to wait our turn.

Victoria, conversely, is not just David's Beckham's wife. She has amassed a personal fortune and worldwide fame. She has not made the choice to walk one step behind David for the sake of her husband and her children, and does not seem likely to do so, at least not for the foreseeable future.

CHAPTER SEVEN

PAINTING THE
TOWN RED

Professional footballers are major celebrities in Manchester and Cheshire. Their appearance in the nightclubs immediately draws a crowd, and they are the centre of attention wherever they go. If Ryan Giggs, Nicky Butt or Dwight Yorke are spotted enjoying themselves there is a buzz of excitement, but it is nothing compared to the frenzy which was created when David Beckham made an appearance. In the ladies' room, the best place to hear all the hottest gossip, women could be heard screaming, 'Oh my God, David Beckham, I've just seen David Beckham,' and there would be an unseemly rush for the door as the word went out that he was standing at the bar or with a group of friends. He became the premier celebrity attraction wherever he was and whatever he was doing. Securing David's presence at a club opening or special function became the ambition of every promoter. In the winter of 2000, David and other members of the

United team were guests of honour at the private VIP opening of Manchester's Buddha Lounge which I also attended. It was the first time I had seen David since our initial meeting a month earlier.

There weren't a lot of people there – maybe 100 – but enough for my face to melt into the crowd and for him not to remember me, which is exactly what I thought would happen. I couldn't have been more wrong. He was over by the bar and caught my eye as I walked in. As soon as he saw me, I saw his face light up. 'Hi,' he mouthed at me across the noisy room, 'how are you?'

This, I thought to myself, is really weird. In my mind I was still trying to dismiss the idea that he was in any way interested in me, and yet there he was, smiling at me as if we were old friends. 'Fine, thank you,' I mouthed back. 'How are you?'

He nodded pleasantly, and I turned back to my friends. We chatted for a few minutes before Lisa quietly turned to me and said, 'Have you noticed that David Beckham is constantly looking this way? He can't take his eyes off you.' I turned round to look, and saw she was right. David was staring right at me – not an aggressive stare, or a leery stare, but just the quiet confident look of a man who has something in his sights which he doesn't intend to let go. He's got a wife, I told myself. He's got kids. And yet the look he was giving me was unmistakable: friendly, flirty, and yet with a hint of arrogance. Maybe it was that arrogance that made me react the way I did.

The spark was there; there was no denying it. At the same time, however, I was very far from being overwhelmed. To everyone else in the club, this guy giving me the eye may well have been David Beckham, but to me he was just another footballer. Famous, yes. Rich, yes. Talented, of course – but at the end of the day not so different from the many footballers I had met in the course of my life. If he wanted to start flirting, it was a game I knew how to play – and I wasn't going to give him the advantage by going weak-kneed in the face of his celebrity. I gathered my things and made to leave.

David looked at me in complete disbelief. I'm here, his expression said, I've been staring at you for however long, I've made my interest perfectly clear, and you're *leaving*? I smirked at him, waved and walked out. As I did so, a little voice in my head said, 'Stupid girl! You should have stayed.' But at the same time, I felt immense satisfaction: if he wanted me, he was going to have to try harder than that. It was like a game of chess, and I had just made the better move. I didn't think at that time that the game posed any danger; it was harmless fun – he had Victoria, the kids, people all around him. It could never go further than an innocuous flirtation.

I certainly never expected to find myself in checkmate …

Players from Manchester City, Everton, Blackburn Rovers and many other northern clubs, as well as Manchester United, come to take advantage of the city's growing reputation as the party capital of the north. But there are very few places that they frequent. They will only go to clubs and restaurants where they feel comfortable and know that they will not be hounded by people and drawn into situations in which they can be threatened or compromised. Given the appetite for stories in the tabloids and gossip magazines about the peccadilloes of football stars, and the recent advent of mobile phones with cameras, any incident, no matter how trivial, can land them in hot water with their clubs and perhaps even the football authorities. The bars they favour have bouncers who they know will look after them if trouble breaks out. They also know that the bouncers will not let the press inside. Here they rub shoulders with soap stars from *Coronation Street* or *Hollyoaks*, and they can be seen, admired and paid homage to by the public all from a safe distance.

In this respect very little has changed since my father's day. Players who liked to go out to nightclubs would congregate in discotheques like Time and Place and Blinkers. Blinkers was below ground in a huge cellar, owned by millionaire bookmakers Selwyn and Harvey Demmy. When Mum and Dad and their friends used to arrive there at eleven o'clock on a Saturday night, there would be lines of customers around the block waiting to get in; being a celebrity meant that Dad never had to queue. There was a strict dress rule: men had to wear a tie; but Dad would never wear one, so Selwyn kept one in his office ready to hang around his neck when necessary. There was a square dance floor in the middle of the room and a revolving disco ball light in the centre for atmosphere. Tables were arranged around the outside for patrons to sit and drink or eat – usually chicken in a basket which was considered the height of sophistication.

The girls who flocked to Blinkers hoping for an eligible catch would not look out of place in today's clubs. They had long blonde straight hair (often boosted by wigs rather than hair extensions, and hair defrizzed with the help of an iron and brown paper), miniskirts up to the thigh, or hot pants and knee-length platform boots. False eyelashes and beige lipstick completed the look.

One episode, which everyone who witnessed it will never forget, happened when George Best was in Blinkers with his fiancée, the striking Danish blonde Eva Haraldsted. George had courted her in very unusual circumstances, on a pre-season trip with United to Copenhagen. She had asked him for his autograph, and he could not get her out of his mind. He launched an appeal in the Danish press for his 'dream girl' to contact him. George proposed to Eva when she came to Manchester, but he soon became tired of her. He had his own way of getting this message across to Eva. George asked the DJ who was in a kiosk at the side of the dance floor to play her a request. He chose the Beatles hit 'Get Back', with its chorus line 'Get back to where you once belonged'. The story made the papers the next day. George broke off the engagement and Eva sued him for breach of promise, which was settled out of court for £500.

Apart from these select clubs, there were very few other 'respectable' places footballers could go. They could enjoy a meal in only a couple of restaurants: one was called Blinkers French, the other Arturo's, and both were in the city centre. George Best and the Manchester City forward Mike Summerbee began to congregate with their friends at a rough pub near the Granada TV studios in Quay Street called the Brown Bull. It became George Best's favourite drinking venue because it had had a very relaxed attitude to the licensing laws and he could drink there any time of the day or night. The interior was, in the words of one customer, 'shabby and a little squalid'. Situated under a railway bridge, it shook every time the trains passed over. It was the bane of Matt Busby's life as he tried to discipline his wayward star, though he often had difficulty remembering its name, referring to it as the 'Brown Cow' or 'Black Bull' on occasions.

Outside the city centre, Best drank in a private club which was effectively a house in the suburb of Whalley Range, called Phyllis's after its proprietor. Phyllis was the mother of the rock band Thin Lizzy's guitarist and singer Phil Lynott, who died tragically young after a long struggle with heroin addiction. Later, when George had effectively finished playing football for United, though the club still held his registration, he set up his own nightclub and restaurant in Manchester city centre with two friends, Malcolm Wagner and an associate who owned other clubs in the city, Colin Burne. He bought run-down premises in Bootle Street, also the site of a police station, which he refurbished and opened as Slack Alice. He branched out further, opening a second, far larger club called Oscars, which was on four floors. These clubs would attract a large number of TV celebrities from the nearby Granada studios. The drink of the trendiest people in the late sixties and early seventies was Cuba Libre – Bacardi and Coke. This demonstrated that you earned enough money to be able to holiday in Spain, preferably in Marbella, in the days before cheap holiday packages had really taken off.

Although the 'Madchester' scene which began in the late eighties made Manchester cool, its real revival has been far more recent. In the last ten years the city centre has undergone a startling transformation. Restaurants, bars and clubs have proliferated. The number of licensed late-night premises in the city has risen from 160 in 1996 to over 500. The IRA bombing in 1996 left the rather ugly 1960s central shopping complex badly damaged. It presented an opportunity for the remodelling of the area, with the creation of squares and piazzas on the continental model, and new stores. As part of this inner-city regeneration, old warehouses, factories and other buildings which testify to Manchester's Victorian industrial prominence have been converted into apartments catering for those who have the inclination and the money to live a sophisticated metropolitan lifestyle.

Manchester is (courtesy of the Ship Canal) a port, which explains the three-masted sailing ship which sits proudly on top of the red devil on the club crest. Developments like Salford Quays rise up from the waterside, all sparkling chrome, glass and white concrete. People flocking to the centre for a night on the town, made accessible by the Metro tram system, are spoiled for choice. There is Castlefield, a canal-side district where the popular bars Atlas and Barca (once part-owned by Simply Red frontman and Manchester United fanatic Mick Hucknall) are tucked into restored railway arches. The latter has a sign by the door asking customers not to pester the famous for autographs, an injunction which is usually ignored. A large cluster of bars around Deansgate and Peter Street includes Manchester's top venue for celebrities, the Living Room. The Village, centred around Canal Street, which achieved national fame in the Channel 4 series *Queer as Folk*, attracts both a gay and straight crowd, while the area around Piccadilly (the site of Manchester's main train station) is up and coming. Some United players like Wes Brown have discovered a quiet four-star hotel called

Rossetti near Piccadilly. The northern quarter has more intellectual and artistic pretensions.

The three clubs in Manchester where today's United men are chiefly to be found are The Living Room, The Sugar Lounge and Reform, though the latter has fallen out of favour somewhat with the players recently since coming under new management. Five or six years ago when they were going for a night out together, the team might meet up in one of the Deansgate bars like Henry's, or Mulligans, a small Irish pub tucked away in a backstreet nearby, but this began to carry too great a risk, despite the fact that the team was accompanied by bodyguards. In 1999, when United were chasing the treble, Roy Keane found himself spending a night in the police cells when the team went out on a drinking session which began in Mulligans and ended in Henry's. Two women and a man had been following them, and, when one of the girls interrupted Roy's conversation with Ryan Giggs and asked him to buy her a drink, the two players ignored her. When the group persisted and the man became abusive, Roy left them in no doubt that they weren't wanted. 'Piss off and leave us alone,' he warned. Then a glass was thrown which narrowly missed his eye, but still succeeded in cutting his face. There was a general melee, showing how soon situations can escalate into fights.

The two women immediately left the bar and phoned the *Sun* newspaper and then the police, claiming that they had been assaulted by Roy Keane. Though the bar manager confirmed that Roy had been the target of unwanted harassment, he was still arrested and detained all night. The charges were dropped, but not before Keane had faced a barrage of publicity and the wrath of his manager, to whom he had some explaining to do in the morning when he was released on bail.

The Living Room, situated in Deansgate, is a large club and restaurant where the Manchester United players held their 2003 Christmas party, to which Lisa and I were invited. Downstairs there is a huge bar on the left which is the first thing you see when you enter. There is a seating area on the left with room for about forty people to gather around circular tables, with a beautiful wooden floor. Fashion TV is shown there all the time, usually women's fashion, and more often than not the models are clad in lingerie or bikinis. On the right is a restaurant. Victoria and David would go there together to eat and would take their acquaintances like Justin Timberlake for a meal. On one occasion, Lisa and I were eating there and David and Victoria were at a nearby table. Though there is a private area on the second floor, reached by a spiral staircase, which can be hired for private parties, David and Victoria were happy to eat in the open restaurant area as it was protected by bouncers. But it was noticeable that they hardly addressed a word to each other. I kept out of sight – I had no reason to, but something told me it would be inappropriate for me to talk to David in front of Victoria. They sat there for more than an hour, speaking to people if they came up to them, but not once to one another. I could tell from their body language that they were not comfortable in each other's presence.

Another place the couple was seen out together was The Sugar Lounge. This is to be found just on the outskirts of the city centre in a development of Manchester's canal side called the Locks. Formerly a very unlovely, derelict set of railway arches, some used as lock-ups by all manner of folk, the Locks is now home to a row of stylish bars, though in recent times the clientele has become more downmarket. The Sugar Lounge is a bar rather than a restaurant, with modern decor and wooden floors. Downstairs is a bar with an open space in the centre, and couches and tables are arranged round the outside of the room. Upstairs you will find a big bar with a DJ, and couches at the back where people can chill out and talk. It is another favourite venue for football clubs' Christmas parties. I was invited to a Manchester City players' party there, and the United wives hired it for their festive gathering.

The Sugar Lounge has a tremendous atmosphere. There is always funky, soul-orientated music playing, and a cosmopolitan mix of hip clubbers. In the absence of a VIP area, stars and ordinary punters mix together. It was a favourite haunt of Dwight Yorke, Manchester United's biggest party man, who loved to dance there. Ryan Giggs and Nicky Butt were also often propping up the bar together, and Lisa and I would watch the girls falling over themselves to attract their attention. Footballers never need to go up to girls and talk to them. Even if the players are out with their girlfriends, a steady stream of hopefuls will march up to them, interrupt their conversations and try to chat them up. When they are out alone, the players appear to lap up this attention as waves of the most eligible girls in Manchester (and the not quite so eligible ones) throw themselves at them shamelessly.

The press wait outside these Manchester clubs every Friday and Saturday night, hopeful that someone will obligingly stagger out drunk in front of the photographers' lenses. Fans also gather, sometimes for hours, for a glimpse of their heroes and an autograph. Compared with London, Manchester is more of a 'village', and it is impossible for players and other celebrities to venture abroad without being under the watchful eyes of half the city.

If David wanted to let his hair down, then it was at the Braz that he chose to do it. He was very friendly with one of the managers, Karen Wilson, and he was always looked after when he was there. Victoria hardly ever came in with him. I think I only saw her once in the downstairs restaurant. If David was in the Braz, a crowd would gather around the edge of the VIP area, straining for a glimpse. As the men's toilets were outside the cordoned-off section, this was the chosen spot for Beckham fans to congregate. Once we watched as he made his way through the crowd signing hands and arms and, in one case, a girl's chest. David looked very proud of himself after managing that particular autograph. It was all very rock and roll.

Dwight Yorke is also a regular in the Braz, living just around the corner from the club, and my circle became good friends with him. He hired the whole of the club at Christmas 2002 to wet the baby's head and belatedly celebrate the birth of Harvey, his son by Jordan. About 150 people were there, actors from *Coronation Street*, *Holby City* and *Brookside*, as well as a host of famous footballers. Jordan, for reasons which were not explained, didn't make it to the party.

Dwight was often there with his cousin Conor, a pleasant and amenable man. Conor was his cousin, his best friend and his minder all rolled into one, and they formed something of a double act in the Braz and around

Manchester. Conor was chatty, Dwight a man of few words who tended to say little and smile a lot, though he very much enjoyed being the centre of attention. Dwight's love of the party lifestyle was to bring him into conflict with Sir Alex Ferguson and eventually lead to his departure from United. His weakness for women is well known, and an evening out with Dwight would always entail plenty of alcohol and girls. He has, like many professional footballers, an athletic glow. Despite his rather silent persona he has an aura about him which automatically attracts female company. Victoria certainly wouldn't have been happy if she had known that David was on an evening out with Dwight. I don't think it was something that David did very often, although I was there to witness just what a bad influence Dwight could be, even on someone as well behaved as David. (David does occasionally have too much to drink without Dwight's prompting. One notable occasion was in the company of the Spice Girls, Ryan Giggs and Dave Gardner when the girls had finished recording their album in 1999. Very much the worse for wear after indulging in tequila slammers, David lost his wedding ring, which was later found by a hotel cleaner. But, in the context of the well-documented 'drinking culture' that is endemic in British football, David is a very moderate imbiber indeed.)

It was a relatively quiet night in the Braz. I was upstairs with Lisa and some friends, and as soon as we arrived the gossip circulated that David had been downstairs drinking red wine with Dwight since the afternoon, and he was rather drunk. Then there was a loud noise on the stairs. Two steps from the top, Dwight missed his footing and fell flat on his face. Then David, who was close behind, collapsed on top of him. Dwight dissolved in a fit of the giggles, and David lifted his head up just in time to see our table burst into laughter. He looked at me, a bit embarrassed, but soon saw the funny side and joined in with our laughter. It was some time before the two of them could manage to disentangle themselves and get up off the staircase. They went to the bar, but Dwight, in a rare moment of restraint, realised that they had had far too much to drink. Within two minutes he had taken David out of the club and they were gone.

It was March 2001, not long after I had walked out of the Buddha Lounge to David's amazement and my satisfaction. I was downstairs in the Braz with Lisa and my friend Lizette. A live band was playing, and we were having a good time; suddenly David walked in with his best friend Dave Gardner and another guy who I didn't recognise. David sat at the table opposite me and, by coincidence, both our phones rang. We didn't realise that we had the same models, and we flicked them both open at exactly the same time; as we did so, we caught each other's eye and started laughing.

We finished our conversations, and once more he mouthed 'hello' at me. I just nodded, playing it cool. There was no way I was going to give too much away. By chance there was a spare chair next to him; predictably a girl seized the opportunity to sit there, and started talking to her hero. David didn't even look at her – he was too busy staring at me. She carried on chatting, and he rolled his eyes at me in an amused way before the management came over and asked her to leave.

Each time I saw David, I could sense that the attraction

between us was becoming a little more intense. I knew he wanted more but it was difficult for him to do anything because there were always people around him. His private life was not his own, his every movement was recorded in the press. Surely he wouldn't be so brazen as to make some kind of move on me. Would he?

After a few minutes, I got up to go to the ladies', which was upstairs. He saw me go, and I am sure it was not coincidence that, as I walked back down, I saw David coming up the stairs. Both of us were being bustled along by the people behind us, so our encounter on the staircase that evening was tantalisingly brief – just time enough to exchange the most succinct of pleasantries before each of us was whisked in our respective directions. If David was disappointed that he did not have the opportunity to engage me further, it was fine by me. I left the club that night surer than ever that I was being actively pursued by the world's most famous footballer. Little did I know that our next meeting would leave a sour taste in my mouth …

It was once more in the Braz, but this time it was a Thursday night. If I'm honest, I have to say that I half expected to see David: he had a bit of a pattern in his social life and, if he was playing on a Saturday, Thursday was a good night to go out, and Thursday nights at the Braz were quite funky – there was a live band, but it was more of a nightclub atmosphere. If you want to bump into someone on the Manchester social scene, Thursday nights at Braz were a good time to do it. I'm sure David knew that as well as I did.

I was wearing my customary party outfit – a short miniskirt and long boots. As I was standing with my friends, I overheard someone saying, 'David Beckham's here!'

'Really?' I said. 'I haven't seen him.' I turned around and there he was, staring as always. He had clearly seen me, and he had just as clearly had a few drinks. Slowly, and without any attempt to be subtle, he looked me up and down, from head to toe and back up again. He gave me a sexy kind of look as if to say, 'Yes, I'm looking at you,' and then his gaze returned to my legs. He stared at my legs ... and stared at my legs ... and stared at my legs ... It got to the point that his friends had noticed that he had dropped out of the conversation, and turned round to see what he was looking at. One by one, they all started looking at my legs too. One of David's friends said something to him, then he whispered back and they both eyed me up again.

I felt sick. All the attention was on me, and I didn't like it one bit. I was suddenly self-conscious and embarrassed; I didn't know where to look and the club was so crowded I could hardly move somewhere else. And still they stared, and still they smirked and chatted about me in the way lads will.

Gradually their attention wandered – all but one. David had not lifted his gaze from me all evening. He realised what he'd done, and was revelling in the discomfort it made me feel. 'You keep walking out of these places when I have made my feelings towards you perfectly clear, miss,' his actions told me, 'and now it's my turn to get you back.' If I had made the better opening moves in this game of chess, he seemed desperate to prove himself a grandmaster.

David was enjoying himself. He continued drinking red wine, and giving me the eye. Once more – again, by design rather than accident, I am sure – we met on the steps. 'Hi, how are you?' he asked, his voice and body language dripping with flirtation.

I wasn't going to let him get away with this. 'Fine,' I said in as offhand a manner as I could muster while still sounding reasonably friendly. 'Anyway, have a good one.' And off I sauntered, leaving the tension between us electric – yet still unspoken.

Rio Ferdinand also came to the Braz, even before he was transferred to Manchester United from Leeds. We wondered if he had been invited by friends or was checking out the attractions of the area before he committed himself. Lisa and I are friendly with Dawn Ward, wife of Ashley Ward, the ex-Manchester City player who currently plays for Sheffield United, and one night we had arranged to meet Dawn, Rio Ferdinand's girlfriend Rebecca and Wes Brown's girlfriend for a drink downstairs in the Braz where there was a live band playing. This was one of Wes Brown's girlfriend's first nights out after the birth of her baby. Dwight came in later, accompanied as usual by Conor and his entourage. He sent over a tray of shots for our table, and Rebecca replied in kind. I had the impression that Rebecca rather liked Dwight and that this was a flirtation between the two of them. Conor motioned me over to their table and then invited us all back to Dwight's for a party. Normally we would shy away from a party at Dwight's because of the rumours of what this might entail, but I thought on this occasion I might be doing Rebecca a favour. 'Well,' I said, pointing at Rebecca, 'I know one of our group will be very happy. I think she really fancies Dwight.'

When I rejoined the girls I felt quite proud of my matchmaking. 'I've just set you up with Dwight Yorke!'

Suddenly I noticed that Dwight and Conor were laughing loudly. Rebecca screamed, 'I'm Rio's girlfriend, I don't fancy Dwight!' She was utterly horrified, especially as Rio, away with the England World Cup squad in London, had been sending her text messages all night, asking her what she was doing and telling her not to enjoy herself too much.

Rio did get to hear about what had happened, and showed he had a sense of humour when he was introduced to Lisa in the Braz by Rebecca. 'I hear your friend tried to set my girlfriend up with Dwight,' he announced. Then, when he began to laugh and revealed that he and Dwight had enjoyed teasing Rebecca about it, I thought it was safe to come over and admit all.

Dwight used to refer to Lisa as his 'salsa partner'. He was in the Braz with Ryan Giggs and his girlfriend when the DJ played a salsa tune, and Dwight asked a girl to come and dance with him. Unfortunately, though Dwight is a very good dancer, she wasn't familiar with salsa steps, so Lisa, taking advantage of the time-honoured salsa tradition by which women can ask men to dance, took Dwight on to the dance floor. After that he would walk past her and ask knowingly, 'Are we salsaing tonight, Lisa?'

Dwight liked to make fun of his own naughty reputation as a womaniser. While he was an Aston Villa player, he and Mark Bosnich had made a videotape of themselves having sex with two women, and a major scandal erupted when it was 'found' – supposedly in a skip – and made widely available on the Internet. Later, when Lisa danced a salsa with another friend, Dwight came over and said, 'I'm relieved. I thought I might have to dance with you when I heard the music.'

'So you didn't feel like dancing, then, Dwight?' she replied.

'No.' He grinned. 'But I like to watch!'

We witnessed one of the more notorious incidents involving a Manchester United player at the Braz, which led to Nicky Butt being charged by the police. We were in the VIP area on a very busy Saturday night when the midfielder pushed into a woman who stumbled and fell. It was accidental, although Nicky had obviously been drinking. The situation soon escalated when the woman's husband remonstrated with Nicky, who lashed out in his direction. There is a Braz regular who lives in Marbella, who was standing behind Nicky. He put his arms round him and lifted him off the floor so that Nicky's legs were bicycling in mid-air. He put him down, hoping that this had calmed him, but Nicky went to rush forward again. 'Mr Marbella' repeated the treatment. Still Butt lunged forward. This happened three times in all until his anger subsided. Apparently the woman had been caught by one of Nicky's flailing arms, although I didn't see this personally, and this was the reason for the police prosecution, which was later dropped.

Drinking and being seen are only part of the attractions of these nights out for players. Meeting beautiful women who are drawn irresistibly to their side is the other lure. For some, like Dwight and Ryan Giggs, women were their Achilles heel, though even David was linked with several women while he was engaged to Victoria. The most high-profile allegations came from Emma Ryan, usually described as a page-three girl from Stockport in Cheshire.

While Victoria was away on a Spice Girls world tour in the winter of 1998, David was supposed to have met the blonde glamour model for a few dates, even securing a ticket for her to come and watch him play at Old Trafford. David and Victoria always talked for hours on the phone every night when they were apart. Indeed, David claims that this was how they have built such a strong bond despite the long separations that their respective careers have entailed. Talking with Victoria, if only for a few minutes, can give him a sense of perspective and help to resolve even major crises. So it must have been very threatening for Victoria to read in the Sunday newspapers that David and Emma had enjoyed long, romantic, late-night phone calls. The most shattering claim was, however, that David had suggested that he pay for a hotel room for the both of them, but could not go through with it because of his love for his wife.

In her autobiography Victoria describes how this story plunged the relationship between herself and David into utter turmoil. The timing could not have been worse. Victoria was five months pregnant. There had also been a kiss-and-tell story which made it on to the cover of the *Daily Star*, revealing details of David's love life with one of his former girlfriends before he met Victoria, which the Spice Girl found uncomfortable reading. Then, a few days later, David made what must have been one of the most difficult calls of his life to Victoria, to break the news that he had been warned that Emma Ryan's allegations would be appearing in print.

Victoria describes her reaction as 'hysterical'. It was so pronounced that the gym owner (she was on a running machine at the time) pushed her into a storeroom to hide her from the other patrons. There David phoned her back to explain that none of it was true and that the blame lay at the door of one of his friends, Tim, who worked in a Manchester clothes store. Tim had given Emma Ryan his own phone number, but when Tim's fiancée found out he 'offloaded the story on to David'. This explanation hardly served to calm Victoria, especially when hot on the heels of this bombshell came more revelations that David had also been seeing another girl, Lisa Hames, whom he had met in a wine bar in Southport.

Bad luck, so the saying goes, always comes in threes, and so it was that a third story was printed in the tabloids. This time David had supposedly been ogling a lap dancer in Stringfellows nightclub; he allegedly invited her for a private dance and offered her a ticket to go and see him play against Juventus. This final allegation was easier for David to deal with than the others: he had never been to Stringfellows.

The Beckhams are not afraid to use powerful legal muscle to quash tabloid speculation. The lap dancer story could be – and was – challenged legally on the basis of factual accuracy, whereas the other claims were less easy to dismiss because they depended upon two conflicting individual versions of events for which there was no other corroboration. The stories in themselves were only of temporary interest. David's stardom in 1998 had by no means reached its peak. And, more to the point, he was a footballer, and his alleged bad behaviour was relatively unsensational, however much Victoria had felt hurt by it.

While David was becoming Manchester's most famous face off the pitch, following the breakthrough 1995–6 double-winning season, he was fast cementing his reputation on it as well. The 1996–7 season was, in terms of his performances for Manchester United, one of his best. The club's video magazine *Manchester United on Video* boasted proudly that Beckham was 'running his own personal goal-of-the-season competition'. He scored eleven goals for United, which does not sound a particularly large total until it is compared with United's other strikers. Top of the United scoring charts was Ole Gunnar Solskjaer, the modest Norwegian who was one of five new purchases at the beginning of the new term, and the only one who was to have a long-term career at United. The new scoring sensation had netted nineteen. Eric Cantona followed him with fourteen goals, but three of these were penalties. David was third in the list, with a very respectable tally for a midfielder. What isn't shown by the statistics is the sheer quality of his strikes that season. But he was proving himself far more than a goal-scorer. His long cross-field passes and corners were creating opportunities upon which the other strikers fed gratefully.

United fans were disappointed that the Blackburn Rovers and England superstar Alan Shearer had, at the eleventh hour, signed for Newcastle instead of United. They did not find 1996–7 an easy season to begin with, not hitting their form until the end of December. But David had no such problems, grabbing everyone's attention in the very first Premier League match. Much has been written about 'that goal' against Wimbledon at Selhurst Park, which gave United a 3–1 victory. Though United were the dominant team, they had only a one-goal lead as the match drew to a close, and the instructions from the bench were to keep possession of the ball and waste as much time as possible. Wimbledon had a reputation as the ultimate party spoilers, able to beat even the best teams by a combination of aggression and committed team play.

David, in the number 10 shirt vacated by Mark Hughes, had obviously not heard the instructions, as, standing on the halfway line, he looked up, saw the Wimbledon goalkeeper Neil Sullivan (who now plays for Chelsea) was out of his goal, and launched the ball into the air. The kick was a high, looping chip which drifted slightly and spun in the air. It seemed to take an age to come down, as Sullivan haplessly scrambled back to try to intercept it. Then it curled across into the right-hand side of the goal. Sullivan stayed for some time with his back to the pitch, his fingers laced in the goal netting, as David stood with his arms wide open in celebration. The ball had taken three seconds to travel fifty-five yards at a speed of thirty-eight miles per hour. It was an audacious goal which demanded vision, accuracy and power to achieve.

The publicity was immense. BBC commentator John Motson asked, 'Have we just seen the goal of the season, on the very first day of the season?' What is forgotten, overshadowed by this opening salvo, is that some of David's goals that season probably bettered this remarkable effort, and were certainly more important in spearheading United's championship and European challenge. United came back down to earth in their next match against Everton, finding themselves two goals down by half-time. David sparked the revival in the seventieth minute, creating chaos in the Everton defence with a wickedly high swirling cross from the right, which Jordi Cruyff headed in. Against Derby at the Baseball Ground he won the lacklustre United a point with a first-half equaliser. He latched on to the ball in midfield then took control of the situation, turning and making a charge until he was thirty yards out in the centre of the pitch. He launched a screaming shot with his right foot which ended up in the right-hand corner of the Derby net; he was christened 'the boy with bullets in his boots'.

Against Leeds on 7 September, the fourth United goal came courtesy of another Beckham cross which Eric Cantona put away from close range. David scored the only goal of the game in a close-fought tie with Liverpool after a nicely worked move with Solskjaer. His vision and marksmanship had played no little part in keeping a stuttering United in fifth place in the Premiership table, which was topped by Arsenal. United began their Champions League campaign with a 1–0 defeat by Juventus, but David made an important contribution to the club's progress in the competition by scoring the second goal against SK Rapid at Old Trafford.

However, United's season appeared to be sliding into disaster when they conceded thirteen goals in the next three games, including drubbings by Newcastle (5–0) and Southampton (6–3). It was also in this period that the club lost its proud record of never having conceded a European tie at home, defeated by a single goal in a disappointing performance against the unfancied Turkish side Fenerbahce. It was not until 20 December that United really caught fire, beating Sunderland 5–0 at Old Trafford. Against Nottingham Forest on Boxing Day, David opened the scoring with a wonderful shot. This time roles were reversed as Solskjaer turned provider, crossing from the left to Beckham, who steadied himself on the edge of the box before looping the ball over the goalkeeper. This was a remarkable effort, considering that he was limping badly from an ankle injury and was on the verge of being substituted. United went on to hit another three goals without reply.

David saw in the New Year by staking his claim to become United's dead-ball specialist. His perfectly placed free kick which curled around goalkeeper Ian Walker in the FA Cup game against Spurs secured the United win and brought gasps of admiration from all quarters of the game. After the match he stayed in London with Sir Alex to represent United at the Sky Sports Awards. United didn't win anything, and Ferguson was furious that the audience, many of whom were drunk, heckled the United pair throughout the programme.

David's contribution to the team was made all the more important because of injuries to key United stars like Andy Cole, who had broken his leg twice and was unable to play for eleven and a half weeks, and Roy Keane, who had missed fifteen out of United's first twenty-three games. Eric Cantona, United's talisman, had, when judged by his own incredibly high standards, been suffering a dip in his form. The range of David's goals and his frequent assists meant that, by the beginning of February, United had weathered the storm of the first half of a torrid season and pulled their way to the top of the Premiership, while qualifying for the second stage of the Champions League.

At the end of February, Victoria Adams came to Stamford Bridge at the prompting of the Spice Girls' svengali Simon Fuller, but she missed seeing David pouncing on a defensive mistake by Chelsea's Frank Sinclair and volleying a tremendous goal to secure a 1–1 draw, because she wasn't wearing her glasses. It was to be

David's last goal of the season, though it would be unfair to blame this on the distraction of the whirlwind, long-distance courtship which began in earnest with their subsequent encounter in the players' lounge at the home game against Sheffield Wednesday.

United's greatest performance was in the European competition. On 5 March, the Portuguese champions Porto came to Old Trafford for the first leg of the Champions League quarter-final. David's powerful cross from the right set Pallister up for the first goal, though it was an electrifying display by Ryan Giggs which was the main driving force behind United's sensational 4–0 victory. When they clashed with German side Borussia Dortmund in the semi-finals, United seemed to have their best chance ever of replicating the achievement of Busby's 1968 side; but it was not to be. Two very disappointing performances saw United eliminated. It was no consolation that Dortmund went on to win the trophy in May, defeating Juventus.

Four days prior to this, United had played what turned out to be the most important match of their season in the Premiership. Their most realistic challengers were Liverpool, although Newcastle United could also beat them to the title. At Anfield on 19 April, the two bitter northern rivals met in what was called the 'Premiership decider' by the media. Usually matches given this appellation are anything but, but this time the hype was justified. United won 3–1, and once again David Beckham had a considerable influence on the victory. A powerful, accurate Beckham corner found the head of Gary Pallister, the united central defender who was not noted for his aerial attacking ability. He scored, then John

Barnes equalised. Another corner, a second Pallister header, and United were once again in front. Andy Cole added a third in the second half to secure the win.

United's success on Merseyside seemed to break the spirit of the Liverpool players, who lost the belief that they could win the league. Despite United's own less than convincing end-of-season form, the title went to Old Trafford when United weren't even playing. Liverpool lost to Wimbledon, Newcastle could only draw with West Ham – and United were the champions.

David had other honours to collect: he was voted the PFA Young Player of the Year in recognition of his fantastic season. That August, the *Sun* named him the best-looking man in the world – Giggs only made thirty-fourth place, a fact which the lads in the dressing room enjoyed enormously. David was beginning to realise that his football and his fame would always be interdependent. Excellence on the pitch goes hand in hand with his superstar status off it.

CHAPTER EIGHT

MODEL
BEHAVIOUR

Head closely shaved apart from a longer central strip, knitted khaki-green close-fitting shirt with sleeves pushed up to reveal tanned forearms, one hand pulling it up to show off his washboard stomach streaked with trails of what appeared to be blood, David Beckham glared out forbiddingly from the magazine cover. His modelling assignment for style magazine *The Face* in July 2001 generated a storm of controversy. Cut specifically for the shoot, and because he fancied a change, it was meant to be shaved off the next day; but, as he really liked the look, inspired by Travis Bickle, Robert De Niro's psychotic vigilante anti-hero in the film *Taxi Driver*, David kept it, even though he was about to captain England in a vital World Cup qualifier against Greece.

The photographs which comprise this notorious spread showed David Beckham in a very different light. Brian Clough, the outspoken ex-Nottingham Forest manager, described his look as 'more like a bloody convict than an England captain'. The Beckham who looks out from magazine is cold eyed, statuesque, his shirt torn, mopping his dirty, blood-smeared face with a towel. There is a simmering undercurrent of suppressed violence. Other shots show him bare chested, or are close-ups of his head with copious rivulets of blood running down his nose and the side of his face, dripping off his chin. He is unadorned, aside from the Hindi tattoo of Victoria's name on the inside of one arm, and the two diamond-encrusted crosses in his ears. The 'blood' was actually a bottle of soy sauce, which David obligingly poured over himself. The haircut, wrongly dubbed a Mohican by the press who are not always well versed in such matters, but which was later properly identified as a Mohawk, made the headlines for days.

This was only David's sixth photo shoot ever, and demonstrated his interest in experimenting with and manipulating his own image in order to achieve a cool look. The session was very much in the sometimes controversial style that *The Face* had made its own. Its espousal of the look known as 'heroin chic', with wasted, pallid models made up to look bruised, had caused an outcry before. But it was something of a shock to see the mild-mannered, beautiful David presented in such bleak and uncompromising terms. When asked what he thought his clothes said about him he replied, 'That I'm relaxed in whatever I wear. I'm not afraid to wear something different.' Questioned about why he did these sessions and whether he fancied himself as a model, he was quick to deny it. 'I definitely don't fancy myself as a model, definitely not. I'm not good looking enough for that. I'm not! I just like it! I think you've always got to have something outside of your job. Shoots like this I enjoy, it's an honour. Even though I'm all soy sauce.'

It was these kinds of modelling assignments, as well as David's promotional work for a range of companies, that led those who were looking for the reasons why David went to Real Madrid to conclude that Beckham's 'extra-curricular', non-footballing activities had created such a circus around him that they were in danger of damaging his concentration, and ultimately his game. They certainly assumed that Alex Ferguson had had enough of it. But is there any real proof that David's 'something outside of his job' was detrimental to his football career?

My father was someone who, even in the seventies, was very well aware of the possibilities that being a football star presented, and how his fame could be exploited. Through his agent, Stephen Reubel, he ventured into a variety of different activities. David has never released a record, although he must have had hundreds of offers from producers and songwriters. Not being able to sing a note is no handicap. Kevin Keegan, perhaps the closest to Beckham of his day, put out a single 'Head Over Heels in Love', and had the confidence to perform it live on television. Glenn Hoddle and Chris Waddle's 'Diamond Lights' charted, and Paul Gascoigne scored a hit with his version of the Lindisfarne Geordie anthem 'Fog on the Tyne'and, like 'Hod and Wad', appeared on *Top of the Pops* to promote it. David has managed to resist these temptations, wisely. My dad did not have any part in the making of the single which bore his name, a working of the 'Willie Morgan on the wing' chant. It was arranged by Graham Gouldman (who was later to become a massive international music star with the group 10CC) under the name 'Tristar Airbus'. Dad's enduring moment of pride from this offering, which was a very average pop tune, was that he now had a record released on the same label as Elvis – RCA.

More serious were the modelling offers which came his way. I remember there always seemed to be a camera crew or photographers following him around the home. But his other work involved major advertising campaigns. Adam Faith had starred in the very popular ITV television series *Budgie*, in which he played a likeable small-time wheeler-dealer and loser of the same name. His character wore distinctive denim suits with tight-fitting jackets and flared trousers, usually partnered with stack-heeled boots and the ultra-fashionable 'feather cut' hairstyle, layered short on top with long wispy strands at the back and sides. Dad was asked to be the face of the 'Budgie Suit' promotion by Barry John, the company that produced them. He also modelled leather and light suede clothing for the Naviede company. One of the photographs I have of Dad's modelling at that time pictures him with two top female models, Gail Marsden and Paula Dean, and the Manchester City striker Mike Summerbee in order to cater for Manchester's two main football allegiances. The girls were wearing that summer's hot look – polka dots, Gail in a red-spotted cotton dress and Paula a blue-spotted blazer from the trendy women's chain Bus Stop. Dad and Mike are modelling Frank Rostron shirts. Mike's looks rather conservative, but Dad's is a very tight swirling paisley-patterned number, which he wears unbuttoned down to his chest. Dad's most important contract was for adidas, modelling their Arena range of products.

In 1964, before he came to Manchester United, he had opened his own clothes shop, as several footballers did in the sixties: the splendidly named Willie Morgan Supa-Teek. The boutique was the idea of Mike Edelson, who is at present one of Manchester United's directors and who was then in the fur business. Brian O'Neill, another Burnley player, went into partnership with Dad in the shop situated in Burnley town centre, which sold women's as well as men's outfits, but they would only put Dad's name on the shop front as he was the star. It was closed four years later, about the time Dad moved to Old Trafford.

David continues to make enormous amounts of money from his various enterprises. The figures filed at the beginning of March 2004 by the company formed to handle his commercial work, Footwork Productions, demonstrate the value of his sponsorship and advertising deals. Its principal activity is listed as 'provision of the services of David Beckham'. Over the past year his commercial activities generated £8.7 million, and David earned £5.7 million from this, with an additional dividend from the business, which brought his total non-football earnings to £6.7 million. This is a rise in earnings from those declared in 2002 of 148 per cent.

For the time, though not in the same league as David, Dad's work was very profitable, but he never received a penny of it. One day I remember my father seemed agitated. He told us that he was going round to see someone who worked for him, because he was not answering the telephone. The offices were empty. This chap, who arranged all the work for him, had absconded with the profits, never to be seen again. Dad thought he had chosen someone whom he could trust absolutely, avoiding the numerous hangers-on who swarm around the young men with lots of money at football clubs. As he says, it did not take a genius to recognise the wheeler-dealers. 'They would come up to you, most of them with a big sign on their foreheads to tell you that they were on the make. They wanted to buy you champagne then pitch their scheme. They all had an angle which was going to make you a fortune and just needed you to hand over most of your cash to them. There were very few footballers who didn't just get rid of these characters.'

The chief danger to the careers of players in this country remains alcohol. Dad played alongside perhaps football's most famous alcoholic, George Best, whose well-documented problems with drink, even after a liver transplant in 2003, continue to see him hit the headlines. Dad is still, to a certain extent, mystified that George's alcohol problem became so severe. He remembers the young Irishman as only a very moderate drinker compared with some of the players whom he knew at United. George also could count on a very loyal group of friends. People writing about Best have described him as prey to hangers-on, but Dad would argue to the contrary that George was very lucky to have the close-knit circle around him, which protected him from the worst problems of his superstar status. George's undoing, in Dad's eyes, was that he did not marry until relatively late for a footballer. He had his own house, but no one to make it a home and keep his socialising in check.

The trajectory of David's promotional work and his increasingly outré image in his photographic sessions is highly revealing. The 1997–8 season was a traumatic time for him, and he admits that he has done his best to forget it. The first and most influential of David's hairstyles emerged during that season, the hair shaped to his head at the sides and the back with sideburns, and a blond-streaked floppy fringe swept to one side. His first magazine spread of any note came courtesy of his relationship with Victoria in March 1999, in British *Vogue*. It was entitled 'Life is Sweet', with the introduction, 'She's the member of the biggest girl band ever. He plays football for England's most successful team. Together they're worth about £18 million. And they're still in their early twenties. Meet Victoria Adams and David Beckham, the most famous couple on the planet.'

The photographs show them as a loving couple, Posh proudly displaying her pregnant belly as David cradles her in his arms and she bites his finger, or lying on the floor (somewhat bizarrely in a hotel corridor, with bemused staff looking on from the laundry alcove nearby), her head on his chest and one hand cupping her stomach. David's other assignment of that summer was for men's magazine *GQ*, whose readers had voted him Sportsman of the Year. Dressed all in black in a leather suit, David looks very beautiful. No gimmicks have been employed by the photographer, who concentrates on picturing his handsome features to best advantage. He turned up to the shoot with baby Brooklyn and Victoria, who spent the whole afternoon on the phone making arrangements for their forthcoming wedding.

The Beckhams' wedding, enshrined as the apogee of bad taste in the annals of style with its two golden thrones and purple theme, was the height of David's pretty-boy phase. His all-white wedding suit with cravat and fitted waistcoat truly marked him out as Prince Charming. His hairstyle and taste in clothing was to remain relatively unchanged until 2000. He and Victoria did another joint photo session for *Vanity Fair*, shot by the famous photographer Annie Leibovitz; this was more raunchy, picturing them as a couple united by desire as well as love. David was, however, ready for a drastic change of image.

Beckham ran out on to the pitch at Old Trafford against Leicester City on 18 March 2000 with a shaven head, a cut which made the front pages of even the broadsheet newspapers. It had cost £300 and was done by his favourite stylist Tyler at Victoria's parents' house in Goff's Oak. David explained the reasons behind this transformation as being very simple. 'I shaved my hair initially 'cause there were so many people with my sort of hairstyle.' He had merely wanted to be different from the many wannabe David Beckhams in the streets.

It was not until 2001 that David began to really push the boundaries of what might be expected from a modelling session involving a famous sportsman. *The Face* photo shoot was the first example, but the following year, in the Autumn and Winter 2002 edition of *Arena Homme Plus*, he was, in the words of the *Independent* magazine style analyst Colin McDowell, 'Posed most assuredly as a bit of rough; a rent boy whose masculinity was available – at a price.' There have been no other footballers prepared to present their sexuality in this ambiguous fashion. The cover shot has David staring broodingly into the camera, clad only in a pair of white underpants and a heavy leather wrist strap. Inside he poses in US military-style chic in camouflage combat fatigues, bare chested or wearing a padded sleeveless jacket or khaki-green vest. He is pictured in very ordinary surroundings, a small room with a cheap sofa, sitting on top of a chest of drawers. McDowell argued that this was to make him appear available to the gay men at whom the shoot, in his opinion, was targeted. But, when David finally did appear in the gay magazine *Attitude*, he was posed in an altogether softer manner. In the June 2002 edition, David's by now longer spiky hair is teased out into a fluffy, platinum cut, which in some of the shots frames his head like a halo. He wears heavy Indian-style brocaded shirts with loosely fitted jeans in some pictures, sprawling in a relaxed mode. In others more is made of his athleticism. Wearing a white T-shirt bearing the capitalised name 'ROCKY', he spins a ball on his fingertip, balances it on his forehead or holds it while staring directly at the camera.

David Beckham's final 'gender-bending' shoot while a Manchester United player was for *GQ*. His pose on the cover is controversial in itself. He stands with arms outspread along a cross of St George painted in red on a white brick wall, bare to the waist, torso glistening with oil. Its quasi-religious symbolism offended some. The imagery of martyrdom was carried further inside, with a picture of Beckham in white baggy cotton trousers and a sleeveless white T-shirt, again with a red St George's cross on the front. David holds his arms behind his back. The T-shirt is spattered with simulated bullet holes. A lionheart (an image suggested by an animal skin that is draped over one shoulder in another shot), he is ready to die for England if necessary. But what really caught the media's attention were the more sexually suggestive shots of David in a white suit, again with a gleaming, oiled, bare chest, his fingernails coloured with plum nail varnish.

David appeared in another ground-breaking photo shoot when he became the first man ever to appear alone on the cover of women's magazine *Marie Claire* in May 2002. He was chosen for this honour because of his new-man status, and his commitment to fatherhood was discussed at length in the accompanying interview. He was also asked whether he thought he was vain or not, which he sidestepped neatly. 'I just like to look good. I don't love myself and I don't think I'm vain.'

The interviewer followed up with another highly pertinent question about the impact of his love for fashion. 'The way you look garners so much press attention – you'd have a much quieter life if you toned it down sometimes.'

'But I like nice clothes,' David answered, 'whether they're dodgy or not. Sometimes it looks right and other times it doesn't, but everyone goes through that.'

Though his rare photo sessions shape and promulgate David's media image, and are obviously something that he really enjoys, most of the money he earns outside football comes from his highly lucrative product endorsements. These began before he became part of the Posh and Becks partnership. In 1997 he became the fresh young face, or rather head of hair, behind the relaunch of the Brylcreem range of hair-styling products. In the forties, fifties and early sixties, Brylcreem was the must-have male hair product. Sportsmen were Brylcreem's chosen endorsers. Post-war, Denis Compton, the debonair, dark-haired international cricketer and Arsenal footballer, was the original Brylcreem boy. The attention that David was starting to excite, particularly among a younger audience, made him perfect for the new generation, and Brylcreem's

e autograph that David signed for my son, Alex, the first time I met him.

David and Victoria in happier times.

...ne of the infamous Manchester United Magnificent Sevens.

...ove left: Steve Coppell.

...ove right: Bryan Robson, one of Beckham's footballing heroes.

...ow: The irrepressible Eric Cantona.

Above: My band, 90% Angels, when there were five of us. We're pictured here with the legendary Alex Ferguson. *From left to right:* Lisa Watts, Belinda Barnsdall, Jackie Ashworth, Lizette Roberts and myself.

© Jean Havil

Below: The current band line-up, *from left to right*, Luisa Jordan-Killoran, Lizette, me Lisa.

© Sandi Hodki

above: Relaxing with my son, Alex, at Mere country club.

© Maura Williams

below: Dad with his great friends Johnny Mathis (*left*) and Howard Keel (*right*).

Above: Teddy Sheringham with the Angels! © Maura Willi

Below: My dad and my son are as thick as thieves. Alex has even begun to follow in his footsteps (*inset*).

© Maura Williams and Jason Van-B

ove left: With Dad at Old Trafford, the venue for one of our 90% Angels gigs.

© Joanne Ellis

ove right: A night out with my good friend Scott Wright.

ow left: With my good friend Steve Pinder, who used to play Max Farnham in *ookside*.

© Jean Havilland

ow right: With Simon Gregson, who plays Steve Mcdonald in *Coronation Street*. Simon I had an on/off relationship for about a year.

© Jean Havilland

Manchester United and me.

Main picture from the Sensua Collection by McGillicuddy Lord of K

Inset © Nick J

sponsorship continued even after David shaved his head.

It is not unusual for footballers to have very profitable 'boot deals'. These contracts not only provide free boots and other sports equipment for players, but also command large sums of money for high-profile players. Ryan Giggs endorses Reebok; Michael Owen, Umbro. David's deal with adidas (the same company as my father endorsed) earns him in excess of £1.25 million a year. They first sent him a pair of the Predator boots, which he still endorses, in the summer of 1996. These boots, designed by an ex-Liverpool player, are meant to increase control and swerve while shooting, a feature that David is perfect to promote. David claims that the Predator boots he was wearing when he scored his wonder goal against Wimbledon in 1996 were originally intended for Charlie Miller, a young Scottish player at Glasgow Rangers. On the tongues of the boots was stitched the word 'Charlie', something that the wags in the dressing room immediately noticed and took full advantage of. He likes to wear a new pair of boots every game, as he prefers them to fit tightly so that he can have maximum control of the ball at all times. He also has his boots customised to his requirements by adidas, with Brooklyn's and later Romeo's names stitched on to them.

At the back of David's latest autobiography, the bestselling *My Side*, along with a summary of his personal details, career statistics and notable moments, is a list of his current personal sponsors. This is a long and varied set of names: adidas, Castrol, Marks & Spencer, Meiji, Pepsi, Police sunglasses, TBC, Tsubasa Systems, Upper Deck and Vodafone. Some of these are very familiar to western consumers. The Marks & Spencer deal was signed in 2001 and involved David endorsing a range of boyswear. It was hoped that David's star power would revive the flagging M & S share in the children's clothing market. For Pepsi, David is one of an ever-changing group of famous footballers (including his Real Madrid teammate Roberto Carlos, Barcelona's Brazilian wizard Ronaldinho and Juan Sebastian Veron, now with Chelsea, but once one of David's rivals for the United midfield berth) who appear in expensively shot and amusing scenarios demonstrating in a tongue-in-cheek manner the reviving power of the world's second most popular soft drink.

Despite the ingenuity invested in finding novel scenarios to set these ads, the most effective was probably also the most low-key advertisement which traded upon David's rapport with children, and his personal humility. David is apparently substituted during a game, and walks disconsolately along the tunnel. He spots a young boy drinking from a can of Pepsi, and asks for some. The lad suggests a swap: the Pepsi for David's number 7 shirt. Beckham readily agrees, but the boy merely uses it to wipe the lip of the returned can before discarding it. This was a nice gloss on the evanescence of fame, as well as the sponsor's message that Pepsi's allure never fades.

Advance shots of David's March 2004 Pepsi ad were misinterpreted by the British press who thought that David and his fellow players were dressed as Roman gladiators, complementing the one which featured Britney Spears, Pink and Beyoncé Knowles dressed as female gladiators in the arena. In fact, David appeared as a medieval knight, freeing a town from the ravages of a marauding band of ruffians who had seized all the inhabitants' cans of Pepsi, which they had tried to conceal to no avail. There is an interesting subtext: the Pepsi hoard is liberated when a 'free kick' smashes the lock of the caged wagon into which the robbers' booty has been stashed. This is not one of David's 'specials', but the work of Real Madrid's other dead-ball specialist Roberto Carlos. David's role is to play long accurate passes to his *compadres*, who include no less than six La Liga players, a comment on the somewhat different role he has occupied in the Spanish team. He is supposed to have liked his costume so much that he asked if he could keep the leather armour and take it home with him.

David is the perfect model for Police sunglasses. Besides his superstar celebrity, he has very evenly placed ears and a perfectly shaped nose which ensure that he looks fabulous in their eyewear range. He first fronted their British advertising campaign for a fee of £1 million in 2001, doubling their sales in that year; they were happy to raise his fee to £3 million when the contract was renegotiated.

Other names on the list of sponsors are less familiar. TBC arranged the promotional tour that took Victoria and David to the Far East in summer 2003. Tsubasa Systems are a leading Tokyo-based producer of specialised computerised systems for the automobile, machine tools, agriculture and office sectors. The company summarises its corporate credo in the slogan 'Be a one-of-a-kind company with a spirit to challenge.' Meiji is a Japanese chocolate manufacturer, who makes delights such as Hello Panda biscuits and Almond Choco sweets. They were responsible for designing and making the three-metre-high chocolate statue of David that was encased behind glass on public display and later presented to

Beckham. David would find it very difficult to promote chocolate or any other kind of confectionery in Britain. He has, along with the face of the highly successful Walkers crisps campaign Gary Lineker, come under criticism for being part of a marketing strategy which uses sport to promote junk food to children. Ian Campbell, chair of the National Obesity Forum, claimed that, by accepting sponsorship from food companies, stars risked undermining messages from other sources about what constitutes healthy eating. 'The manufacturers want to be associated with these stars, but I cannot accept that by advertising these products they are helping.'

Though Castrol is a major worldwide brand of lubricants, the deal that David signed with the company in April 2002 was specifically to promote its oils in the Asia Pacific region. The chief executive officer of Castrol for that area revealed the thinking behind employing Beckham. 'David Beckham is one of the most recognised and admired sporting figures in the world, playing one of the most popular games on earth. The combination of Beckham's visibility and leadership in the sporting arena makes a natural fit for Castrol as the world's leading lubricant company.' Castrol's research showed that consumers in Thailand, Vietnam and China associated both David and Castrol with words and phrases like 'world class', 'powerful' and 'winning'.

Do David's modelling and endorsements harm his football? Were they, as some people have suggested, the reason that he was forced out of Old Trafford? Stan Hey, writing in the *Independent on Sunday* shortly after Beckham's transfer, certainly thought so. In an article entitled THE BOY WHO GOT TOO BIG FOR HIS BOOTS, he thought that shoots like the *GQ* assignment where David appeared covered in baby oil with purple fingernails would have been an affront to Sir Alex's no-nonsense Glaswegian masculinity. However, it is very unlikely that Alex would have any serious objections. He is supposed to have suggested to David that he abandon one of his more elaborate hairstyles to avoid exciting too much attention from the press, but endorsements and modelling have been part of a footballer's life for decades, and will continue to be so. Gary Neville did point out that, at the busiest times of the football season, when the pressure from the number of games is intense and tiredness is a big issue, all United players were told to cancel their promotional work so that they could rest as must as possible and avoid distractions. However, this is not a rejection of the practice in general, but a common-sense response at a specific point in time. Dad is particularly scathing about suggestions that any promotional work might blur a professional's focus. 'Football comes first,' he says. 'Everything else fits around it. When Beckham is in a studio, he's not in a pub or gambling.' Alex Ferguson agreed. 'From the moment he has arrived he has been an example to others of the value of practice and it has shown in his performances. You don't get that from going to discos.'

Despite David's handsome earnings from his commercial activities, commentators have been quick to stress that he is not in the same league when compared with the giant sums commanded for the use of their image by American sports stars like Tiger Woods and Michael Jordan. However, in March 2004, adidas unveiled Beckham's very own logo, a stylised figure with one arm outstretched and its leg drawn back about to take a free kick with his right foot, mirroring David's stance. The image is at the heart of a huge new deal with adidas and was designed by Eric Vellozzi who said, 'We captured the unique nature of his free kick.' The *Daily Mirror* saw it as confirmation of Beckham's status as a world superstar and 'a sign of just how far he has come. There was a time after the 1998 World Cup when the nation might have chosen a two-fingered salute as the most appropriate symbol for the Real Madrid player.'

The 1997–8 season, the one that David would prefer to have forgotten, was, in terms of his United career at least, unspectacular. After the first few games, his place in the starting line-up was secure. He was almost ever-present in the United team, avoiding serious injury, and played the most number of full matches. David also racked up the same goal tally as he had done the previous season, eleven. However, his overall scoring contribution was not as significant. Andy Cole netted twenty-five goals, and Teddy Sheringham had the second-highest total of fourteen. David scored two of his goals in the FA Cup, in a fabulous performance against Chelsea which showed the heights that this United team could hit on its day. The rest were scored in the Premiership – none in Europe.

David's season had a stuttering start. Given a place in the squad for a friendly international tournament along with Paul Scholes, the Nevilles and Nicky Butt, the United men were largely responsible for the England victory in the Le Tournoi tournament in France in the summer. But Alex Ferguson, always alive to the extra pressures placed upon his United players by international duties, was not very keen on so many of his young stars being selected to represent England in what was effectively a friendly competition, especially after the rigours of the 1996–7 season. David did not go on United's pre-season tour of the Far East. When the new term kicked off with the Charity Shield, David Beckham and Gary Neville were not included in the team. Neville said later that Alex had told both men well before the game that he would rest them so that they would have more time to recover after the summer's exertions. 'He started to plod a bit at the end of last season,' Ferguson opined. Despite this, there were widespread rumours that David was in fact being punished rather than rested, a warning about his increasingly high-profile celebrity lifestyle. TAKE A BECK SEAT, was how one newspaper saw it. The mutterings became louder when David, now the holder of the number 7 shirt as new signing Teddy Sheringham became United's number 10, was named as a substitute for the first three league games of the season.

One report of the home match against Southampton on Wednesday, 12 August declared the policy a success, whatever the reasoning behind it. 'The tired jaded figure has once again been replaced by the player we've come to know.' David came off the bench in the sixty-fifth minute to replace Paul Scholes, and, when Ryan Giggs, easily United's best player in the game, skipped past the Southampton full back and put in a cross, David met it with a header to give United the win. Alex Ferguson commented, 'David did very well to take the goal. But it didn't matter to me who took it, I was just so pleased to win.' But the manager had been more impressed than he was prepared to show, as Beckham was restored to the starting line-up for the next game. David scored another header against Everton at Goodison Park from a Paul Scholes cross in the twenty-ninth minute, a goal which signalled the start of United's dominance of the match which they eventually won 2–0.

United's form in the first part of the season was inconsistent. The team was drawing too many matches. During the tie with West Ham at Upton Park, a 1–1 draw, David was subjected to some disgusting chants about Victoria. When Roy Keane equalised, he ran over to the West Ham fans and David followed along with Gary Neville. The newspapers claimed that David alone was inciting the crowd in revenge. Neville wondered how David managed to cope with the abuse. 'Becks knew he was going to get the press attention going out with Victoria,' he said. 'But why should he be slaughtered like this?'

United capped a disappointing run by losing 1–0 to bitter rivals Leeds United at the end of September. It was during this game that Roy Keane ruptured his cruciate ligament and, although he tried, amazingly, to play on even though he had 'felt something snap' in his knee, the injury was so serious that it ruled him out for the entire season. The loss of United's driving force in midfield was to have a disastrous effect on their prospects for success, although in the short term the team rallied and ironically began to play some irresistible football. At the same time, Beckham-baiting was, worryingly, starting to become a national sport. David was stung by allegations in the press that he had sworn at some children who had asked for his autograph, a charge which he hotly denied.

Old Trafford saw one of the team's finest performances in the Champions League against Juventus. Alessandro

Del Piero put the Italians in the lead after only nineteen seconds, but the Reds refused to be demoralised. Giggs, who was having one of his best starts to the season, cut through the Juventus defence time and time again. David was tireless, playing in a reshaped midfield in Keane's absence with Nicky Butt and central defender Ronny Johnsen. Teddy Sheringham equalised in the thirty-eighth minute with a header from a high, looping cross from Giggs, then in the second half Paul Scholes put United in front after evading the Juventus defenders and going around the goalkeeper Angelo Peruzzi. Ryan capped an electrifying performance which won him Man of the Match by scoring a fabulous third goal. The delirious crowd was momentarily silenced when Zinedine Zidane made the scoreline 3–2 in the last minute of the game, but the roar when the final whistle blew could be heard for miles.

The Juventus game galvanised the team, which suddenly could not stop scoring. David was an important part in this bravura football, but he felt that United were not exploiting his talents to the full by sticking him out wide on the right wing. In an interview in the official Manchester United magazine, he said that he saw himself as a central midfielder, though obviously he was happy to play in any position to secure his place. He did admit that the spectacular goals had dried up. Although he had just doubled his total with his two goals against Wimbledon, at the same point last year he had scored seven. He put this lack of goals down to the fact that opposition defenders now recognised the threat he presented and were denying him space. But, if he was not scoring goals himself, he was making them for other players.

Perhaps his lack of goals could also be down to the fact that, with target men like Sheringham, Andy Cole and Ole Gunnar Solksjaer, he was required to be a provider rather than a finisher. David's assists, mainly his hard-driven, pin-point crosses, were feeding the strikers in the very prolific spell which followed. Barnsley were humiliated 7–0 with a Cole hat-trick and two from Giggs. In the 6–1 pounding of Sheffield Wednesday, then led by the flamboyant former United manager Ron Atkinson, a right cross from Beckham made the third goal for Cole. He also put the ball in from the right so that fellow Londoner Sheringham was only required to stoop slightly to head in the sixth. At Selhurst Park, United scored five to beat Wimbledon 5–2, all seven goals coming in the second half. David was a substitute, but within forty seconds of him coming on to replace Gary Neville, who by his own admission was having 'an absolute nightmare from start to finish', David latched on to a ball rolled across the penalty area by Paul Scholes from the left and smashed it with his right foot through the goalkeeper's open legs to make the score 2–0 for United. Wimbledon equalised with two quick goals. Then Phil Neville passed the ball to Butt, who sent it to Beckham. David looked up, squared himself for the shot and from thirty yards out he drove the ball low and hard and it was deflected into the net.

United's winning streak was crowned by a 3–1 victory over Liverpool, wins over Blackburn Rovers, Newcastle and Everton, and qualification for the quarter-finals of the Champions League. At Anfield, Andy Cole gave United the lead with a brilliant solo effort, only for Fowler to equalise from a penalty won by Michael Owen. David restored United's advantage with one of the searing free kicks which had been missing this season. As the ball left his foot from a position on the edge of the D, it curved around the wall from the right to bend into the top left-hand corner and hit the underside of the crossbar to beat the stranded Liverpool goalkeeper David James. A Becks cross from the right was headed in by Andy Cole to beat Newcastle, and the first goal in the 2–0 victory over Everton came courtesy of a fantastic Beckham corner. He sent over a curling, floating ball which caused mayhem in the Everton defence before it dropped for Johnsen to play it in, and for Henning Berg to score.

United were top of the league, but the Beckham-baiting intensified. The Dutch club Feyenoord complained that Beckham had deliberately tried to maim Giovanni Van Bronckhorst. In the return tie their players taunted and kicked him throughout the match. Gary Neville described how he was appalled when 'their left back booted Becks up in the air. I ran over to David. "Look out," I said. "I can tell by the way he kicked you there he wasn't going for the ball. If there's a fifty–fifty ball, don't go in for it. It's not worth getting injured."

'Becks replied, "He's already told me, 'You've put two of our players out of the game, and now it's your turn.'"'

The worst tackle was reserved for Denis Irwin who was sidelined for over a month after Jan Bosvelt lunged at him with his studs showing towards the end of the game. Ferguson told his team not to swap shirts at the end, so disgusted was he with the way that Feyenoord had behaved.

The New Year held out the tantalising prospect of a treble of the Champions League, the Premiership and the FA Cup when United turned in another of their best performances ever to beat Chelsea 5–3 in the third round of the FA Cup at Stamford Bridge. David was again on top form, scoring twice in the twenty-third and twenty-seventh minutes to put United 2–0 up. Andy Cole passed the ball to Sheringham, who flicked it on to Beckham to fire the ball into the net. His second came from another great free kick which he whipped in low and hard. Amazingly, sloppy play at the end allowed Chelsea to score three goals in the last ten minutes, which flattered the London team. But the United bubble began to deflate. A 1–0 defeat by Southampton, who scored right at the start of the game and then survived a host of missed United chances, began a dip in form.

Before training on Sunday, 25 January, David told Gary he had asked Victoria to marry him the previous day and asked him to be his best man. Another defeat followed, 1–0 to Leicester. Injuries to key players were starting to take their toll.

From 18 February until 19 March, United had a total of nine games to play, six away from home. David broke the deadlock at Aston Villa in the eighty-second minute with a superb individual goal, winning the ball in midfield, playing a one-two with Sheringham off the outside of his foot, dribbling round the defender and blasting the ball past Bosnich the Villa goalkeeper. He was so relieved that he dived into the crowd to celebrate, closely followed by the whole team. In the next match against Derby, which United also won 2–0, Ryan Giggs, who had been so important for United this season, tore his hamstring. The medical room was packed with casualties. A rather makeshift United side were knocked out of the FA Cup by Barnsley.

Ironically, it was to be the first leg of the Champions League quarter-finals away against AS Monaco which, with hindsight, effectively finished United's chances of holding any trophy at the end of May. The Monaco pitch is built on top of an underground car park and is bone dry and hard. The match ended 0–0, but the already tired United players completed the game with stiff legs, torn calf muscles and tight hamstrings. United's depleted squad could not cope, losing the crucial home game to their nearest challengers Arsenal. United were six points clear in the Premiership, but it was a false position, as Arsenal had three games in hand. Though David did his best to keep United in Europe, playing in central midfield when they faced Monaco in the return at Old Trafford, he was one of seven United players on the pitch that day with minor injuries, and they were eliminated from the competition. Peter Schmeichel, Ryan Giggs, Gary Pallister and of course Roy Keane did not even start. By the start of April the situation had eased, but by then it was too late. David scored United's equaliser against Newcastle, but the 1–1 draw meant the title race was over. In the last match of the season, the Leeds United fans taunted Beckham again. When he scored, all the United players ran over to celebrate in front of them.

It was a highly disappointing end to a season which had promised so much, though David had the biggest summer of his football career so far to look forward to. When the England squad was announced for the friendlies before the 1998 World Cup, from which the final twenty-two players were to be selected, he, Nicky Butt, Paul Scholes and Gary and Phil Neville were all included. He could not expect that the summer would end the way it did: being labelled a national disgrace, and with an unexpectedly early first step into fatherhood.

CHAPTER NINE

WILLIE MORGAN'S DAUGHTER, DAVID BECKHAM'S SON

I felt my blood run cold. Flicking through the paper I had come across a brief story about how Romeo, the Beckhams' youngest son, had begun crying when they were on board a plane. His older brother Brooklyn turned to comfort him with the words, 'Why are you crying? You mustn't cry, our dad is David Beckham.'

Most people would not bat an eyelid at this comment, thinking it was a very sweet child's observation. However, I knew what these words actually meant to Brooklyn, because this is exactly what I used to believe. I thought that I had been born into a special kind of life, a protective bubble. Everyone wanted to talk to my dad, wanted to meet him because he was just such a great person. There were always people surrounding him – press, photographers – and everybody idolised him and talked about him as if he was absolutely wonderful. As a child you absorb all of this as if it is the truth. You believe that your father is invincible, some kind of a god, an idol that excites near worship in complete strangers. You come to think that nothing can hurt you in this world because of your proximity to this fabulous individual whom everyone adores.

My father did not create this idea; it was a fantasy that my brother and myself invented based on the words and behaviour of other people. We grew up with it, and Dad never noticed because he was away so much. We internalised the unreality of the attention given to a celebrity, and I believe absolutely that Brooklyn and Romeo will do the same. I do not see how they can do otherwise. Both their parents are idolised to an enormous extent. The consequences will, I believe from my own family's experience, be some kind of emotional trauma. My brother was driven to try to take his own life, I starved myself to the point where my health was threatened, and we at least had one parent at home with us to provide an emotional centre. It does not matter how much money you have, or how well you are looked after. What you have in life cannot protect you from the negative effects of being a celebrity child. Their lives will be an emotional roller coaster, and the pressures that those boys will face in their own minds will be with them as long as they live.

Brooklyn and Romeo can never have a normal upbringing, no matter how hard David and Victoria strive to ensure it. Until recently they have eschewed the services of a nanny, hoping that grandparents and relatives will be able to provide the care that their busy lifestyles mean they cannot always be there to give, but this is not a substitute.

The bonuses of a celebrity lifestyle are many, but ultimately they do not compensate for the psychological scars it inflicts. There will be a defining moment in both boys' lives when Bubble Beckham bursts. This does not have to be a major incident. Something happens that forces you to face up to the fact that you will not be protected from hurt or difficulty all your life just because your dad is famous. And Victoria and David, just like my own father, will not realise this as they are so busy. The Beckhams will think that, because they have the money to send them to the right schools (as my parents did), take them on the best holidays that money can buy (again, as my parents did) and mix with the right people, their sons will be fine. But those things do not matter. They give an illusion of normality where none exists.

In a footballer's family, it seems inevitable that the boys suffer more because of the obvious comparisons that can be made between their own and their father's sporting ability. My brother Scott is even more forthright about the trauma of growing up in a famous family. He told me once that he considered it 'a horrible burden to carry, Gaynor, and one that I wouldn't wish on my worst enemy'. He wrote a letter to me setting out his thoughts, and I am going to quote from it at length here, because what he said is so compelling.

> I would like to try to get across how fickle people's perceptions can be. And really how hard it is to get ahead in life when someone you know and love is famous. I haven't always been the perfect son, and could not profess otherwise even though I have the most fantastic, loving and supportive mum and dad in the world and a family most people would die for.

It has been desperately hard for me as an individual to get on in life. I would have willingly given up all the material things we had to have the chance to grow up without being looked upon as the son of a famous footballer. In no way would I ever blame my parents for anything as they tried everything that was humanly possible to make my life as normal as they could. My parents have never put pressure on me to achieve anything, just wanting me to be happy. The problem lies with the expectations of other people.

I love playing sports, from tennis to football, but always I was expected to be better than everyone else because of my dad. I used to play for a local football team when I was about eight years old and, without being conceited, I was their star player, but as far as I was concerned I was just enjoying playing football, being part of the team and helping them to do well. As far as the rest of the boys were concerned, I was one of them. No one had made the connections between Scott and Willie Morgan. Then, one day, someone who did know that my dad played for Manchester United came along to watch the game, and shared this information, not realising the effect the news would have. There was an immediate and dramatic change of attitude, from the kids, their parents and the coaches. I was made an outcast. Suddenly I was not a little boy having a good time. I was no longer expected to be their best player, I was supposed to be superhuman, aged eight. If we lost a game it would be Morgan's fault, even though, as happened once, I scored all six of our goals. I was made to feel that I did not belong, and this was something that I have had to live with all my life. I could not cope. Three months later I left.

The best way I can think of to describe some people's attitude was that they wanted to see me fail. If you succeed, then it is not because of any merit of your own, but because everything has been gifted to you on a plate. Throughout school I was subjected to a level of bullying and harassment that was unbearable, from teachers as well as the other children. The ten years I spent at the same school were the hardest time of my life. There was not a single day where I was not reminded of the fact that my dad was famous. I was the butt of everyone's jokes and made to feel different, when all I wanted to be was anonymous and to fit in quietly.

I could write a book about the things I had to put up with at school, but one incident will suffice to illustrate what I went through. One day I was hit in the eye with a stick and the pain was excruciating. My eye was bleeding and I had splinters in it and would later require surgery to remove them. I begged to be allowed to go home, but instead I was locked in a room for three hours until the school bell went for the end of the day. The teacher simply would not listen to what I was saying about the pain I felt. Her response was on the lines of, 'Shut up, you spoiled little brat, you deserve what you get!' Thankfully the doctors were able to save my sight. I had two nervous breakdowns while at that school from the constant bullying and the physical punishments which the staff inflicted upon me.

Away from school the pressure was no less. I remember having a summer job to earn some money myself for the summer. It was stacking food on to trays for airlines. For two months I did the job happily, getting along well with the people I worked with. Then a boy I had been at school with arrived, told people who I was and as usual things changed. There was a rule that you weren't allowed to work in the freezers for longer than an hour, but I suddenly found myself on permanent freezer duty, for up to eight hours at a time. And I became frozen out in another sense, as no one would give me the time of day. My line manager actually kicked me when I asked why I had been consigned to the freezer. I was determined not to be forced out of the job, but the last straw came when one of the girls approached my dad when he came to pick me up one night and told him I had got her pregnant. I didn't even know who she was.

My suicide attempt came in my mid-twenties because I had made a successful career for myself, but I was falsely accused of having achieved that success by drug dealing. When things began to go wrong it all became too much. I tried to end my own life as the only way out, but I also know umpteen people who have a famous parent who have been in prison or are still there, having reacted to the pressure in a very different way.

I find Scott's words very distressing. I knew a little of what he was experiencing, but never realised how close to utter despair it had brought him. In fact, Scott made two attempts on his life that I am aware of. The first time he slit his wrists, and I can still visualise clearly the whole scene that we discovered. As a family we tried to work through it all to find out why he had become so desperate. The second time there was no one there. He connected the ignition pipe of the car to a hose, and the only reason he is still alive today is that a passer-by noticed the pipe, thought something was amiss and opened the car door and dragged him out. The memory is still very vivid of the phone call that my father took in the middle of the night, telling him that Scott had tried to kill himself.

The child of a famous person often feels threatened, whether it is the threat of being ignored as a person in his or her own right, or the threat of physical danger. In the Christmas 2003 ITV documentary, *The Real Beckhams*. Brooklyn could be heard crying as the Beckhams' car was mobbed on the way out of the Bernabeu stadium and fans banged on the windows. David was very calm, reassuring him, 'They can't get in the car, Buster.'

People can lose all sense of what they are doing in their anxiety to get to the famous. One family day trip to the ice rink near our home became a nightmare for Scott and myself. Dad decided to take us for some lunch before we went on the ice. No sooner had we sat down at a table when a man called loudly to his friend, 'Look, there's Willie Morgan!' Suddenly the place seemed to erupt. I was too frightened to take in much of what happened next, but a crowd descended upon us and began to climb over Scott and me to reach my dad. He did not know how to react at first, and was bemused by the level of attention. I was stamped on and crouched on the floor, covering my head with my hands in a vain attempt to protect myself. Luckily the staff retrieved us from the crush of bodies and escorted us to our car, shaken and bruised. I suspect the people who behaved in such an idiotic manner, with no regard for the safety of two small children, would not be able to explain why they reacted so excessively to the sight of someone famous. A kind of herd mentality seems to take over.

David has always tried to give Brooklyn a taste of 'normal life'. He often used to bring him to the David Lloyd centre when he was in Cheshire, maybe sometimes as often as three times a week. Usually he drove his son there in the Ferrari with a see-through engine, which he would park in the ambulance bay. David would always take Brooklyn through the main doors into the lounge, just the same as any other visitor. By contrast, if Victoria came there she would go by a route that avoided the possibility of contact with the public, up a flight of stairs to a walkway. David would sign autographs if he was asked, but if anyone met Victoria she would refuse. David would bring Brooklyn in and sit him on the reception counter and talk to the receptionists. Upstairs there is a large landing between the beauty salon and the changing rooms, and David would play there happily with Brooklyn, rolling a tennis ball or a football patiently at him so that he could try and kick it back. The message he seemed to be trying to get over to his young son is that he could be around ordinary people if he wished, and there was nothing to worry about.

However, ever since Brooklyn was born in the Portland Hospital in London on 4 March 1999, he has been subject to intense media and public interest which shows no sign of waning. As I write this chapter, Brooklyn has just celebrated his fifth birthday, and over the previous few weeks there has been a plethora of stories about him and, to a lesser extent, his little brother Romeo, in the press. In the *Daily Mail*, Victoria's least favourite newspaper, for which she has become something of a hate figure, Brooklyn's celebrations prompted an article which spelled out the heavy cost of being Posh and Becks' son: 'A £10,000 birthday, 24-hour bodyguards, a nanny she vowed he'd never have, and a hero dad he seldom sees ... the price of being Posh's pampered prince.' According to the article by Geoffrey Wansell, Brooklyn has never enrolled at the English-speaking Runnymede College close to where the Beckhams have rented a mansion in Madrid, but is being educated in Hertfordshire. Victoria defended this decision recently as being taken because 'I couldn't send him somewhere where he wouldn't fit in. People recognise him, and I want him to go to a small school where he isn't going to feel he's Brooklyn Beckham.' As Scott's experience shows, that is a vain hope. He will always be Brooklyn Beckham, and sooner or later he will find out that people's response to his name will not always be positive.

David has, as he told me, high hopes that Brooklyn will follow him into a career in professional football. Victoria would prefer him to become a golfer, because she recognises the pressures that trying to live up to David will put upon him. The little boy has already shown signs of having inherited some of his father's sporting abilities. When he took his first few steps he kicked a teddy across the floor. He has excellent balance and strikes a ball well for his age. It has been reported that Brooklyn has been playing football in a scheme at White Hart Lane, where David also trained for a time. But will he ever be allowed to step out of the shadow of his father's footballing fame? Once he reached a certain age Scott could not play football any more, even for enjoyment. Jordi Cruyff, the son of the great Dutch player Johan, who joined United in 1997, apparently asked for the name on the back of his shirt to be changed from 'Cruyff' which had been added automatically when he signed, to Jordi, so that there would not be an instant association with his father.

I once met David when he was in the Trafford Centre shopping with Brooklyn, but there was a jarring note to what should have been a happy family scene. Brooklyn was being swung in the air, but one of the people holding his hands and swinging him backwards and forwards was a minder. Brooklyn has not just been the centre of attention since he was born; he has also been targeted in more sinister ways that required the Beckhams to engage twenty-four-hour security protection for their sons. There have been accusations that they are paranoid about the threat to the boys, even that they have deliberately exaggerated it for their own purposes. I think that any parent will refute that suggestion. Neither David nor

Victoria can afford to accept even the slightest risk of danger for their children. Any celebrity's child can recall a number of times when their family was threatened in some way. I certainly can.

The first time I remember anything really sinister happening was when I was about eleven years old. I came home from school and noticed that our golden Labrador, Magill, whom we'd had since he was a pup, failed to come pounding up the garden path to lick my face as usual. It was almost as if he liked to see me safely inside the garden gate. I let myself into the house and headed straight for the kitchen. Magill's basket, which took up the whole corner, was empty. Mum was sitting at the kitchen table with her head in her hands. A crumpled piece of paper lay in front of her. It was a ransom note. Magill had been snatched from the garden, and a scrawled message left that if we wanted to see him again we would have to pay a ransom. Mum and Dad called the police, but our pet was never returned. I cried myself to sleep, wondering what had happened to him and how frightened he must have been. For my parents the ordeal must have been far worse. The family had lost a beloved pet, but what if one of their children had fallen prey to kidnappers?

If they had known what happened to me not long afterwards, I don't know what the consequences would have been. My horse, Jackson, was stabled on a farm at nearby Dunham Massey, and every morning before school I would ride my bike over there, as well as at weekends, to groom him and muck his stall out. It was something I enjoyed doing, and the farm hands who worked there were very nice to me, as they were to all the children who came to the stables to ride or to care for the horses. One morning I had a flat tyre, so Dad offered to drive me. A couple of the farm workers saw Dad drop me off. They obviously recognised him, but that did not worry me. After that they began to change their attitude towards me. They were no longer friendly; indeed sometimes I thought they were quite aggressive.

Next Sunday I arrived early at the stables on my bike in my usual routine. I was approached by one of the men with a request to help him untangle a length of rope that was full of knots. I was anxious to be helpful and followed him to the coil of rope which I noticed had a loop on one end. Then all hell broke loose. Another man appeared out of nowhere and flung the loop of rope over my head and pulled it tight around my chest. I screamed, absolutely terrified by what was happening. I heard the noise of an engine being started. I threw my head around and couldn't believe what they were doing. They had tied the other end of the rope to a motorbike which they accelerated suddenly towards the farm gates, throwing me off my feet. They dragged me along the ground, laughing at my screams, enjoying my obvious terror. 'Enjoy the ride, you spoiled bitch,' they shouted.

I had my explanation for this unprovoked assault. They had seen my dad. The pair of them could not have cared less about my pain and fear. I have no idea how long this went on for, but it seemed as if they dragged me along the ground for miles. I was convinced that I was going to die, until the bike ground to a halt. I looked up and saw that they had come to a road and stopped the motorcycle to allow a car to pass. I pulled off the rope, lifted it over my head, and ran as fast as I could, sobbing bitterly. My attackers must have come to their senses, as they didn't try to follow. I walked and half ran the several miles back to the house. As I made my way to home and safety I had already decided that I was going to conceal this from my parents.

Just as Scott had covered up much of his suffering, I did the same. You might ask why I responded in this way, but children do sometimes make the choice that it is better to remain silent. I was worried that Dad might get himself into trouble once he found out. I knew that there would be an enormous amount of fuss about it, that the police would be called, that Mum would be distraught. Restrictions would be put on my movements, but most of all I would be alienated even more from those around me.

The Beckhams have already faced three major kidnap threats that have made the press. There are probably more that have never been made public and have been checked out in secret by the police. In the summer of 1999, when Brooklyn was about six months old, Victoria came back to the house in Sawbridgeworth from a screen test for a part in the film *Charlie's Angels* to discover that there had been a kidnap threat. The police felt that it might be a hoax, and the message had indeed come to the Beckhams in a very convoluted way. The threat was made from an untraceable mobile in a call to the shop in Manchester where David's friend Tim (the one who had been involved in the Emma Ryan affair) still worked. As he had Victoria's mother's number, he was able to contact the family to pass it on. According to Victoria, this convinced the couple that they needed their own in-house security rather than occasional police surveillance. A man who had chauffeured the Spice Girls gave Victoria a contact who recommended an ex-SAS man, Mark Niblett, who was prepared to offer twenty-four-hour protection. Niblett became a trusted employee, an important part of the Beckham lifestyle, booking hotels, flights and restaurant tables and even babysitting Brooklyn once or twice.

The danger to Brooklyn seemed to heighten when, in early September, Victoria was working on the third Spice Girls album and David was away with the England squad at the FA's training headquarters, Burnham Beeches. This was, on the surface, a far more serious threat, as the police themselves contacted Victoria, informing her that they had had a tip-off from what they felt was a reliable source that Brooklyn would be the subject of a kidnap attempt the next day and taken to a house in Hampstead. This could not have come at a worse time. It was the night before an England game, and normally wives were strongly discouraged from making contact with their husbands. However, Victoria called David, who went to the England manager Kevin Keegan for advice. Keegan, the England masseur Terry Byrne and David all drove to the Beckhams' Hertfordshire home in the early hours of the morning. Keegan was incredibly sympathetic, reassuring Victoria and telling her that he and his wife had received death threats while he was playing in Germany. Kevin took the whole family to Burnham Beeches and the Beckhams got about four hours' sleep, with Brooklyn in between them in the bed.

For the next nine months, as Victoria describes it, the family were in a state of virtual siege. The security system in the house was extensive, with panic buttons, a twelve-minute response to the alarm from Scotland Yard, and security cameras. Niblett advised the Beckhams that it was not even safe for their little son to go out into the garden to play. As she graphically described it, 'We all lived in this bubble of fear.' Later the Beckhams' suspicions were raised about Niblett's trustworthiness, tracing a number of leaks about their personal arrangements to their security men, and dispensed with his services, taking him to court to retrieve tapes and personal papers which he had acquired.

The most contentious of the publicised threats to Brooklyn happened in December 1999. In July, David had been caught speeding in Alderley Edge, and was due to come before the magistrates for the offence. As he already had ten points on his driving licence, there was a very strong possibility that he would receive a ban from driving. Given his lifestyle, this would be very inconvenient to say the least. David's defence was that he was avoiding an unidentified photographer who had been following him for ten miles in an intimidatory manner. The pursuit, he alleged, had almost caused a serious accident as the photographer swerved to overtake David's Ferrari while still taking pictures. The magistrates, however, based on police testimony that they had no evidence of such a pursuit, banned him from driving for eight months and fined him £800.

Beckham immediately appealed. Two days before his appeal was due to be heard, there was an incident outside the top London store Harrods, where the Beckhams had been Christmas shopping, which garnered a great deal of public sympathy, as well as illustrating that the family did face real threats to their safety. As the Beckhams left the store and pushed their way through the waiting crowd of photographers, according to the *Sun* the following day,

Victoria had knocked down an individual who had tried to snatch her son from David's arms.

There has been much cynicism about whether this was genuinely an attempt to grab Brooklyn. Andrew Morton, author of the bestselling *Posh & Becks*, expressed his doubts, citing the facts that the incident was not captured either on the Harrods CCTV cameras or by the waiting photographers. Ned Kelly, who was in court with David as his case was heard, is far more uncompromising in his opinions. At the 1999 players' New Year's Party, he had spoken to Mark Niblett about the kidnap attempt. He said that nothing had happened. Kelly believes that Niblett served the Beckhams well and accepts his version. David certainly used the story of the kidnapping at his appeal hearing, when the judge overturned the earlier verdict.

Whatever we may think of the reliability of the witnesses, it may very well be that Victoria and David did believe that there was a threat to Brooklyn. Given that they routinely have to protect their children from dangerous melees wherever they go, as parents they have the responsibility to decide when and if their offspring are under threat. What might seem nothing to an outside observer may seem very different to those at the heart of the crush, who only have a split second to interpret the level of danger and take action.

On 3 November 2002, the *News of the World* carried a sensational exclusive story headlined IF BECKHAM DON'T PAY UP, SHE DIES: POSH KIDNAP. It revealed the greatest threat to the Beckham family yet. The plot, formulated by an 'Eastern bloc crime syndicate' was to ambush Victoria's car as it pulled out of the drive of her London home and sedate everyone inside with a 'chloroform-type spray ...

brought in from Italy'. The gang was, according to the report, incredibly well organised, and the plan had such a level of detail and planning, as well as recruitment and funding, that it was a world away from 'the usual loose criminal fraternity talk of kidnapping a celebrity'. Victoria and, the gang hoped, three-year-old Brooklyn and two-month-old Romeo would be transferred to another car by the nine-man abduction team and driven to a house in Brixton, south London, where a 'reinforced room' had been prepared for them. A staggering £5 million would be demanded in ransom.

Details were given of the various meetings the undercover reporters, who were supposed to be providing a getaway driver and also pretended to be interested in buying stolen goods from Sotheby's auction house, had attended. One of the gang took out his 8mm handgun and showed it off. At another meeting the men bickered over whether it would be better to go for a smaller sum in ransom as it was more likely to be paid. Another of the gangsters added chillingly, 'If the kids are with her, it's even better. We ask David Beckham for £5 million. It's one hundred per cent he pays. But if something happens and he don't pay, Victoria is going to die.'

Victoria and David were informed of the plot, and the police brought in. On 2 November, armed police surrounded the gang which had been lured to the car park of the Ibis Hotel in London's Docklands on the pretext of selling some of their stolen art treasures. The *News of the World* reporters described graphically how, after a pre-arranged signal had been given, two dozen officers from Scotland Yard's elite SO19 firearms team leaped out of a white van screaming, 'Armed police, get on the floor.'

Detective Inspector Ian Horrocks, of Scotland Yard's kidnap and specialist investigations unit, thanked the paper with the words, 'You've done a fantastic job and taken on dangerous criminals. We're extremely grateful for your information.'

Victoria expressed equal gratitude. She told the paper, 'I'm stunned by what has happened today. It's clear these people were serious and that has, of course, scared the life out of me. It's terrifying to think that someone would want to do that to you and your children. I'm in absolute and total shock.' David, about to play in a match against Southampton, later made a statement in which he said that he and Victoria would be reviewing security arrangements at their homes in Hertfordshire and Cheshire. 'The first role of a father and husband is to keep his family safe.' Manchester United added that it was 'very concerned', but that its security arrangements were 'under constant review'.

Almost immediately, however, other sections of the press began to express concern that the alleged gang members would not receive a fair trial, and that their pictures had already been printed in the paper. The revelation of the plot was perhaps the most dramatic in a string of such scoops from Mazher Mahmood, whom the *Guardian* labelled 'the King of Sting'. He had posed as the 'fake sheikh' to whom the Countess of Wessex had made remarks about her PR firm's royal connections. She was later forced to resign. Mazher claimed that his exposés had led to 119 convictions. However, the Beckham kidnap case did not add to that number. Though the plotters were brought to court, a judge threw out the case in June 2003 after ruling that one of the main witnesses, Florian Gashi, described as a 'Kosovan parking attendant with criminal convictions for dishonesty' was an unreliable witness. But the *News of the World* was also exonerated from acting improperly in the case by paying £10,000 for the initial details.

None of this would have spared the Beckhams the hours of worry and anxiety they faced. As David said, his first duty was to protect his family in the best way he could. Celebrity assassination is a reality, as the killing of the newsreader Jill Dando showed.

One of the ways in which celebrity children find it hard to cope in the real world is in their friendships and personal relationships with the other sex. I was fortunate in my friends, but I did learn to censor my conversations. Even though I attended a private school, Loreto Convent Grammar School, a traditional Roman Catholic establishment that has become popular with the well-to-do Cheshire set, I learned that it was not a good idea to tell people that, for example, Sean Connery's son Jason was staying as a guest. When it came to boyfriends I found it impossible to work out who was genuinely interested in knowing me, or which of my suitors were more interested in Dad's fame and his money. I was too trusting and, as I'll readily admit, a very bad judge of character. I had no idea the dangers that my position might lead me into.

I met a young man whose family ran a hotel, and he invited a few friends and me over on Christmas Day for drinks in the evening when it would be closed. I went along with a male and a female friend I had known for a while through tennis. The evening was very enjoyable, and my boyfriend kept supplying the drinks. I must have passed out, at least I could not remember anything the next day – apart from vague memories of trying to wake up, being unable to move and having a strange light in my face. The next morning I came round, feeling absolutely terrible. I was in one of the hotel rooms with my two friends, with no idea how I got there, and there was no one else anywhere to be found in the hotel. It was a very weird scene.

A few days later I still had not heard from my boyfriend. Then a letter arrived in the post. I recognised the handwriting, and as I tore the envelope open a photograph fell out. It was a picture of myself and my two friends, completely naked on a bed, comatose. There was a note which said that this was one of many, and unless I paid a huge amount of money for the pictures he would post one a week to my dad. Looking back, this was all pretty amateurish, an obvious set-up. However, in my inexperience I panicked, desperately trying to think where I could get the money in order to keep this from my parents. Eventually, I opened my heart to another one of my male friends, hoping that he would be able to help me. My friend was furious and he told me to leave it with him. The next day he brought me the photographs and the negatives and said that I should forget all about it. 'Don't ask any questions, Gaynor,' he told me. 'No one was hurt and you have all the photographs to destroy.' That was the end of the matter in terms of the crude attempt at blackmail, but its impact on my self-esteem was shattering.

I now wondered if every boy I met was going to try to abuse my trust. Were they really interested in me, or did they see me as an easy route to my family's wealth? When

I did meet boys whom I thought could be genuinely interested in me, they were often overwhelmed at meeting my dad, and were nervous and tongue-tied in his presence. Others seemed jealous of Dad and his celebrity status, and resented the fact that as a family we have famous friends. Brooklyn and Romeo, and any other Beckham children, will face this predicament even more because they have two famous parents, the intimate details of whose life is known to millions worldwide.

I did eventually meet someone who was different from the rest. When I was tennis coaching I met an intelligent, good-looking man called Andrew Grayson, who seemed to want me, rather than just Willie Morgan's daughter. We decided to marry and at first were very happy; after a couple of years we had a son, my pride and joy, Alex. In retrospect I can see that my five-year marriage to Andrew was doomed from the start, and that I married too young, trying to find a quick solution to my insecurities. Our relationship gradually fell apart, a victim of the gulf between us which was caused by my close relationship with my family and Andrew's difficulties in dealing with the pressures which Dad's fame imposed upon it. I have the suspicion that he resented my dad's celebrity and the way that he succeeded in sport. It is a difficult act for any man to follow.

After our marriage broke up, I tended to date celebrities – professional footballers, sportsmen or actors. It was much easier: I understood why they might not be able to see me when they were training, or why they were always checking for photographers and press and might ask me to leave separately. I knew that I might have to wait while they signed autographs, or that people might interrupt us during a drink or a meal and monopolise their attention. For a time I went out with the actor Simon Gregson, known to millions of *Coronation Street* fans as Steve McDonald. Our relationship made the headlines in the national press, but I accepted this as part of the lifestyle. My upbringing in a celebrity household had prepared me for it. But it was never going to be a long-term, serious relationship, and I confess that I did enjoy a dalliance with another Corrie star, Johnny Wrather who played Joe Carter, whom I met at the Howard Keel Golf Classic in 2002. The confusion between fiction and reality in a celebrity's lifestyle is neatly demonstrated by the fact that, at one time, Johnny and Simon's characters were also involved in a love triangle in the soap.

This lies in the future for Brooklyn and Romeo. Brooklyn's inseparable companion is Victoria's sister Louise's little girl Liberty, who is older than Brooklyn, and has been his playmate since his earliest months. Louise and 'Bibby' often accompany the Beckhams on their holidays, and Victoria has bought a home for Louise close by her own in Hertfordshire. The Beckhams have also reportedly employed a governess for Brooklyn to educate him when he is taken out of school to stay with his father in Spain.

Perhaps the last word on this subject should go to my father, who has experienced the problems of being a man in the spotlight who was often away from home, and trying to bring up two children at the same time. As I was talking about our upbringing, he said to me, 'It is only with hindsight that I understand the impact that our life had on my children. I had no conceivable idea that either you or Scott would suffer because I was playing football.

I know it will be the same for David and his wife, no matter how much they try to protect the boys. Other people will create problems for their children. People will give them plenty of advice about what to do, but the biggest danger is that you cannot see what is happening. You just can't see that you are doing anything wrong.'

CHAPTER TEN

LIONHEART

I could hardly get into the Braz. It was completely packed with people celebrating. I walked up to the VIP area. I noticed that one of the bouncers was positioned there, and immediately recognised whom he was protecting. David Beckham normally shines, but this night he positively glowed. His elation was clear to see. I was with my boyfriend Darren Proctor, then a DJ on Key 103, one of Manchester's top independent radio stations, and also Dr Fox's stand-in on his Radio 1 show. In March 2004 he made the move to one of the hottest new radio stations in Manchester, Century FM. We hadn't been going out long and, although we have remained the best of friends, our relationship was not to last. When David saw me coming up the stairs his face broke into a beautiful, gleaming smile and he waved me over as Darren went off to get our drinks.

'Gaynor, how are you doing?' were his first words.

'Absolutely fine, David,' I replied. 'No need to ask how you're feeling!'

After all, he had just scored the goal which meant that England had qualified for the 2002 World Cup. In fact, he had virtually dragged the team into the competition finals, in a second-half performance of such drive and energy that Glenn Hoddle later described him as 'playing in the positions of three men, all over the pitch'. All seemed lost when the Greeks scored first at Old Trafford, and England were sluggish, unable to play with any fluency. Then David took control. The England equaliser came from a Beckham free kick on to the head of Teddy Sheringham, but the Greeks immediately plunged the crowd into despair as they took the lead again. In the dying minutes of the match, Teddy won another free kick, and the stadium fell silent as David waited for the whistle. The kick swirled and bent, flying into the net. Sky's commentator Martin Tyler summed up his performance brilliantly. 'David Beckham has done it, big time! He said he wasn't a natural leader. Well, David, we all disagree with you now. You are our Captain Fantastic!'

David grinned again. Then he asked me what he really wanted to know. 'Did your dad watch the match? What did he think?'

I'm afraid I had to disappoint England's hero on this one. 'David, Dad is Scottish. Of course he didn't watch the match. He made a big point of going to mow the lawn while it was on!'

David burst out laughing. So there was at least one person in England who wasn't glued to the box that night. He tried again. 'So what did you think?' Another big smile.

'Erm, sorry, David, but I haven't seen the game either.

I'm waiting to go home and watch it on tape! I was booked to go to a charity function and didn't want to let people down.' I was wearing a low-cut, very formal ball dress, so I think he'd worked this out already. He laughed again. He was just about to add another comment when he was completely surrounded by adoring fans. While I'd been talking to him, people kept trying to pull him away, tugging at his arms and T-shirt. Normally the bouncer would have stopped this contact, but David had obviously given instructions that for this night only it was all right if people wanted to get up close to him to express their joy at the result and his own fantastic performance.

Later on that evening, Darren asked me if I would introduce him to David. I can't deny that it was almost out of a sense of mischief that I agreed. I walked over. 'David,' I said with an enigmatic smile, 'I'm here with my *boyfriend*, Darren. He works at Key 103.' He looked at me with one eyebrow raised. 'You know, the radio station.'

David nodded slowly. 'Yeah, I know.'

'He'd *love* to meet you, David,' I said.

Again he nodded slowly, and without taking his eyes off mine he said, 'OK, Gaynor. Bring him over.'

'Actually,' I replied, 'he's just here!' Darren stepped out from behind me. 'David, Darren. Darren, David. I'll leave you to it.' And off I walked. They chatted for about five minutes before Darren came back completely buzzing. I looked over at David and smiled, as if to say, Thank you, you've made his day. He inclined his head politely.

Not anyone can just walk up to David Beckham and have a conversation, but people had seen me talking to him that night and realised that it was something I could do. Almost inevitably, a tall, model-type girl came up to me and said in her squeaky little voice, 'Could you introduce me to David Beckham?' I looked her up and down. She was very attractive, with the longest legs you've ever seen. Normally I wouldn't even have entertained the idea of making the introduction, but on this occasion I thought to myself, Well, you made me feel uncomfortable last time we met. Maybe I'll have a little fun at your expense this time!

'Of course!' I exclaimed, taking her by the arm. 'Sure! No problem! Come with me!' I walked her over to where David was sitting. 'This is Mickey,' I said to him. 'She's *dying* to meet you. I *know* you won't mind. David, Mickey. Mickey, David.' I looked at him, winked and walked off.

His face said it all: I'm going to kill you. I'm absolutely going to kill you. I'm not going to ignore her, because you brought her over, but at the same time – I'm going to *kill* you! The girl stayed for about thirty seconds – she couldn't think of anything to say. David just about gave her the time of day, but no more. She toddled off and I didn't see her again.

Once more, the frisson was there. I had to be careful because I was with Darren, and I couldn't put myself in a situation where David and I were exchanging too many meaningful glances across a crowded room, but it was clear to me that that was the night David decided that something was going to happen between us. I'm David Beckham, I imagine he thought to himself. I've made it obvious that I want something to happen with this girl, she has just walked in with a guy who is supposed to be her boyfriend, and she's just introduced me to a tall blonde. What the hell is going on? This *is* going to happen.

The endgame was approaching.

David Beckham's growing reputation as one of the best footballers in the world has been built not just on his play for Manchester United, but primarily on his performances in an England shirt. His participation in the national side has brought him perhaps his greatest personal satisfaction – and an OBE, which he received from the Queen in 2003. But it has also exposed him to some of the worst abuse that a footballer has ever had to suffer. His England career has been a roller-coaster ride. It has even been suggested that his superlative performances for England were another factor in his departure from Old Trafford. Some critics have said that he never put in the same effort for his club as he did for his country.

David has been an England regular since his call-up to the national team in 1996. Apart from one particular, and very controversial, decision by Glenn Hoddle to leave him out of the first two games of the World Cup against Tunisia and Romania in 1998, he has been an automatic choice in the four major England international campaigns between 1996 and 2004. More than that, he has become England's talisman, the man upon whom the success of the side depends.

My father played for Scotland in one World Cup, in West Germany, and rates it as the greatest experience of his career. Like David, he knows what it was like to play a major part in a crucial qualifying game. In September 1973, in front of a staggering crowd of 100,000 fans at Hampden Park, he made the second and winning goal in a 2–1 win over Czechoslovakia. The *Daily Record* encapsulated the joy which swept Scotland as the winner was scored: 'Audacious Willie Morgan got the ball out on the right and with a diving header that will be remembered for all time, tall Joe Jordan [who also later played for Manchester United] hurled himself at the ball to give us the goal which will take us to Germany.' Scottish celebrations were made all the sweeter because England was knocked out of the competition by Poland.

Tommy Docherty was the manager who deserves the praise for taking the Scots through the qualifying rounds to West Germany in 1974. He had the vision to overcome the prejudice against 'Anglos', Scots players who were based in England, and they dominated his squad. The Doc could not continue as Scotland manager when he took over at Manchester United. Willie Ormond replaced him, and changed the team dramatically, but Dad was one of only three players who survived in the relatively young new squad. However, he was omitted from Scotland's first match in the finals against Zaire. This was a grave error and probably the reason why Scotland did not go on to the second stage. They won the match 2–0, but the group was eventually decided on goal difference and Scotland had needed more goals in this game to progress. Wingers could have exploited Zaire's obvious problems in dealing with crosses into the box. Yugoslavia didn't make the same mistake, and scored a record nine goals in their match against the African team.

Dad thinks this was one of the best Scottish international sides ever. They were eliminated even though they were unbeaten, becoming the first country ever to suffer that fate. The next two matches were hard-fought draws against Yugoslavia and Brazil, but it was not enough to go through. The team was given a hero's reception when it arrived back in Scotland in recognition of what it had achieved.

David's debut for his country came when England's international fortunes were undergoing a revival. Under Terry Venables, England had automatically qualified for Euro 96 as the host nation, and had done exceptionally well. When Venables resigned at the end of the tournament, Glenn Hoddle gave up his job at Chelsea to become England's youngest-ever manager at thirty-eight, and he awarded Beckham his England call-up. He said he had spotted David's potential at an early stage, even though the papers thought that David's sensational goal from the halfway line at Wimbledon had given him a hint he could not ignore. 'I came across David a couple of years ago when I took Chelsea to Old Trafford, and I earmarked him down as a great talent even then.' David's debut was on 1 September 1996 in a World Cup 98 qualifier against Moldova in Kishinev. His performance was considered promising, rather than spectacular. As Henry Winter of the *Telegraph* put it, 'David Beckham settled in quietly, showing occasional touches of real quality, and will clearly feature regularly in Hoddle's squads.'

Not everyone was thrilled by David's call-up. Alex Ferguson thought that he could handle it, but warned that 'David is very young and there is a long way to go yet.' But he played in every qualifier in the campaign, making a goal for Alan Shearer against Poland in October with a glorious diagonal pass on to the striker's head. Hoddle had a dream start to his new job. Except for a defeat against Italy, which was no disgrace, England won all their first-round games. Despite this success, there was much agitation in the press for David Beckham to be moved into central midfield, a debate which still rages about where he can be most effective. Hoddle took the opportunity of a very prestigious friendly tournament, the Tournoi de France, which featured Italy and Brazil as well as the host nation, to try David out in what many thought would be his best role. Hoddle was about to usher in what became known as his 'revolution', an influx of young, fresh blood, primarily from Manchester United, and David, Gary and Phil Neville, Nicky Butt and Paul Scholes, as well as Andy Cole, went out to France. Alex Ferguson was faced with the sight of six of his first-teamers having their rest period in the closed season seriously curtailed, and he was not happy.

During this tournament the Manchester United men shone, particularly Paul Scholes in the first game against Italy, with Becks alongside him in central midfield. David was booked in this match, and again against France, thereby missing the final encounter against Brazil. Hoddle ticked him off in public for his response to his yellow card. 'Beckham needs to understand that when he has been booked, whether he agrees or not, he cannot afford to stand there arguing.' Despite losing to the Brazilians by a single goal, England won Le Tournoi, and David posed proudly with his winners' medal. Following the summer break, Hoddle further experimented with David's position, playing him as a right-wing back against Moldova at Wembley, where he created a goal for Scholes, and in the heroic 0–0 draw against Italy in Rome which saw England go through to the World Cup finals as winners of their group. He never solved the Beckham conundrum: wingers spend most of a match isolated on the flanks and find it impossible to dictate play as David, and many analysts, thought he should. But in central midfield, David's swerving, accurate crosses from the wing could not be exploited.

When the World Cup squad was named in 1998, Nicky Butt, Phil Neville and Andy Cole were all deeply upset by their omission. David, Gary Neville and Teddy Sheringham had made the team. Hoddle's selection caused considerable controversy: Paul Gascoigne was inconsolable and reportedly wrecked his hotel room. Hoddle's decisions during the tournament were also to attract enormous criticism, none more so than David's omission (in an echo of my father's World Cup) from the first game of the finals against Tunisia, an easy 2–0 victory, and also from the starting line-up for the Romania match which England lost 2–1. Hoddle justified leaving David out by claiming that he sensed that Beckham had 'lost focus', a statement which he has since often repeated, but never fully explained. Pictures of David sporting a sarong on his pre-tournament holiday had been splashed all over the tabloids in June, but otherwise his preparations had been immaculate. David was asked to attend the press conference which followed the defeat, and he could not hide his disappointment. 'You never really get over something like that because I am the sort of person who wants to play in every game. I was desperate to play in that game, even the last five minutes, just to get on. But it's up to the manager.' Alex Ferguson exploded after witnessing the conference, claiming that a 'distraught' Beckham had been thrown to the 'jackals' of the press, more ammunition for his belief that an England call-up was not beneficial either for his young stars or Manchester United.

In the next game, David answered Hoddle's doubts by scoring a magnificent free kick in the 2–0 win against Colombia, a wicked curling ball which tucked inside the post. It was later chosen as one of the best goals of the tournament. David was particularly fired up during the game. He seemed, as he always does when he pulls on the England shirt, to be trying to win the World Cup on his own, but his efforts had a manic edge. All was now set up for the match against England's old rivals Argentina in the second round. Everyone knows what happened to David in this game. He was sent off for an innocuous retaliation against a bad challenge from the Argentine captain, Diego Simeone, a mere flick of a boot which did no harm. The match was drawn 2–2, and England were knocked out of the tournament on penalties.

The press reaction was unprecedented. David was universally held responsible for his country's exit. This was the beginning of a hate campaign which was to last nearly a year, whipped up to ridiculous levels, and involving crude death threats and constant abuse at away matches. With hindsight, most observers would agree that David did not deserve to be sent off. Even a Scotsman like Dad was furious with the referee, shouting, 'No way, no way!' as the red card was shown. It is particularly ironic when you consider some of the incidents which weren't punished. Holland's Dennis Bergkamp walked on Yugoslavia's Aleksander Mihailovic. Zinedine Zidane, France's captain, also received a red card for raking a Saudi player with his studs, an offence which hardly bears comparison with David's. Dad also points out that it wasn't David who missed a penalty in the shoot-out, and that England still had as much chance as Argentina of going through when that test of nerve began.

What is significant is that the abuse directed against Beckham had already begun long before he was sent off. The clutch of United players called up for the national side were roundly jeered at internationals in the 1997–8 season. 'Stand up if you hate Man U' and 'We only hate United' were directed against them as they were playing their hearts out for their country, usually by fans of southern clubs (or so we believe in Manchester!) who had very few players in their first team eligible to play for England.

The ludicrously exaggerated abuse following the World Cup did have one big bonus for David. Though he had a relatively quiet and certainly disappointing season with United in 1997–8, Manchester United's fans took him to their hearts after his experiences in the 1998 World Cup. Some United supporters have a very ambiguous attitude towards the English national team. To start with, many are not English. But in recent times there has been a debate which is usually described as 'club versus country'. As the most successful club side in England with, since 1995, a relatively large number of English-born players in its team, United has had to try to satisfy the need to have its strongest team available for domestic competitions, as well as responding to frequent England call-ups for its stars. David Beckham was welcomed back to Old Trafford as a hero and, as the fans had done for Eric Cantona during his time of trial, they sang his name at every opportunity.

During the 1998–9 season, David's goal tally was lower than his three previous totals: he was fifth in the table of United's goal scorers with nine, six in the Premiership.

The top two, Dwight Yorke and Andy Cole, shared fifty-three goals between them. One of the more important and spectacular Beckham goals came from a perfect free kick which briefly gave United the lead against Barcelona in the Champions League in September, though the match finished 3–3. The club's official review describes this game as one of David's 'most compelling performances'. But, if David was not scoring goals, he was making them for United's highly potent strike force. For the first goal, he took the ball on the right from Yorke, feinted to go inside Barcelona's Sergi, but fooled the left back by cutting to the outside. Still running, he put in an early cross with pace and swerve towards Giggs at the back post. Ryan then leaped high above his marker to power his header across the goal past the Barcelona keeper. On twenty-five minutes, Beckham found Yorke whose overhead kick rebounded off the Barcelona defence for Scholes to crash home.

United's Premiership season had its customary slow start, with three consecutive draws. David saved the first match against Leicester City when Sheringham touched his shot past the keeper for the first goal, and he scored with another fabulous free kick three minutes into stoppage time. But by January the team was back at the top of the table, and in February 1999 David orchestrated an 8–1 demolition of Nottingham Forest, four of the goals coming from substitute Ole Gunnar Solskjaer in the last ten minutes. In the crucial matches which gave United their historic treble, Beckham's assists and goals were vital, the midfielder scoring the first goal against Arsenal in the pulsating FA Cup semi-final replay and the equaliser against Tottenham when United won the

Premiership on the last day of the season. Roy Keane headed in a Beckham corner to start the United fight back against Juventus in the second leg of the Champions League semi-final in the Stadio Delle Alpi in Turin. United had gone two goals down in the first ten minutes, and the match looked as if it was over before it had really begun. Finally, on a wonderful night in May in Barcelona, David took the two corners from which the goals came which won the Champions League so dramatically at the last gasp. The 'Beckham on the right or in central midfield' debate was further muddied by what happened in the final at the Nou Camp. Jesper Blomquist took Giggs's place on the left wing, Giggs switched to the left and David was in central midfield. The impact of his crossing was effectively nullified, and United suffered; only towards the end of the game was he sent wide and began to assert his influence.

Qualification for the 2000 European Championships, to be held jointly in Belgium and Holland, began in October 1998, but without David who was serving the suspension from his World Cup sending-off. By the time he resumed his England duties, two poor results had demonstrated how much he was missed, which was some help as he faced the ordeal of returning to the England ranks. England lost 2–1 to Sweden, and drew 0–0 with Bulgaria in the opening games of group five. In the latter tie, the Beckham-less team was booed off the pitch. Once he began to lose matches, Hoddle also began to lose the respect of the press, who pilloried his eccentricities, including the inclusion of his personal guru, faith healer Eileen Drewery, into the support team for the players, and the publication of his indiscreet World Cup diaries. In an interesting twist, Alex Ferguson was being widely tipped to be Hoddle's successor.

David's reintroduction to the England team altered its fortunes, though the 3–0 defeat of Luxembourg's team, with its large proportion of part-timers, did not give much grounds for optimism. By the time he played his next Euro 2000 qualifier, Hoddle had been forced to resign and Howard Wilkinson had taken over temporarily until the new manager, the emotional and mercurial Kevin Keegan, took over, appointed initially for only four games, as he did not want to leave his job at Fulham. David and Victoria instantly warmed to Kevin, finding him approachable and supportive where Hoddle had been enigmatic and aloof. Keegan's arrival galvanised the team. They beat Poland 3–1 at Wembley on 27 March 1999, all three of England's goals scored by Paul Scholes. David gave credit to Keegan, describing how his enthusiasm had lifted everyone. 'He inspired you about what you could do as an England player.'

Keegan, in an effort to solve the problem of where to play David to best advantage, adopted a compromise. The England midfield would use a diamond formation, and Beckham would play 'inside and out', going wide on the right, but also tucking back in to bolster the midfield when necessary. Unfortunately, when this strategy was first employed, against Sweden in June, David looked confused by this role. Hakan Mild, the Swedish defender, commented after the disappointing 0–0 draw, 'Beckham is a very good player, but he is not a player who dribbles effectively and we blocked him out.' David played most of the match closely marked by two Swedes, Pontus Kaamark and Arsenal's Freddie Ljungberg, a tribute to the danger he posed for his opponents. The result effectively ended England's chances of automatic qualification and the team was now dependent upon a 'back door' route into the finals via a play-off. Four days later, looking fatigued after a long, hard season, the weary England men could only manage a 1–1 draw against a Bulgarian team which, according to one reporter, was full of old-timers with spreading waistlines.

In September 1999, revived by the summer break, England romped to a 6–0 win over Luxembourg. David was in central midfield to accommodate Newcastle's pacy wing back Kieron Dyer on the right, and played a part in setting up three of the goals, despite the fact that the night before the drama of the kidnap threat to Brooklyn meant that he managed only four hours' sleep. Kevin Keegan, whose support had meant everything to the couple, offered to allow David the choice of staying in England to protect his family, rather than flying out to Poland for the next key game. David was determined not to let Keegan down and took part in the dismal 0–0 draw, which left England's chances of progressing on a knife edge. Agonisingly, the nation and the players had to wait for two months before Sweden's victory against Poland set up a play-off with Scotland.

Allegiances in the Morgan family were divided when the teams met on 13 November for the first leg. David was jeered by the Scots crowd from the outset; this wasn't anything to do with his sending off in France – the whole of Scotland was very grateful to him for playing a part in England's World Cup exit – but more a twisted compliment to the man they feared most. The two goals came courtesy of Manchester United players. Paul Scholes scored both, heading the second in at the near post from a fast curling cross from David. Though England, to the delight of my father, lost the second leg 1–0, his hopes were dashed as they went through on the aggregate score over the two games. Qualification was now assured for the Euro 2000 finals in June.

There was little optimism about England's chances in the tournament, given the way that they had scraped through so far. Kevin Keegan has always been criticised for his tactical naivety as a manager and, even though he had been persuaded to give up his job at Fulham and assume the England managership full time, it did not protect him from the savaging in the press that all recent England managers have experienced. David and Manchester United's season had been successful but, as ever where United were involved, controversial. The team had lifted another Premiership trophy, but David had also had his dispute with Alex Ferguson about missing training to care for Brooklyn.

England's critics looked as if they would have to eat their words when the team raced into a two-goal lead against Portugal within seventeen minutes in their opening game in the group stage of the finals on 12 June in Eindhoven. Again, the first goal was scored by Scholes and made by David. Phil Neville played the ball down the left to Alan Shearer, who laid it back to him to cross over on to the right flank. David, with the vision to spot an opening that was a fast-developing part of his game, despatched a speedy, curving cross which found Paul Scholes's head and flew into the Portuguese net. Gary Neville started the move which led to the second goal with one of his long throws from the right (his sister

Tracey was an England netball international, so it runs in the family), which Michael Owen controlled and turned inside to Becks. He then landed a perfect cross on Steve McManaman's head which even a player with as little skill at heading the ball as Macca could not fail to put past Vitor Baia in the Portuguese goal.

Unfortunately this early elation was soon wiped out as Portugal came back with two goals before half-time. Much of this recovery was the work of their star right-sided player, Luis Figo, now one of David's new colleagues at Real Madrid. Portugal scored a third in a second half during which the England supporters had been largely silent. However, a small, drunken minority had found their voices to abuse Victoria and her father before and after the game. David's wife had been promised a seat in a secure area, but she found herself instead in the crowd where she was jostled as well as insulted. As David came off the pitch, bitterly disappointed that the team had let their lead slip away, another group of about six men began to jeer and shout insults about David, his wife and Brooklyn. David's response was to stick his finger up at the crowd and this gesture of defiance was captured by a photographer and splashed across the papers the next day.

Though there was the usual attempt by the tabloids to make more of it than it deserved, there was a general feeling that David's reaction was justified. One writer humorously dubbed the gesture 'half Churchillian'. Kevin Keegan defended his player unequivocally in the press conference afterwards. 'I heard the abuse,' he told reporters, 'and I was ashamed. There were more than David Beckham upset by the abuse. It was ferocious.' He also praised David's contribution to the match. 'He covered every blade of grass for us. That was his best performance in an England shirt.' In the next game David was very encouraged by the mass singing of his name in support.

The team gave the perfect answer to this undeserved abuse by inflicting England's first defeat of Germany in a competitive international since the World Cup final of 1966. The German midfielder Dietmar Hamann (now a Liverpool player) had said before the match that the key to victory was 'to keep Beckham under control'. David again played in Keegan's preferred midfield diamond formation and, as Hamann had warned, he was closely marked all game. The single goal which clinched the game, from Alan Shearer, was the result of a foul on David near the touchline. He took the free kick that was awarded, and bent it across the goal mouth where Alan Shearer was waiting to head it home gratefully.

Phil Neville was to find himself the second United player to become a scapegoat for England's exit from an international competition when he gave away a needless penalty in the final minute of the last group match against Romania which secured England's defeat. The final score was 3–2, and England had once again surrendered a lead. Alan Shearer, England captain and the third-highest goal-scorer ever in an England shirt, announced his international retirement after the game and gave his succinct, if harsh verdict on England's performances. 'We got what we deserved, which was an early plane home.' The Belgian authorities were not sorry to see the England fans going home early too, after ugly scenes of hooliganism.

Shearer was not the only one to retire unexpectedly. Kevin Keegan was to become despondent about his ability to give the England team the leadership it needed. The schedule of international qualifying games is now unrelenting. The disappointment of the Euro 2000 exit had barely had time to sink in before it was time to begin qualifying for the 2002 World Cup. England has a habit of being drawn in a group with Germany, and this occasion was no different. Albania, Greece and Finland completed the list of England's opponents. The October 2000 match was to be the last one to be played at Wembley Stadium, where demolition was to start the next Monday to make way for the new National Stadium. The Germans began the demolition early, scoring in the first few minutes after a mistake by David Seaman. Beckham was substituted with a knee injury near the end and he limped disconsolately off the pitch in the rain which had fallen constantly throughout the game.

Keegan had been on the receiving end of criticism shouted by the fans as he left the dugout at the end of the game. David described how the manager had walked into the dressing room and announced he was going to resign. The immediate reaction of those around him, including David, was to try and persuade him to change his mind. The timing of the announcement was particularly bad as there was another World Cup qualifier against Finland in a few days' time. Howard Wilkinson again took charge, and presided over a 0–0 draw which left England bottom of their group. Wilkinson's inexplicable tactics were roundly condemned. David was not available for selection because of the knee injury he sustained against the Germans; Michael Owen was fit, but was dropped to the bench as a substitute. Though England was desperately in need of a striker, he warmed up on the touchline for most of the match without coming on.

The FA had already decided that they were going to take the unprecedented, bold step of appointing a foreign coach to head the national side, the Swede Sven-Goran Eriksson. In the meantime, the Leicester manager Peter Taylor replaced Wilkinson as caretaker for a friendly game against Italy in Turin, and he had a surprise for David. He took the opportunity to bring in a group of new young players, but also to find a replacement for Alan Shearer as captain. David was staying at Gary Neville's house when the phone rang at eight in the morning. Taylor broke the news that he felt David was exactly right to wear the captain's armband. It was an audacious move. David's character was still not entirely rehabilitated, but there were also concerns that he was not a natural leader like the previous incumbents of the captain's job, Shearer and Tony Adams.

The most trenchant argument advanced against his elevation was that he had no experience of captaincy. In his autobiography, David says that he had only captained one side, the youth team that won the Milk Cup in Ireland in his first year at Old Trafford. In interviews at the time he also joked that he had captained United for one match when Keane was unavailable: he had picked up the armband from the dressing-room bench, put it on and 'walked past the manager who did not notice'. England lost the friendly by a single goal, but David was prepared to defend his claim to the job on a more permanent basis. 'A lot of things were said about me,' he said, 'but I have got my head down, played football, enjoyed my football, won trophies and now I am England captain. Two years on it is astonishing that I am captain of England.' To charges that he was not a natural leader he replied, 'I am not going to be one of those captains who shouts his mouth off, like Bryan [Robson], Roy [Keane] and Tony [Adams]. I will be quieter than those. But part of being a captain is geeing the players up ... I will talk to them. But the biggest influence I can give to players is what I can do with my feet, not my mouth.'

David Beckham was to be true to his words. As England captain he has led his team magnificently by example. Assuming these responsibilities has, according to many analysts, added something more to his game. The man who knows his playing capabilities best foresaw that this additional dimension would transform his young protégé. At the beginning of the season, Sir Alex Ferguson had outlined his hopes for the millennium in an extended interview with the official club magazine. He said of his treble-winning players, 'The '94 team influenced other players with their strength. This team has developed along those lines, and that same strength is coming out. Keane and Stam influence people. Beckham influences the game. Eventually, he'll influence others. And then we'll have some player, won't we?' The week before the Greece game he made Beckham captain of United for the first time in a match against Spurs.

Eriksson had left David in no doubt that he would continue as captain in the foreseeable future. The urbane, softly spoken Swede could not have been a greater contrast to Keegan. His appointment had been made on the strength of his managerial experience with a host of top European clubs, including Benfica, Roma, Fiorentina,

Sampdoria and Lazio. David rewarded Sven in his first match in charge, the qualifier against Finland at Anfield, by creating the equaliser and scoring the winner. Gary Neville had unfortunately deflected in the cross which gave Finland the lead, but then collected a clever pass from Beckham, who had robbed a Finnish defender of the ball. Neville drove it low across the goal for Owen to shoot home. For David's winner, Scholes squared the ball to the unmarked Becks who blasted a shot into the far corner of the goal with his right foot. Amazingly, it was his first England goal from open play.

The new England manager was warm in his praise for David after the match. 'He's just twenty-five,' he pointed out. 'He really wants to perform as captain. And he did that today.' Paul Hayward, writing in the *Telegraph*, was typical of the press response when he opined, 'Though he is the essence of everything Man Utd, he is starting to be known primarily as the England captain, a leader not by mouth so much as deed.'

Under Sven, the debate about which position David should play became irrelevant because of the selection of Paul Scholes and the Liverpool midfielder Steven Gerrard in the centre. The Swede's tactics were simple: players should play in positions they were familiar with, and where they were a success for their clubs.

For the next qualifying game against Albania, Eriksson fielded seven Manchester United players during the game: David, Nicky Butt, Gary Neville, Andy Cole, Paul Scholes, Wes Brown and Teddy Sheringham. It was the biggest single club representation for England ever, beating the six Liverpool men who won caps in 1977. Michael Owen scored the opening goal in the 3–1 win, then Scholes got the second and Andy Cole netted his first international goal for the third. Sven had reversed England's losing streak, and David was already seeing the impact of the captaincy on his play. 'There is a new authority in my game, and that is something I needed.' Sven revealed that he had asked Becks to sign a number 7 shirt for his teenage daughter, Lina, who was a big fan.

David continued to make a telling contribution to England's new-found success in a torrid game in Greece. David was pelted with missiles every time he took a corner, but he was still a driving force, eventually making the victory secure when he won a free kick three minutes from the end of the match and struck one of his curling balls into the goal. The summer break followed, and September would begin with a game in the Olympic Stadium in Germany which has already gone down in history as one of England's greatest performances ever. The 5–1 drubbing of Germany was achieved with five goals from Liverpool players, and it was a match which David doubted he would be fit enough to make because of a muscle tear. He was morose for a week until his fitness was confirmed. The England physios talked him into wearing cycle shorts to protect the injury, but he couldn't bear the restricted feeling they gave him. England went a goal down almost instantly and David stripped off the extra shorts, another moment captured on camera. In a pulsating second half England overturned the deficit and couldn't stop scoring. At the final whistle, David raised his arms over his head and made a double thumbs-up gesture. The referee, the distinctively bald Pierluigi Collina, widely rated as the best referee in the world, asked for David's shirt, and he returned the compliment.

Despite this fantastic result, England still had work to do to nullify the effects of the disastrous results in the first few qualifiers and go through to the World Cup finals in Japan and Korea automatically. A long break in the qualifying programme followed, before it resumed in June 2001. Then Owen and Robbie Fowler scored the two goals against Albania which brought England to the top of the qualifying table for group nine. Eriksson stressed the importance of David's defensive contribution in this game. 'Beckham's a complete player. When people think about Beckham it's not only the right foot, he's hard-working, very fit and strong and takes up good positions when defending. It doesn't matter whether the ball comes to him high or low. When you have such a good first touch, your second touch is ready to pass or shoot. That's a great, great thing in modern football where you never have space or time. And he behaved like a captain. I am proud of him.'

Automatic qualification was still not secure. The final game was at Old Trafford against Greece, and it is probably David's greatest performance so far in an England shirt. He pulled the team back from a 2–0 deficit by sheer will and determination, scoring the equaliser with his ninth free kick of the game, kicks which had been getting closer and closer, until this one left his white-booted foot at 64.8 miles per hour, travelling 29.6 yards. Teddy Sheringham had tried to take the kick instead, but David refused, settling himself with a few deep breaths.

In a friendly against Sweden he added another string to his bow, taking his first England penalty, which he scored. Before David could go to his second World Cup finals, he had a season with United to negotiate. It was in March, in the second leg of the Champions League quarter-finals against Deportivo La Coruna, that Aldo Duscher, the Argentinian midfielder, derailed David's World Cup preparations by lunging at him in a two-footed challenge with studs showing. It broke a small bone in David's foot. The whole country became familiar with the position of the second metatarsal bone as various experts, physiotherapists, orthopaedic surgeons and doctors, speculated about the timescale for recovery. Uri Geller tried to harness a wave of psychic-healing energy by asking the nation to concentrate their minds on the ailing right foot. Although David had already been told that he would probably be able to play the first game in the finals, Sir Alex had decided that he would not be recovered in time. 'But he's young,' he said, in what was meant to be consolation. 'He will play in the World Cup again and play in the European Cup again.' Gary Neville, who had broken the same bone a week later, was largely ignored.

David was able to play, thanks to a very carefully planned programme of rehabilitation, but also very much because he is young and able to heal quickly. But he was not able to train and build up his match fitness. This was to be a crucial factor given the high temperatures and humidity in which the games would be played. The bonus for England of the finals being held in Japan and Korea was that they had enormous support from the indigenous population. David had his own massive personal following cheering his every move, and the crowds were full of fans sporting his latest hairstyle, the 'fin', where his hair was brushed into a ridge in the middle of his head. By contrast, England's opponents in Saitama on 2 June made the opening game particularly piquant for Sven. He was hoping to defeat his fellow countrymen, the Swedes.

Every time David took a corner, the stadium lit up with thousands of camera flashes. After twenty-five minutes, one of those special Beckham corners was headed in by Sol Campbell, but Alexandersson equalised in the second half from a bungled clearance by Danny Mills. David tired badly, had to be substituted and the match ended as a draw.

The second match was the one which the England players had been waiting for, as they faced Argentina in Sapporo. Owen won a penalty, much to the disgust of the Argentinian players, who claimed he had dived. Michael Owen could have taken it, but it was the captain's decision that he would do it himself. David began to lock himself into focus with fierce concentration – afterwards Sven described him as 'ice cold'. Cavallero, the Argentinian goalkeeper, tried to put him off, gesturing to show David where he should strike the ball. David blanked him totally. Then Simeone, the player who had ensured that David was sent off in France, tried to shake his hand, but Nicky Butt and Paul Scholes pulled him away in a gesture of Manc solidarity. He hit the penalty low and true. 'It was nice,' said David later, with massive understatement, 'to finally put the memory of four years ago to rest.' Nicky Butt was Man of the Match: he stamped his dominance on the midfield so well that Juan Sebastian Veron was taken off at half-time. Butt's form was no fluke – Pelé later rated him one of the best players of the tournament. At the end of the game, which England won by that single goal, the Argentinians refused to swap shirts and shouted abuse at Paul Scholes as he boarded the team coach.

The match which took England through into the second

stage was against Nigeria in Osaka. David described it as 'ninety minutes of hard labour'. The heat was searing – thirty-four degrees – but the result, a 0–0 draw, was enough. Denmark now stood in England's way for a place in the quarter-finals. The fans danced a conga in the stands as England scored three times without reply. But England's biggest challenge awaited: the quarter-final itself against Brazil.

Dad had faced a very different kind of Brazilian team in the 1974 World Cup finals: they played cynical, negative football. David and his teammates knew that they were facing some of the most talented individual footballers in the world: Ronaldinho, Rivaldo and Ronaldo. But there was optimism that this was not the strongest Brazilian team, and many of the big seeds had been knocked out of the competition already. Would David be lifting England's second World Cup ever? Achieving the dream came closer when England took the lead, but Brazil equalised just before half-time with a goal from Rivaldo. David believes that this goal killed the spirit of the England players. The team had failed to score in the second half of any of their five games in Japan, and was exhausted by the heat. Brazil was reduced to ten men in the final thirty-three minutes, but Ronaldinho settled the match with a free kick which left Seaman stranded. Depending on your point of view, it was either a freakish stroke of luck, or an audacious streak of brilliance. England were eliminated, bitterly disappointed. David came back to Old Trafford from the heat of a family holiday in Barbados to an unexpectedly chilly reception.

CHAPTER ELEVEN

A NIGHT OUT WITH DAVID BECKHAM

I was out with some friends in The Sugar Lounge one Friday night in 2001 when I bumped into Dwight Yorke and his cousin Conor. Conor asked me if I'd like to go to Manchester United's Christmas Party the next weekend, and gave me some tickets. I was not sure if I wanted to go, but when I spoke to Lisa she assured me it was one of the most sought-after invitations in Manchester, and the rest of the girls from the band were keen. As I had a couple of tickets left over I invited two friends from Key 103 whom I had met when I was dating Darren Proctor – two rising DJ stars, JK and Joel, who have since moved to Radio 1 and are tipped to be the new Ant and Dec. On the night, Joel phoned to say that JK had split up with his girlfriend and did not feel like going to the party, but he would still love to come himself and would meet me at the venue, Manchester's exclusive Reform Club.

The party started early at seven o'clock, so we dressed in a bit of a rush. You could describe our outfits as daring: I wore a short red miniskirt and a black top which fastened with one button, leaving my midriff bare. Black knee-length boots completed the ensemble. Lisa was all in black, and her trousers had cut-out squares along the sides of each leg. Lizette, the third of the Angels and a tall blonde, also wore black trousers, with a red, asymmetrical top with one bare shoulder.

The Reform Club is in one of Manchester's most beautiful Victorian Gothic buildings. The interior is very luxurious, with chandeliers, heavy scarlet drapes and plush furniture. That night there was more security on the door than I had ever seen before. 'You'd think the Queen was in there,' Lisa joked.

'She might be,' replied Lizette.

There were five or six security men outside who checked our bags, then we walked up the fabulous spiral stairway into the bar area on the first floor. The music was pumping out, funky soul inviting people to dance. There is a huge circular wooden bar, and standing on it, dancing as only he knows how, was Dwight, the party animal who craved the limelight and loved being the centre of attention.

Lisa was flabbergasted. 'Every pretty girl in Manchester must be here tonight!' she announced. She had exactly summed up the sight which met our eyes. The room was crammed with girls. The United team was there too, but without partners – there is a strictly no wives or girlfriends policy. Indeed, one year the wives gatecrashed the Christmas party, so suspicious were they of what might be going on. I do not blame them for their suspicions. I had watched the way women lusted after my father, and how they still run after him today. This arrival of the wives was not very well received at all by the players as this was their main night in the year to relax and let their hair down, and from what I heard their partners were marched out and home.

The players looked to be having a great time – they had been warming up for the party all day. The girls were dancing, and there was a relaxed atmosphere. Joel was sitting by the antique fireplace and we went to meet him. Almost immediately, David Beckham strolled past to say hello, which gave me a real buzz inside as I knew every girl in the place was hoping merely for a glance from him. He was dressed casually, in a grey knitted hat, jeans and a white T-shirt, topped with a grey-green cardigan. He caught my eye and we smiled at each other. Joel, who is a massive United fan, naturally wanted an introduction. As this wasn't the Braz, I thought I had better check with David first if this was acceptable. I knew he would ask me how I was, and so he did. 'I'm fine thanks,' I said. 'Great party! Listen, I've got a friend with me, a DJ from Key who wants to meet you. I know what it's like being hassled so I wanted to check if it was allright to bring him over in a bit.'

'Of course it is, Gaynor,' he reassured me. 'Any friend of yours, bring them over any time.'

A DJ by trade, Joel knows how to talk. It's often hard to get a word in edgeways, but when I brought him to David he was speechless. He just did not know what to say. In fact, we witnessed the unaccustomed sight of David Beckham saying far more than Joel to keep the conversation going. I decided to leave Joel to fend for himself with David – a bit cruel really, but it would be fun to watch how he reacted. I knew how much he likes the sound of his own voice, though, and I thought he would chat away for a while. To my surprise, he was back with us a minute later. By this time he'd found his tongue. 'That was absolutely fantastic,' he announced. 'But I couldn't think of anything to say to him. So I ended up saying something really stupid like, "If you are ever at Key 103, David, come over and say hello."' This is yet more evidence of the power that David's celebrity exerts over people. Joel meets stars on a daily basis, but he was totally in awe of him.

Lizette looked at the elaborate clothes, hairstyles and make-up of the girls on the dance floor and turned to me with the observation that we should have made a bit more effort. 'They look as if they've spent days preparing for this. We just combed our hair and slapped on a bit of blusher!' There were plenty of friends I recognised from the Braz, and I enjoyed myself chatting to them.

About an hour went by, and I was standing with a drink in my hand talking to Joel and Lisa. Suddenly I felt someone come up behind me and put his arm around my neck from behind, pulling me down. I went crashing on to the floor, and found that I was lying on top of Dwight Yorke. A bit the worse for wear, Dwight had decided that it would be very funny to pull me over backwards. But he had miscalculated and I hurt my back quite badly. Joel came to my rescue and he was very unhappy with the way that Dwight behaved, letting him know exactly how he felt. In fact, I had the distinct impression that Joel was going to take a swing at Dwight and I immediately defused the situation by laughing, even though I was in pain. David had seen the incident as well and he was obviously perturbed. I then went to the ladies' room and dusted myself off. The matter did not end there as, for the next six months, Joel kept up a barrage of criticism about Dwight on his radio show. This was funny at first, but then after a while it was undeserved: Dwight meant no harm, and Conor sent me a lovely text the next day in apology.

When I went to get some more drinks with Lisa a little later, David was standing nearby and when he spotted me at the bar he came over. He took my hand and asked if I had recovered from my fall, at which point Lisa stood back and gave us some space to talk – she realised that getting the drinks was now the last thing on my mind. 'You don't need to ask me if you want to bring anyone over,' he repeated.

'I know,' I replied, touched by his concern. 'But it's still polite to ask. Don't forget that I know what it's like, having grown up with Dad. Everyone wants to say hello and talk about football. I've spent years fighting for his attention. But it's really nice of you to say that, I appreciate it.'

He smiled. 'No problem.'

And then it happened. Almost out of the blue, David spoke a few words that were to put our relationship on to a very different footing. 'I've fancied you for ages.'

My heart stopped. All of a sudden, I was totally focused on what he was saying, oblivious to the noise and the people around me. David had crossed the line that I never seriously believed he would even dare approach. After he said those few simple words, I knew that anything could happen.

'Why did you ignore me the other day?' he asked. I honestly had no idea what he was talking about. 'I saw you when I was outside Starbucks in Wilmslow,' he explained. 'You were in your car at the lights. I waved like mad to you and you ignored me.'

I looked at him in disbelief, amazed that he had spotted me in the car, and that he had bothered to wave, but mainly because he seemed genuinely worried that I might have ignored him. 'No, David,' I reassured him. 'I didn't see you, honestly. I am in a world of my own when I'm in the car. Believe me, I never would have ignored you.' I squeezed his hand and he seemed relieved.

He took off his hat, revealing his shaven head underneath. 'I'm glad we've sorted that out,' he said. 'Are you still in the band? I've not seen you in the papers for a bit.'

It was a subject close to my heart. These were exciting times for the group, which was gaining some very flattering attention. Paul Williams, the writer of some of the world's greatest songs, like the beautiful Carpenters hits 'Rainy Days and Mondays' and 'We've Only Just Begun', had sent us an email telling us how good he thought we were after seeing us perform. He actually said that he would be honoured if we would record a song he had written. This was such a fantastic compliment that we were elated for days. I mentioned this to David, then said, 'We're doing well, but even more importantly we're really enjoying ourselves. It's great fun, and we got to sing with Johnny Mathis live on stage this week.'

At this point I had the distinct impression that David did not know who I was talking about, so I decided it was better to change the subject. David took hold of my hand once again, and looked at me to gauge my reactions. This was totally unexpected. I felt a frisson of excitement as I realised that this was a deliberate and significant action. I tried to look as if what he had just done was the most natural thing in the world, but it took quite an effort to maintain my equilibrium. We chatted on. I can't remember much of what we said, just the special feeling of him holding my hand in his.

Suddenly Dwight appeared and stood right next to us, obviously curious about how engrossed David and I were in conversation. His eyes took in the scene and he stared down at our interlinked hands as if to say, What is going on here, then? We ignored him, but David was unabashed and never loosened his grip. Dwight staggered off, finally getting the message. David and I both burst into laughter. But, as I glanced up to see Dwight go, I saw that he was not the only one whose curiosity had been piqued. A small crowd had gathered around us, wondering why David had spent so much time talking to the same woman.

I felt I had to warn him about the prying eyes.

'We shouldn't be doing that,' I told him.

'What?'

'Chatting like this and holding hands. People will start talking.'

David just laughed. He obviously didn't care what people thought. I really could not believe that our fingers were still entwined. For David Beckham to make any display of affection on any level, in a public place, was incredibly risky. I wasn't complaining, though. I was a single girl and he was a fantastic person and a very handsome man. I savoured the moment, expecting him to pull away at any time. But he didn't. Then I almost gasped in surprise and, I have to admit, pleasure, as he started stroking the inside of my palm with one of his fingers as we carried on our conversation. At any time I could have walked away. He had no wish to impose on me; rather, he was showing me that he wanted to get closer, but only if that was what I wanted too. And it *was* what I wanted, and for a brief while I forgot about the consequences.

Gradually we moved closer and closer to each other. I felt his breath on my cheek and finally we stood so that we were almost touching. The tension I felt is indescribable. We seemed to stand for an age, staring into each other's eyes, though it was probably only for a few seconds. I was intensely attracted towards him and, as I brushed lightly against his skin and looked up at him, the mutual, unstoppable passion that had built up between us became almost too much to control. Still he was gently caressing the inside of my palm with his finger. It was a very warm gesture, almost loving, something you would do with somebody you knew very well. We got to the point where we were completely sandwiched together. It was dangerous, but we were oblivious to it. It was clear to both of us that something was going to happen; and it was clear that it was going to happen *there*. It didn't matter where we were, and it didn't matter if we were in public. It was going to happen. It had to.

The hands that we were holding were by the bar – my left hand and his right hand. Slowly he let go and put his right hand on my thigh. Very gently, he started stroking me. I gasped, unsure what to do – we were being carried away on the tide of our mutual passion. I don't know how long this went on – I lost all sense of time, but the details of exactly what happened between David Beckham and myself at that point will always remain our secret.

Before I knew it, I became aware of someone approaching us purposefully. It was Gary Neville. He took David by the shoulders and said, 'Come on, mate, time to go.' The look he gave me was stern. David didn't seem to want to move. It felt to me like one of those moments when you just want to give someone a hug and a kiss; whether David felt the same I don't know, but the look he gave me suggested it was so. Gary wasn't going to be denied, however, and by this time I had Lisa on my arm. We gave each other a parting smile, and he was gone.

Lisa led me away and sat me down on a sofa. I was in shock, astonished at what had just happened. I kept repeating to Lisa what David had just done. 'I know,' she said. 'I saw it all. We need to go, now.'

And that's exactly what we did.

I was tempted to get in touch; I knew that I only had to say the word and we would have embarked upon an affair which would probably have ruined both our lives: he was married, devoted to Brooklyn, and Victoria was pregnant with Romeo at the time, and I had no doubt that he loved his wife. Perhaps at that moment he was not *in* love with her – and they are very different things – but I had no wish to go down the path of breaking up a marriage, and I certainly didn't want to play second fiddle to Victoria Beckham.

That night marked the start of a very stormy time for me. For a start, it was quite out of character. My dalliance with David was not just an intimate one, but an emotional one too. I had perhaps not realised throughout the months of flirting that David had in fact made me feel quite special with his attention. He has that knack, the knack of making you feel like you are the only person in the world that he wants to talk to. It is a rare gift, but it makes it terribly difficult when you have been on the receiving end of it and are suddenly left with nothing.

As a professional sports person and with my own personal insight into the world of top-level football I am only too aware of the way in which women are sometimes used as sex objects to fuel their team-driven egos. I knew I should have known better after witnessing years of groupies throwing themselves shamelessly at my dad, but totally out of character I got lost in the moment because of the magnetism that had built up between David and myself and, before I knew it, it was too late.

To make matters worse, over the few months that followed, David reached the very peak of his fame. You could not turn on the television or open a newspaper without seeing his face or reading his name. You could not walk down the street without being bombarded by his image. Even my son talks about David Beckham on a daily basis.

Gradually, I started to get realistic. I started to be able to put David from my mind, and a few months after that evening together I ventured out to the Braz. I was in the VIP bar when my friend Jason – a professional footballer who used to play with Manchester City – walked in. We have been friends for a long time, so he immediately walked over and asked me if I would like a drink. We sat down and started chatting. And then in walked David.

Of course, I knew that I would see him again, and in my mind I had played out the scenario any number of ways. Should I go up to him and say, 'Oh my God, we shouldn't have done that'? Or would he come up to me and make the first move? I suppose David had no idea what my relationship with Jason was; for all he knew he could have been my boyfriend, and he is, after all, a very handsome guy. Maybe that's why he reacted the way he did.

Within seconds of sitting down, he was staring at me, only this time it was very different to the looks I'd been used to getting. It was the first time I had seen real aggression in his face. I hoped that Jason wouldn't cotton on to what was happening, but it wasn't very busy that night and David was hardly being subtle. It didn't take my friend long to notice the dagger stares we were receiving. As a professional footballer, he was not overawed or starstruck by David. He turned to me and asked, 'What's his problem?'

I feigned ignorance. 'Who? What are you talking about?' I hadn't told anybody but Lisa about what had happened between me and David, and I wasn't about to spill the beans now – even if the looks David was giving me made my protestations a bit comical.

Jason didn't buy it. 'Gaynor, what is his problem? Because, if he doesn't stop, I'm going to smack him.'

Still I made light of it. 'Don't be stupid, Jason.' And so it went on, but David knew he was making Jason feel uncomfortable; he was being purposefully aggressive towards him. It didn't take Jason long to decide that he wasn't going to put up with this. He stood up to go over. I grabbed his arm. 'Jason, sit down. OK, there's a bit of a history. You're my friend, please don't do anything or say anything. I'm going to walk away now and go home, so please just leave it.'

In that short space of time I had seen a very different side to David Beckham; a side that I didn't like one little bit; he had turned from a flirtatious Dr Jekyll into an obsessive Mr Hyde. That more than anything persuaded me that we needed to draw a line. I was cross with him: cross that he'd put me in that situation, and cross that he had made my friend uncomfortable. I told Jason to go back to his friends at the bar, then I grabbed my coat and left. But that was not to be the end of it.

Two weeks later I went into the Braz for a late drink with some friends, and David was sitting at the same place. The moment I saw him, my heart dropped – I asked my friend to get me a *large* gin and tonic, and did my best to ignore David. I sat down next to Mike, an old family friend with whom I practically grew up. He is a very astute businessman, but in some ways more like a girlfriend – very gossipy. We chatted for about five minutes when he suddenly looked at me quite seriously. 'Gaynor,' he said, 'I've known you for a very long time.'

'Yeah.'

'We're good friends.'

'Yeah.' I wondered where he was going with this.

'Well, I'm a very astute guy, and I've been sat talking to you for ten minutes. Can I ask you a question?'

'Of course you can.' I was confused.

'Can I ask you why David Beckham looks as if he wants to kill me?'

I was very angry. I had no idea that David was doing this with Mike, but it was something that Mike had clearly noticed. In the space of ten minutes he had made his presence – and his feelings – very firmly felt. I stood up, made my apologies and left.

It was the second-to-last time I would ever see David Beckham.

CHAPTER TWELVE

THE REAL DEAL?

Not one of the players gathered together in the Reform Club in Christmas 2001 could have guessed that David would be leaving the club within two years. The circumstances by which they came to be celebrating the festive season in 2003 without one of the mainstays of the team still remain unclear, but some idea of what happened can be pieced together.

In the 1999–2000 season, David enjoyed yet another successful term with the Reds. He describes the buzz in the team which, after winning the treble, felt that it was invincible. David was hotly tipped to win the European Footballer of the Year award in December 1999, voted for by fifty-one international journalists. The Brazilian striker Rivaldo, also nominated, paid David the ultimate compliment when he said, 'Beckham is the only British player who would get into the Brazilian squad.' Though David eventually came third, this was no disgrace. 2000 was also Sir Alex's testimonial year, and he announced that he would retire when he was 60 in 2002.

David scored only eight goals in this season, but he was a highly effective provider. His rating in the Opta statistics, which measure a player's performance by a variety of criteria, made him United's player of the month for September for two goal assists against Liverpool, setting up a goal for Dwight Yorke against Sturm Graz in the Champions League and putting in a first-time cross for Teddy Sheringham to head in against Southampton. In the Premiership, United put in an exceptional performance, finishing eighteen points above Arsenal in second place. The club scored ninety-seven goals, and lost only three games all season. But it could never have been a treble-winning season. United did not defend the FA Cup at all. The club opted out of the competition for the first time in United's history. Instead United flew out to Brazil in January 2000 to compete in FIFA's inaugural World Club Championship.

Manchester United has always maintained that the government, in the form of the then sports minister Tony Banks, put enormous pressure on them to accept the invitation in an effort to help England's bid to host the World Cup in 2006. The FA was asked to allow United to miss out the third round in return, which was categorically refused. United were indeed caught between a rock and a hard place. If they did not take part in the competition, they would be accused of scuppering England's chances of hosting the World Cup. The English papers, particularly the *Daily Mirror* which mounted a campaign to have United banned from the FA Cup in subsequent seasons, blamed the club for conspiring to ruin the greatest cup competition in the world by devaluing it. Martin Edwards, the club chairman, defended the decision. 'We've given England a chance now. You cannot expect our players to play in seventy games.'

United's experiences in Rio de Janeiro were mixed. David was sent off for a high tackle on Jose Milan in the game with the Mexican team Necaxa in front of a crowd of only 2,000 whose voices echoed eerily around the magnificent Maracana stadium. Alex Ferguson was also shown the red card for disputing the referee's decisions from the touchline, and Dwight Yorke missed a penalty before he netted a late equaliser to make the final score 1–1. On a public-relations level the trip was a disaster. The club had arranged several PR events, including inviting children from the Rio slums to train with them, but, when the players arrived after their long journey, they spent their first day's training behind closed doors. This sparked a campaign against the club in the local press. 'The English play football without joy and United are here without any joy. When Brazilian fans tried to greet David Beckham he acted like he was in front of a death squad,' claimed one reporter.

This was not fair to David. He had shown his usual welcoming attitude to the public, never refusing an autograph or a request for a photograph, according to one observer. He particularly enjoyed coaching the children in a session arranged in co-operation with UNICEF, the international children's charity to which the club has given its support.

Though knocked out of the tournament early, the players enjoyed themselves in the sun. Such were their renewed energies when they returned to England that the club was now accused of engineering its own midwinter break by underhand means.

In February 2000, David had his dispute with Ferguson over missing training to care for Brooklyn, the argument that Dad still maintains was the beginning of the end for David's United career. The *Daily Mail* later claimed that, following the incident, Fergie had secretly visited the Barcelona star Luis Figo (a name which would loom large in David's later career) to try to bring him to Old Trafford. David Beckham was to be offered in return in the £37 million deal, so Dad may have been right. However, David stayed at the club, though why he was not sold until 2003 might be more to do with Alex's original intention to retire in 2002, rather than any patching up of differences between the two men.

In his account of why he went to Madrid, David does not recognise that there was any major deterioration of their relationship until 2002. The 2001–2 season was disappointing for the club: United won no trophies at all. They lost the Premiership title to Arsenal by five points, were beaten by the unfancied German club Bayer Leverkusen in the semi-finals of the Champions League, and went out of the FA Cup in the fourth round after a 2–0 defeat by Middlesbrough, now managed by Alex Ferguson's former assistant Steve McClaren. Despite these disappointments, David's goal-scoring form underwent quite a revival in this season, and he struck a total of sixteen, twice what he had managed in the previous year.

The season began with the announcement that the United manager would definitely be retiring at the end of it. Alex's dream was that he would finish his term of office by leading his team out on to the pitch at Hampden Park in Glasgow, the venue for the Champions League final. He would then assume an ambassadorial role of some kind for United. Before then, however, he still had some highly significant decisions to make which demonstrated that, even in his last season, he was in charge. In April and over the summer, he had made two highly expensive signings: the Dutch striker Ruud Van Nistelrooy and Argentinian midfielder Juan Sebastian Veron. Then, following the serialisation of Jaap Stam's autobiography in the *Daily Mirror*, the linchpin of the United defence was transferred with bewildering speed to the Italian club Lazio. Stam had thought that Ferguson had accepted his apology for revealing that the manager had made a behind-the-scenes approach to persuade him to come to Manchester, and that his future at United was secure, but he was very wrong. When he appeared at the press conference to announce his signing for his new club, Stam was still visibly shocked, holding a Lazio shirt limply in his hands. Stam's replacement was Laurent Blanc, a highly cultured French defender who, aged nearly thirty-six, was not a long-term prospect. In January 2002 Alex also signed Diego Forlan from River Plate, but by then he had reversed his decision to retire.

The replacement that United was supposedly lining up for Ferguson was the England coach Sven-Goran Eriksson. According to Michael Crick, who wrote a bestselling unofficial biography of Alex, one of the key factors in Eriksson's appeal for the United board was that David Beckham would respect him. David had been delaying signing his new contract, and a major reason for his reluctance was that he wanted to see who would be Ferguson's successor. David says that he was very happy when Alex decided to postpone his retirement. However, he was not to know how Fergie's attitude towards him was going to undergo a drastic change.

The trigger seems to have been David's commitment to the preparations for the World Cup. Following the fracture of the metatarsal bone in his right foot, Ferguson wanted David to stay in Manchester and work with the United physiotherapists in the training complex at Carrington. But Becks had been invited to Dubai with the rest of the England squad and their families to begin the preparations for the tournament. He had the feeling that Ferguson was not happy with the extra responsibility that came with being England captain. The presence of wives and children at this camp would also be a distraction from his recuperation. David did not take Ferguson's advice, and he suspects that, in Alex's mind, this meant that he was prioritising his England duties over his responsibilities to his club.

After his exhausting summer schedule, David arrived back at Old Trafford feeling unprepared for the 2002–3 season. He made a lacklustre start, going through the motions, and was actually relieved when he sustained bruised ribs in a Worthington Cup game with Leicester City on 5 December. He had privately hoped that he might be rested for this tie, but he played and opened the scoring with a penalty. Operating in central midfield, he was an inspirational force in the match, creating the second goal with a searching cross for the young substitute Kieran Richardson to head in. He was named Man of the Match for his remarkable performance. David now believes the injury did him a favour. The mental and physical exhaustion that he experienced after returning from Japan had never left him. Now he had no option but to take the rest he so badly needed. Before going on a brief holiday to Barbados, he joined up with the England squad for a get-together in an international week, when the league programme was suspended. The players had been invited to Buckingham Palace for an audience with the Queen, which David attended, as everyone would expect him to do as England captain.

David returned to Old Trafford refreshed, but found the atmosphere distinctly unwelcoming. In what my father would describe as the sort of psychological tactics a manager employs, sometimes unconsciously, to begin the process of easing a player he has decided to dispense with out of the club, Ferguson began to give David the cold shoulder. When this had gone on for a month without any sign of improvement, David confronted the gaffer, asking Alex if he had a problem with him. Eventually Alex gave Beckham a reason for his behaviour. David should not have gone to the palace to meet the Queen, but flown out for his holiday immediately. Once again, David, to Alex's way of thinking anyway, had put England before United. According to Beckham, Ferguson told him, 'When I saw you turn up there, I questioned your loyalty to Manchester United.'

As he had done when Brooklyn was sick, Alex had chosen the wrong issue about which to take Beckham to task. As England captain, he had no option. To fly off to Barbados, and be pictured sunning himself on the beach when he should have been talking to the Queen, would have been interpreted as a snub. But Alex refused to admit that David had any justification for his actions, and Becks left the manager's office with nothing resolved. In fact, speaking his mind to Ferguson had exacerbated the situation. He became a target for the manager's criticism in training, which he found both personal and humiliating. When he wasn't criticising David, the boss was ignoring him. David describes those three months as the worst he'd ever known at Old Trafford. Victoria, coping with their new baby Romeo, had to bear the brunt of her husband's depression. He missed having a buffer between himself and Ferguson at the club, someone like Brian Kidd, Steve McClaren or Eric Harrison who could give him advice about how to deal with what was happening. Carlos Queiroz, Ferguson's second in command at the time, was not that sort of figure.

Again David decided to confront Ferguson head on, but he denied that he was treating Beckham any differently from the other players. However, the tension did seem to lift, and he began to feel happy again.

Then United drew 1–1 with Manchester City at Old Trafford on 9 February. City equalised late in the game, after United had dominated the match and should have won convincingly. Ferguson again singled Beckham out for criticism in the dressing room, saying that he had given the ball away too often. Inwardly David seethed at what he perceived to be unjust blame, though he accepted the accusations without comment. On 15 February, United's opponents in the fifth round of the FA Cup were Arsenal. United lost 2–0, but the match is remembered now for what happened after it rather than the events of the game. Ferguson rounded on David for being responsible for the second goal. Rather than agree with his manager this time, David swore at him, something he admits was wrong. Then Alex aimed a kick at a boot which was lying on the floor. It hit David just over the left eye and he 'went for' Ferguson, but was restrained by Ryan Giggs, Gary Neville and Ruud Van Nistelrooy. Alex did apologise to him later, but David refused to answer and went into the players' lounge to meet up with Victoria and tell her what had transpired.

Just how the story got into the papers is unclear. United was angry because they suspected that Arsenal had broken one of the unwritten rules of football by leaking information about what had gone on in the privacy of the inner sanctum of the dressing room. But David was not prepared to conceal his wound. He walked out of his house the next day with his hair pulled back from his face with a flexicomb headband, clearly showing the two Steristrips which the Manchester United club doctor had applied when he had been called to the Beckhams' home the night before as the cut had reopened. Pictures of David driving in his car, again openly displaying the gash, were splashed across every newspaper and made the main television news. David was accused of deliberately parading his cut, but it was United's manager who had the explaining to do. However, when he faced the press he was not prepared to admit either that he was wrong, or that he owed his player an apology. In fact, he tried to minimise the incident, calling it a 'freak of nature'. He also attempted to defuse the crisis with humour, and did raise a laugh by saying that he was not a good enough footballer to have hit David with the boot deliberately.

United's season was now really warming up, in more ways than one. Arsenal enjoyed an eight-point lead at the end of February, though United had a game in hand. The Reds had also lost the final of the Worthington Cup to

Liverpool. But March was a turning point. United won all of their three league matches that month, and Arsenal lost to Blackburn Rovers, the second time they had done so that season. David set his mind firmly on football matters, showing once again his strength of character. Both United goals in the 2–1 win over Leeds at Old Trafford came from Beckham crosses, though the first one was an own goal by Leeds defender Lucas Radebe. David scored the single goal to win United's away game against Aston Villa, squeezing in front of Alan Wright to knock Ryan Giggs's cross into the net. As one report commented, 'He may have scored more sexy goals, but in the long run few will have been more important.' A Van Nistelrooy hat-trick defeated Fulham. The gap was down to two points and there was a growing belief that United could catch and overtake Arsenal. Manchester United were now also the only British team left in the Champions League, having won through to the quarter-finals. The highlight of their group stage was a terrific 3–0 win against Juventus. However, in the second stage they had drawn Real Madrid, and would need to be on top form to overcome their formidable opponents.

David had a sore hamstring and did not start the next Premiership game against Liverpool, though he came off the bench to help create the last two of United's four goals. The aim was not to aggravate his injury before the first leg of the Champions League quarter-final at the Bernabeu. United were taught something of a footballing lesson in this game and were 3–0 behind, before Ruud van Nistelrooy scored with a header at the end of the game to give the team some hope for the second leg at Old Trafford. David did not play well. Most commentators explained his rather anonymous performance as the result of Roberto Carlos's knack for closing him down and nullifying his influence. But there was a more prosaic explanation: David's hamstring was still giving him problems, and restricted his freedom of movement. The injury kept him out of the next Premier League fixture against Newcastle, and Ole Gunnar Solskjaer took his place on the right wing. There were eight goals in the match, six of then scored by United after Newcastle had taken the lead. Solskjaer equalised, Paul Scholes bagged a hat-trick, and United were top of the league, though Arsenal had played one less game.

It was then that David learned he would not be in the team for what had turned out to be one of the most crucial games of the Premiership season, the away game against Arsenal at Highbury. The match ended as a 2–2 draw, but United looked as if they were winners by the final whistle, and Ferguson came on to the pitch and punched the air with delight in a gesture redolent of victory. Arsenal's challenge was finally halted on 4 May when Leeds United beat them 3–2.

Before the season drew to another successful close for Manchester United, they had to face Real Madrid with a two-goal deficit. When David learned that he was only a substitute, he felt sick and was bitterly disappointed, but the hurt turned to frustration when he discovered that Juan Sebastian Veron, who had been out injured for seven weeks, was preferred to him. Beckham's omission was a grave miscalculation. Ronaldo scored a hat-trick, Van Nistelrooy scored a goal for the Reds and Helguera put the ball into his own net to make the score 2–3 to Madrid on the night, 3–6 on aggregate. With twenty minutes left,

David was belatedly called into action to replace an obviously tiring Veron. A big-game player, he rose to the occasion magnificently and scored two goals: one from a fabulous free kick, and for the other he poked the ball over the line. United won the match 4–3, but had needed two more goals to go through to the semi-final.

From the time of the first match against Real Madrid, there had been enormous speculation in the newspapers that David would be joining the Spanish club in the summer. All the parties supposedly involved denied it vehemently. However, there had been moves behind the scenes. Whether it was Beckham's people or United who acted first depends on whose side of the story you accept. What is certain is that United made the first public move, in a manner that worked to the club's discredit. They issued a press release, which David only learned about when his agent Tony Stephens read it out to him on the telephone while he was in the States. 'Manchester United confirms that club officials have met Joan Laporta, the leading candidate for the Presidency of Barcelona. These meetings have resulted in an offer being made for the transfer of David Beckham to Barcelona.'

David was being offered for sale without his knowledge. He did have another two years to run on his contract at United, even though he had refused to sign a new deal before he left for his summer break. He could have refused to leave the club at all, though his position was intolerable. Instead he seized the initiative and spoke to the Real Madrid president, Florentino Perez, on the telephone. By 1 July 2003 he was no longer a Manchester United player, and a new challenge awaited.

I was invited to the 2002 Christmas bash at the Radisson Hotel, but had a prior engagement. The 2003 party was held on 12 December at The Living Room, and we decided that we definitely could not miss the party this time round. I was also curious to find out what the evening would be like now that United had lost its biggest celebrity, and one of the core members of the team. We decided to go along with one of our friends from *Coronation Street*, Trevor Dwyer-Lynch. Trevor is a fantastic character, lively, bubbly and bling-bling, wearing his big diamond cross around his neck. As a former youth coach at Old Trafford he knows everyone at the club – in fact, Trevor just seems to know everyone in general. In his party were other Corrie actors, and we knew that we were really going to enjoy the night, whatever happened.

If anything the security was even tighter than before. The men on the door stripped people of their mobiles and cameras, and these were placed in numbered bags downstairs. The Manchester United team had taken over the whole of the upstairs restaurant. A cordon of ten bouncers blocked the way to potential gatecrashers. Lisa surveyed the scene as we passed through. 'It's the team and ten thousand women,' she remarked drily. The dance floor was packed, with the favoured funky soul blasting out.

Trevor introduced me to the new owner of the number 7 shirt, the dazzling young talent Christiano Ronaldo. He had made a spectacular debut, not afraid to show off his superb close control of the ball. Since then he had come under criticism for overuse of his favourite 'step over' manoeuvre. David had also had to contend with the English preference for the functional, safe option rather than more daring, creative play, which might play the team into trouble if it misfired. He was, as a young player, discouraged from hitting 'Hollywood' passes. I had to ask Ronaldo what it felt like to know that he was following in such illustrious footsteps, but he was very measured in his response. He told me that Alex Ferguson had, in his brusque manner, handed him the shirt and said, 'This is yours, get on with it!' which is exactly what he was trying to do. He had not really thought that the number 7 put any more pressure on him than he had already. His main problem was that he was desperately missing Portugal and his family.

I also renewed my acquaintance with Diego Forlan, and Lisa was meanwhile having a long conversation in the back bar with Roy Keane. Lisa knew Roy's reputation as a drinker and hellraiser, and it seemed to be confirmed when she saw that he was wearing a T-shirt with the motto 'Don't Waste Any Time'. He was surrounded by his three brothers (the youngest of whom looks exactly like him) and friends, playing with an electric shock game based on Russian-roulette principles – you insert your finger into the machine and wait to see who is unlucky enough to get an electric shock. But Roy Keane is a changed man, and was playing the captain's role to perfection that evening. He drank nothing stronger than sparkling mineral water, and was all the better company for his sobriety. He is incredibly entertaining, with a dry, quick wit, always teasing and poking fun at people.

I came to find Lisa, and of course she introduced me to him as 'Willie Morgan's daughter', and that had its usual effect. I was warmly invited to join the group. Then one of the bar staff came over. 'Roy,' he asked, 'do you want me to stop the free bar?'

'What's the tab?' Roy replied.

It was £28,000. Lisa and I could not stop ourselves gasping quietly. That sounded like an awful lot of money, although you could easily see how the total had been reached as there were bottles of Cristal champagne everywhere. Roy was unfazed. 'Make it a pay bar when it reaches £35,000,' he told the barman.

Thinking about it later, £35,000 would not be a huge sum given the wages of the players who were contributing to the bill, but we told Roy that it was very generous hospitality, nonetheless. 'Yes, well,' he said and looked at us with what can only be described as a roguish twinkle in his eye, 'we do expect a little in return.'

A couple of players from United's youth team came over. It became quite clear that these lads had got the distinct impression that we were two bimbos on the make, and they addressed us accordingly. Then Roy told them I was Willie Morgan's daughter and their attitude was transformed. One of them started to sing 'Willie Morgan on the Wing', and, at that point, Roy had to assert his captain's authority, and this put an end to our conversation. Later Roy Carroll, United's second-string Irish goalkeeper, who was very drunk, had got into an altercation with another player. It did not take Keane long to sort it out. Such is his presence no one would argue with him.

Roy Keane's impeccable demeanour could not have been more different from his perceived combative public persona. I don't think any of those people who have built him into some kind of thug would believe that the phrase he kept repeating that evening was 'It's nice to be nice.'

Lisa and I were completely charmed by him. 'Did you realise he was so sexy?' Lisa asked me.

'No way,' I replied.

The party never flagged, but we did, and left at three in the morning. It was another hour or so before the players called it a day.

'I am happy at Real Madrid, I want to stay at Real Madrid, and that's the end of that.'

David Beckham had not yet played a whole season for Real Madrid before the rumours began that he would be leaving to join an English club. There are only two clubs who could afford to buy him and one of those, Manchester United, was already out of the reckoning for very obvious reasons. So it followed that David would be signing for Chelsea, newly made football plutocrats because of the vast wealth of their Russian chairman, Roman Abramovich.

David was so concerned that he acted instantly to quash the speculation about his future. He chose the *News of the World* to put his side of the story, and the paper published his denials on 14 March 2004. He stated that he was intending to see out his contract at Madrid. 'People say there are problems and I want to go back to England but all the speculation surrounding a move back home is rubbish. There is absolutely no question of me putting in a transfer request. Why would I? I have signed a four-year contract with Real Madrid. I want to stay here. I am happy. I am playing great football, everyone can see how much I am enjoying my football.'

If David is so happy in Madrid, why was a move considered such a strong possibility? There is a very familiar ring to the explanation proffered for the imminent, premature departure of the Beckhams from Spain.

Victoria, or so the newspapers claimed, was reluctant to live there and had taken Brooklyn and Romeo back to Hertfordshire, to the house in Sawbridgeworth, close to her sister and her parents. The *Daily Mail* went a stage further with its comments. Despite the Beckhams' insistence that the family would 'always be together in Spain', Victoria was hoping that David would come back to England to be with her and the children, leave the Spanish league leaders and play for Chelsea. A 'family friend' revealed that, 'Real Madrid was fine, but it was only a stop gap in her mind. She'd like him to be at Chelsea by this summer.'

When the Beckhams failed to renew the lease on the private house on the outskirts of Madrid that they had been renting, this added further fuel to the speculation that they had abandoned all pretence of family life there. In an interview with the Sky Sports Spanish football show, *Revista de la Liga*, David said that the intensity of the media pressure he was under in Spain meant that he had not felt able to bring his family to live there. He could not take his children on family outings and it was safer for them to attend school in England. Victoria could not, at that point, live in Madrid because of her work commitments in the US and Japan. David claimed he had not renewed the lease on his rented house because he was planning to buy a property in the Spanish capital.

It is possible to keep your children with you if you travel for much of the time. I know this from personal experience as my brother and I went to the USA with my father when he played in the four summers from 1977 onwards for Chicago Sting and Minnesota Kicks. We were usually taken out of school a few weeks early, but made special arrangements to take work with us so that we would not fall behind. We had an utterly wonderful time in America. The people there could not do enough for us. The accommodation provided and the various activities that were arranged were all of the highest standard. We were treated like royalty. It confirmed Dad's love affair with the States, one which David shares.

Dad must be the only professional footballer who actually had it written into his contract that he would be taken to Las Vegas to meet Elvis. The owner of Chicago Sting, Lee Stern, was determined to do anything to get Dad playing for his team which was managed by the ex-Manchester United player Bill Foulkes. Dad had agreed to go over twice before, but was forced to pull out because of injuries. But during Christmas 1976 there was a knock on our door, and Lee Stern was standing on the doorstep.

'I am Lee Stern,' he announced to a very surprised Willie Morgan. 'I own Chicago Sting. I'm here to make sure that you come over in the summer and won't pull out of the deal. Can I take you to dinner?'

Dad and Mum took him to the Portofino restaurant on Altrincham Downs. Mr Stern was determined to get his man. 'I'll come,' Dad assured him. 'No problem, you have my word.'

This wasn't enough. 'I want a guarantee. What will it take? Do you want more money?'

'Look, Lee,' Dad tried again. 'I've sorted it with Bill. I made an agreement and I'll come.'

Stern was still unconvinced. 'Is there anything at all in America that would guarantee you coming over next year?'

My father's reply was so typical. 'Well, if you can arrange for me to meet Elvis, that would guarantee me coming over every year. Actually, all I need you to do is to get me to Vegas.'

Elvis appeared in Vegas every year, and Lee didn't bat an eyelid. 'I have my own private jet and I will fly you down to Las Vegas with the family to see Elvis's show.'

Dad could then ask one of his friends, Tom Jones or Johnny Mathis, to set up a meeting. He asked Lee to put the arrangement in his contract, which he duly did. Dad went to the States, but in summer 1977 Elvis cancelled all his engagements; he died in September.

David has impressed the people of Madrid and Spain as a whole. He has become known for his 'normality', his lack of ego. His character on the Spanish version of the satirical puppet show *Spitting Image* gets laughs because it is so perfect. One sketch showed Real Madrid's president Perez checking all the players for body odour by sniffing their armpits. They all, Perez pronounced, stank horribly, except Beckham who smelled of flowers. Victoria, on the other hand, is not so well liked. The Spanish know how little time she spends in a country that she once memorably described as 'garlic-smelling'. The newspapers reported that she was only with her husband for 34 of his first 110 days in Madrid.

David was, to all intents and purposes, living as a single man in the city. After training he was often seen with teammates like Salgado, wiling away time in a city-centre restaurant. In the first few months after his move, he lived in a hotel and was spotted in the company of women whom gossips claimed were more than just friends. Meanwhile there were reports that Victoria, who was recording her new album with Damon Dash in New York, had more than a professional relationship with her musical guru. She refuted these claims in *i-D* magazine, in an interview accompanying a provocative photo shoot with what appeared to be a Parisian brothel theme. When asked about her 'affair', her response was typically straightforward. 'Me and Damon? Oh my God! I mean, that is ridiculous. I couldn't even begin to think of him in that way. Me and David are good friends with Damon. Working with him has been inspiring. This talk of an affair is just rubbish and everyone knows it's rubbish.'

The Beckham publicity machine swung into action to counter the accusations that their marriage was faltering. On Christmas Eve 2003, ITV's prime-time evening offering was the glossy, fly-on-the-wall documentary *The Real Beckhams*. The audience was a disappointing 5.5 million viewers, and the reviews were uniformly poor. Far from being an intimate portrait of how the Beckhams were settling into their new life, the show was an extended promo for Victoria's latest single, and a forum for her to push her latest incarnation as 'shrewd businesswoman'. The thinly veiled attempts at image manipulation were too obvious. One discussion of the documentary on a radio show suggested that the main problem with it had been that Victoria dominated, while everyone really wanted to know about David.

The programme was also, it is true to say, quite tedious. In one scene, where Victoria was failing to pack the family's clothes in their hotel suite as the Beckhams prepared to move into their rented house in Madrid, she held up a T-shirt which read 'Bored with the Beckhams'. It might have been a better title for the show. We also learned that Victoria constantly pulls at her hair, which we saw being styled in virtually every scene. The hair extensions which she favours have excited some debate in the papers because they are made from real human hair which is sourced in Russia from prisoners, patients in mental hospitals and orphanages, a practice which is considered to be nothing better than the exploitation of the disadvantaged to satisfy the vanity of spoiled western women. Victoria joked tactlessly, 'I've got Russian Cell Block H on my head,' showing that she is aware of the origins of the hair used in the process. According to the *Daily Mail*, these extensions cost £1,300.

Other segments featured Victoria on the Beckhams' joint promotional tour of the Far East in the summer of 2003, the unveiling of a huge poster of Victoria modelling Damon Dash's Rocawear range in New York's Times Square, Victoria buying diamond earrings for David's anniversary, Victoria recording her double A-side single 'This Groove' and 'Let Your Head Go' at Sony studios and Victoria playing with Brooklyn and Romeo as David holds a press conference for his autobiography in London. Then there was Victoria bagging freebie designer gear at Dolce & Gabbana's London store, appearing at the British Style Awards in September 2003, at a private opening of Harrods for her Christmas shopping and shooting the videos for her singles.

In between this frenzy of Victoria-centred activity, David and 'Tor' moved into the house they had chosen to rent in Spain, or rather that had been chosen for them. David unpacked his clothes and organised them all meticulously – shoes and trainers lined up, outfits hung in orderly rows. Victoria had no clothes to unpack as she was travelling backwards and forwards and 'you only need jeans'. She announced as she walked around the house, which she had not seen before, 'I actually don't want to go back to England now, and I never thought I'd say that, David, did you?' If this was intended to show that the Beckhams were a 'grounded' (a word Victoria likes a great deal) couple with an ordinary home life, it failed. But the show did end with David receiving his OBE, and some charming shots of him getting ready for the big occasion while looking after little Romeo, looking adorable clad only in a nappy. And David told a joke about his big day, saying that the Queen had told him that she had read his autobiography. 'She said she'd bought it at WHSmith as well.'

David also talked about the strain that the persistent rumours about his marriage had caused. 'It doesn't help,' he said, 'when you have to justify your marriage over and over again.' He said that the situation since their move to Spain was no different from the rest of their married life, where they had found themselves apart for long periods because of their jobs.

Potentially the most interesting part of *The Real Beckhams* was the reply that the couple gave when they were asked about why he had moved from SFX, the company which had managed his interests for so long in England. David asked Victoria to answer for him, and she explained that David wanted to set up his own office in Spain and that they were going to merge the commercial side of their careers. David added that he had been at SFX for a long time and done a lot of things with the company, but now it was time to 'move up a level', echoing the phrase that Victoria had just used. 'And, if I'm going to do that, why don't I do it with my wife?'

Earlier we had seen Victoria discussing her return to being managed by Simon Fuller, the man who made the Spice Girls such a success, but whom she portrayed in her own autobiography as a dictatorial control freak from whom the girls had to break free in secret. But the key to the change was that for the next year David would be able to concentrate on the European Championships and Real Madrid's season.

Real Madrid decided from the outset that David should play in central midfield. It was a decision which was in a sense inevitable, because the 'first *galactico*', Luis Figo, occupies the right-hand slot in the team and, in order to finance David's transfer, Madrid sold their central midfielder Claude Makelele to Chelsea. Indeed, initially there were predictions that Madrid could not accommodate both Figo and Beckham, and that one of the two would find himself on the bench. Most opined that David would be the man left out, acting as an understudy for the more gifted Portuguese star. David's switch to the centre has substantially revised the opinions of those critics both in Europe and at home who considered that Madrid had bought a pretty boy with enormous marketing potential, but a rather limited footballer. The Spanish winger Michel, for example, accused him of being 'a typically British player' who 'lacked technical quality'. Beckham, we were told, would be missing training to do promotional shoots because he was a 'commercial' signing. Much of this carping was based on the brief view of Beckham's skills that the Spaniards see on their TVs in the weekly ten-minute package of highlights from the Premiership. Instead, Beckham acts as one of the 'double pivots', one of the two defensive midfielders who sit in front of the Madrid defence. Helguera, Cambiasso and Guti compete to occupy the place alongside him in that role.

No one has been more lavish in David's praise than his 'rival', Luis Figo. In February 2004, before a friendly international between England and Portugal, he spoke about what he saw as a transformation in David's abilities. 'Beckham,' he said, 'has come to Real Madrid and become a complete player. His experience at the Bernabeu has made him a much better player and a stronger leader for England.' And as for his role in central midfield, 'It is a position which suits him perfectly because he is always involved in the game and his qualities suit him playing there in Spain. I cannot remember many other players being able to run and cover as much of the pitch as Beckham. His work rate is like no other player that I have seen. It has helped him as a player because it has given him a new challenge. Not only has he come to a new club but he has played a new position. That is the sign of a great player and I am sure he will play there for England one day.'

David's first three months as Madrid's sixth *galactico* must have transcended even his wildest dreams. He immediately impressed fans and colleagues, scoring after only 126 seconds in his debut against Real Betis. A series of brilliant performances followed which had the Spanish sports press salivating. Spain has four national daily sports papers, two based in Madrid and two in Barcelona, which are dominated by football. A reporter for one of the Madrid papers even went as far as to pay David an enormous compliment, comparing him to the club's greatest-ever player, the legendary Alfredo di Stefano.

Beckham's pinpoint long passes, his free kicks and his goal assists put him top of the Spanish league's statistics by December, giving official proof of what spectators already knew: the Englishman had been the best player. As Carlos Queiroz, Alex Ferguson's second in command who surprisingly followed Beckham to Madrid as their new coach, said, 'David brings intensity, that ninety minutes of complete concentration that characterises English football. Others can learn from his sacrifice.'

His acceptance was complete following Madrid's first La Liga victory in twenty years over their arch-rivals Barcelona. Luis Figo has long been the target of ferocious invective from Barca fans since he changed allegiances by leaving their club in 2000 to sign for Madrid, an act of betrayal which will never be forgiven. In El Derbi the previous year, when Figo went to take a corner he was pelted with missiles, beer cans, plastic bottles, an empty whisky bottle and, bizarrely, a pig's head. David had turned down Barcelona for Madrid, so this year he came in for some abuse from opposing fans. A banner was unfurled in the crowd, which read, in English, 'Beckham is a wanker'.

It is wrong, however, to see David's relocation as something which has been easy for him to accomplish. I will always believe that, no matter how successful he is in Spain, his heart will always be with Manchester United. Dad still describes the moment he had to leave Old Trafford as 'dreadful'. When I asked him about it recently he left me in no doubt about what it had cost him emotionally when Docherty forced him out. 'Manchester and Old Trafford were my life. I never moved away from the city, couldn't move away. I made sure that I signed for clubs within travelling distance because it was my home in all senses of the word.'

He too believes that David will always carry the same kind of feeling with him, but maybe to an even greater extent because David is a Manchester United supporter. 'I wasn't a Manchester United supporter,' Dad continued, 'I was a Celtic fan. And I didn't join the club as a young lad in my formative years. I know he wouldn't have left United if he hadn't been pushed.'

However, Dad doesn't think that going to Madrid has been a disaster for David.

'It was the best thing that could have happened to him. You can't give your best as a footballer when there is a situation between you and the manager. There is always that idea in your mind that he is waiting for you to fail. And I'm sure that those people at United who sanctioned his sale have been expecting him to fail in Spain as well, to justify their actions. Real Madrid have given him a platform to express himself and show the doubters what he is capable of.'

Though I delude myself that I know most things about Dad's football career, he always manages to surprise me. Talking about David joining Real Madrid had jogged his memory, and he turned to me and mused. 'I wonder what life would have been like if I had accepted their offer to join them?'

'Join Real Madrid, Dad?' I said, flabbergasted.

'Well, I never entertained it as a serious possibility,' he elaborated. 'I was only sixteen at the time. I had played in a youth tournament with Burnley in Germany. Ajax and Real Madrid were the other sides involved. After the game, some representatives from the Spanish club came to me and asked me to join them. One of them was their president Bernabeu, the guy their stadium is named after. I said no.'

'Why did you turn them down?' I asked, intrigued.

He just laughed. 'I'd only just found out where England was! When they'd gone I turned to my mates and said, "Where's Madrid?" and someone replied, "It's in Spain." Then I said, "Where's Spain?"'

Dad wonders if David will come back and end his career at Manchester United in the distant future, perhaps as their manager. Stranger things have happened in football. One of those strange ironies has been the involvement of Peter Kenyon, United's former chief executive, in Chelsea's alleged attempt to bring David back to England. Kenyon was, because of his United job, prepared to let David go to Madrid, but was now supposedly trying to bring him to Chelsea, his new employers. Kenyon made a surprise move to work for Abramovich at Stamford Bridge, and was pictured alongside Chelsea's new Russian boss watching David play in the Bernabeu. Victoria was supposed to have invited both men.

Since Christmas 2003, David's form has dipped somewhat and the reports in the press are no longer quite so glowing. He has picked up injuries which he has found hard to shake off, and Real Madrid struggled to beat one of the weaker sides in the league, Murcia. At the end of the match he received a gash on the ankle. He picked himself up to take the free kick which was awarded after the foul challenge, but blood could clearly be seen seeping through his white sock. 'I got caught as I was shooting and it started bleeding immediately,' he said in the post-match press conference. 'I have had to have four stitches.' This coincided with Madrid losing their place at the top of the league to Valencia, though only temporarily. Until 17 March 2004, Madrid were in the running to complete a grand slam of domestic Spanish titles, as well as progressing through into the quarter-finals of the Champions League after two hard-fought and explosive matches against Bayern Munich.

David has also begun to earn far more bookings than he did in England, a consequence of his more combative midfield role. At the end of January this culminated in his sending off at the close of Real Madrid's Copa del Rey quarter-final win against Valencia. He was booked twice, once for dissent and the second for a foul. David was philosophical about his dismissal, which was his first since 2000 in the World Club Championships. 'I didn't think it was deserved because I was running back and I just clipped his ankle as I ran back with him and the referee decided it was another card. I knew I was going off because the referee had been like that all day, not just with Madrid but with Valencia as well. There are things you can get away with in the Premier League that you can't do here. I wouldn't have got sent off in England, but I have no qualms with the referee; it's his decision. I don't know what the first card was for. Even if I had said something to the referee he wouldn't have understood it.'

Injuries and suspension disrupted his rhythm, but David also looked tired when he resumed. After Real's 1–1 draw with Santander in March he was singled out for savage criticism in one Spanish paper, which charted his decline since his earlier sparkling form: 'First of all he played and ran. Then he ran and played. Then he just ran. Now he neither runs nor plays.'

David's first big setback with Real was their defeat on 17 March in the Copa del Rey final by Real Zaragoza. The run-up to the final had been very sombre because of the bomb attacks on commuters in the city which left 201 dead. He could have collected his first major medal (he already has one from the Supercopa, the equivalent of the FA Community Shield, contested by the winners of the Copa del Rey and La Liga) if Real Madrid had been victorious. The club had not won the Spanish Cup since 1993 and David was looking forward to helping them rectify this. 'I hope we can win another trophy for Real Madrid, but it will be a hard and special game.'

It was obvious from the start of the match what a different role David plays for Madrid compared with his previous positions in the United and England teams. He takes up a very deep-lying position in the central midfield and rarely comes forward. Critics believe that he is playing too deep, forced into this by the extra defensive load which he has to carry when he is partnered in midfield by Guti, who does go forward on goal regularly. The pace of the game was very different from the Premiership. Even though this tie was contested at a faster tempo because it was a cup final, it still seemed slow. Madrid's game is based on possession, which they dominated in this match, keeping the ball off the Zaragoza players for long periods. Defence, however, is not the team's strong point. They have been accused of lacking bite and the will to scrap for points at all costs, and David has been praised for bringing a new spirit to the side. He certainly worked hard, tackling, running and even heading a ball off the line.

When Madrid took the lead it was because of a Beckham special, a curling free kick from thirty-five yards of such quality that it was compared with his climactic goal against Greece. Shortly afterwards he nearly repeated the feat, but this time his shot hit the outside of the post. Zaragoza replied quickly, carving open the Real Madrid defence all too easily. Just before half-time Guti, who was having something of a disastrous game, brought down an opposing player with a panicky, unnecessary tackle. Another free kick levelled the scores shortly after play resumed in the second half, only this time it was Roberto Carlos who hit the ball low and hard around the wall to evade the goalkeeper.

The game was littered with yellow cards, and there was, to English eyes anyway, an excess of gamesmanship as players from both sides rolled around in exaggerated agonies at even the slightest touch. At one point the Zaragoza players tried to get David booked, surrounding the referee and aping the gesture of holding up a yellow card. He reacted furiously. Unable to show his disgust in Spanish at this particular practice, which is frowned upon in England, he repeated the gesture, shaking his head, making his meaning abundantly clear. Sensing that David was unsettled, Zaragoza subjected him to a number of crude fouls, but he walked away from them, refusing to rise to the bait. Zaragoza's Cani was sent off shortly afterwards for two yellow cards in quick succession, one of them for fouling David. Only once did we see Becks driving into the penalty area. At the end of the game, when everyone else seemed to have settled for extra time, he ran forward, trying to steal a late winner, as Manchester United had done so often when he was part of that team. His contribution in the match had been some excellent corners, great free kicks, tigerish tackling and incessant running. He played some wonderful raking balls out of midfield for the Real forwards to run on to, but their finishing was not incisive enough. Raul, scorer of so many goals in the previous season, and currently the most popular Real player, was anonymous, and the injured Ronaldo was badly missed. The game went into extra time and Real Zaragoza triumphed, courtesy of a fine shot which came from nothing and squeezed past the Madrid goalkeeper. As the final whistle blew, David dropped his head, utterly dejected and utterly exhausted.

But Real Madrid's season was far from over, and looked as though it would hold more promise than Manchester United's season would. Although they ultimately went on to win the 2004 FA Cup, they were eliminated from the Champions League by Porto and they suffered a run of draws, plus a 4-1 defeat by Manchester City, all in the space of one calamitous month.

In the first few weeks of January 2004, Manchester United had a lead over Arsenal, and while not playing at their best, continued to prosper. Then the papers were quick to point out that the team had not missed David Beckham. Now, as they held the inquests into United's declining form, David's departure was seen as a crucial factor in the collapse of their season. Ron Atkinson, former United manager, stated in his regular *Guardian* column under the headline UNITED STALL WITHOUT THE SPARK OF BECKHAM, 'Manchester United are going through a crisis by their standards, and I don't think it's all down to problems with their back four. I've felt for a while that they have never really replaced David Beckham, and that was obvious again against Porto.' What United missed, according to Big Ron, was not so much David's crosses, free kicks and passes, but his defensive work. United are now too easy to break down on the right, and Beckham used to work hard defensively, in tandem with Gary Neville. Christiano Ronaldo is not yet the man to replace him – Ron described him as 'basically a substitute, someone who can come on and stretch teams. He can get at people in the last third but when the ball changes hands he's not the best at the moment at offering protection.'

Are United missing David Beckham? Well, the answer is obviously that they are. Ruud Van Nistelrooy said exactly that in February on the eve of United's away Champions League tie against Porto. 'Becks is missed here at United as a player as well as a person. And from what I've seen of him in Spain, he's doing really well, which is a credit to him.' But they would not be missing Beckham quite so much if Ole Gunnar Solskjaer, who deputised for him at the end of David's last season at United, had not been out for months following an operation. United were also managing well enough until Rio Ferdinand was suspended for eight months for failing to attend a drugs test. Ferdinand, in the eyes of many United fans and others, was vastly overrated and United had been fleeced when they bought him for £30 million from Leeds United. At least that is what they used to believe – until he began his suspension and it became apparent that he is the linchpin around which the defence is organised. Wes Brown, just returning from his second cruciate injury, was pitched straight back into first-team action to solve United's defensive crisis. Meanwhile Alex Ferguson was reluctant to go into the transfer market to buy a central defender, on the basis that, if he wanted to buy a player who would be eligible to play in the Champions League, he would have to ignore the top-quality players.

Against Manchester City, United gifted their rivals two goals because of embarrassing defensive errors from which they could not recover. They were also without Roy Keane, whom the *Sun* suggested was about to quit United in an article with the sensational headline TORN APART. The paper also claimed that Ruud Van Nistelrooy, who has only just signed a new five-year contract, has fallen out with Alex Ferguson after being omitted for the league game at Fulham which United drew 1–1, falling further behind to Arsenal. Real's coach Carlos Queiroz is a big Van Nistelrooy fan, and the club is reportedly prepared to pay £25 million for him. The *Sunday Express* had a different line: Real Madrid had 'launched discreet moves to try and land Rio Ferdinand, if they can outbid Chelsea, who want Ferdinand to partner John Terry'. And, of course, there has been criticism of United's current favourite scapegoat Ryan Giggs who is, so the rumours say, to be sold this summer. As Dad never fails to point out, with some feeling and from personal experience, 'Wingers always get it in the neck. It's the hardest position to play in, and you get little thanks.'

Roy Keane, by his own admission, has only a few more seasons left as a top player, and it could be said that United will miss Beckham most when Keane finally does leave United and there is a gaping hole in the heart of the midfield. David is currently demonstrating that he is maturing into something that United have craved for some time: a creative midfield playmaker. Alongside a holding player like Nicky Butt (also close to leaving Old Trafford in 2004) he could be the 'single pivot' that Juan Sebastian Veron never succeeded in being. Of course, ironically, this is a dimension in his play that would never have been revealed if he had not gone to Real Madrid and remained on the right wing.

While Manchester United underwent a recovery, defeating Arsenal once again to go through to - and ultimately win - the FA Cup, Real Madrid's fortunes continued to decline as they suffered a shock defeat by Monaco which eliminated them from the Champions League. Without David, who was suspended after picking up a booking in the last minutes of the first game against the French side, Real surrendered a 4–2 lead. Beckham didn't escape criticism. There were accusations that he had deliberately engineered his booking so that he would be sure of playing in the semi-final it seemed certain Real would reach. He also wasn't in Monaco to see his teammates' humiliation. Instead, he was on leave in the French Alps with his family, facing another major challenge to his reputation, this time from a very unexpected quarter.

Billed as 'The story you never thought you'd read', the *News of the World* carried a sensational seven-page exclusive exposé from the Beckhams' former PA, Rebecca Loos. Soon dubbed 'the sleazy senorita', as details of her bisexuality and alleged insatiable sex drive were revealed by an ex-lover, she claimed that she began a steamy affair with David in the months when he first came to Madrid. Hired by SFX, the management company that David has now left, to smooth the couple's transfer to their new life,

Rebecca became David's constant companion while Victoria pursued her recording career in London. Loos alleged that David, at his lowest ebb, wracked by suspicions that Victoria's infatuation with Damon Dash would destroy their marriage, turned to her for sex and company. Their lovemaking was 'highly charged and explosive', but ended when Victoria became suspicious. The proof of this bombshell came in the form of pages of sexually explicit text messages between the two, the more graphic passages censored by asterisks.

As soon as Rebecca's claims were made public, I knew they were true – my own experience showed me that he had that tendency, that he was looking for something that his marriage couldn't give him. I didn't allow it to go any further, but I knew that he had a need to take it further if he found the right person. What had started with me had developed with Rebecca. I knew it would happen, as plain as night follows day.

The Beckhams (accompanied as usual by Victoria's family) took a short break with a skiing holiday in the Alpine resort of Courchevel, where they appeared together as a united family. David had already issued a statement describing Loos's story as 'ludicrous'. Meanwhile, it emerged that she had reportedly been paid £350,000 in a deal brokered by PR agent Max Clifford, and there were counter-suggestions that Beckham had been set up in some sort of sting and that his ex-chauffeur in Spain, Delfin Fernandez, sacked in January 2004 for trying to sell secrets about David, was involved. A further deal with Sky for an hour-long TV interview is supposed to have earned Loos the massive sum of half a million.

Once Loos's story hit the headlines, a string of

allegations about David's infidelity followed. Lists of his alleged conquests appeared in the papers, but the attempt to smear 'Tarnishedballs', as one correspondent called him, as a womaniser was less than convincing. David may have been unfaithful to Victoria with Rebecca Loos, but by her own admission this was on four occasions and only in response to particular circumstances when the Beckhams' marriage was under considerable strain. Some of David's supposed other encounters with women date from this time. Loos said that he spent time with the stunning supermodel Esther Canadas, whom he nicknamed 'Ms Biglips' and also enjoyed flirty texting sessions with her. Frida Karlsson, a Swedish model, declared that she had kissed him passionately, and Loos claimed to have procured a short, blonde tapas waitress to provide him with sexual services in a restaurant toilet.

Other wannabe recipients of Beckham's attention appear to have jumped on the bandwagon. Nuria Bermudez, nicknamed the 'Spanish Jordan' by the English tabloids (a description which is unfair to Jordan), who had already claimed to have slept with half the Real Madrid team, said she had sex with David and also received sexy texts. 'Corrie Beauty' Stacey Wingfield went public with a story that he had begged her for sex as far back as January 1998.

The *News of the World* followed up its scoop with 'Lover Number 2', the 'Malaysian beauty' Sarah Marbeck whose alleged affair with Beckham had lasted two years. Their relationship had begun when they met at a function in Singapore in 2001 on the Manchester United pre-season tour, and David had had sex with her twice, when Victoria was heavily pregnant with Romeo. After that the affair had consisted of texts in which David referred to himself as Peter and her as Tinkerbell. An ex-boyfriend spoke of her belief that she would become the second Mrs Beckham, an idea which at best seems highly optimistic, and she herself said that she had broken her silence because she had spent two years of her life waiting for him.

David and Victoria acted quickly to show that their marriage was unaffected by these stories. Victoria, looking glamorous with new highlighted hair extensions and wearing a black designer dress with long sleeves and cut-away shoulders, appeared in the Bernabeu with Brooklyn to watch David's next game against Osasuna, and to hear the boos of some sections of the crowd as the team lost again. David flew to England to take Victoria to dinner at Claridges in central London for an early celebration of her thirtieth birthday. They happily posed for waiting photographers when they left, hands closely interlocked. In a smart PR move designed to let the furore die down naturally, while dissuading any more unproven allegations, they announced they were considering legal action, while keeping a watching brief.

Questions were asked about why the Beckhams had avoided bringing a libel case against Loos, the implication being that her allegations were true. But one media consultant speculated that they wished to avoid the exposure of yet more details about their family life and the intrusion that such a case would inevitably entail. Rebecca Loos had already spoken about how awful she found Victoria's pushy, 'nouveau riche' parents and how Victoria was often irritable with her sons in private. She went on to say how David hated Victoria's skinny body and was always encouraging her to eat more. Victoria, on the other hand, belittled David in public and, in Rebecca's view, encouraged him to dress like a 'kid' in grunge style.

Only time will tell how far the British public believes these allegations, and whether any significant damage has been done to the Beckhams' image. The furore in this country has largely been ignored by the Spanish press who consider that this is David and Victoria's personal business. They are more concerned by Real's catastrophic dip in form. Here we have grown used to reading opinion pieces warning Victoria of the consequences of leaving her desirable husband alone, and the pages of text messages have created a national sport of guessing what words might fill the blanks. In terms of David and Victoria's relationship, it has been suggested that they have known that these allegations would be printed for some time, and have settled between them whatever problems they may have gone through in the past.

What awaits David in the immediate future, besides cementing his place at Real Madrid, is the 2004 European Championships in June. This will be his fourth major international tournament, and perhaps his best chance of bringing England its greatest honour since the World Cup victory in 1966. David's contribution to the fortunes of the England national side continues to be of the greatest importance, even though, as the last chapter revealed, the 2002–3 season was one of considerable trauma and heartache for the England captain. The first qualifying game took place in Bratislava against Slovakia, on a quagmire of a pitch. Sven-Goran Eriksson's private life had come into the spotlight following revelations in

Ulrika Jonsson's autobiography that they had had an affair, and both Rio Ferdinand and Sol Campbell were unavailable. Their absence proved to be the more decisive factor in the game, as the Slovakians scored first after Nemeth was able to exploit England's defensive disarray. England equalised early in the sixty-fourth minute from one of David's best free kicks for England. From forty yards out on the left he swung the ball high into the penalty area. It evaded everyone and curled into the net. Owen scrambled the winner home to start the qualifying campaign off on a positive note. England would not be playing catch-up from the start as they had done before.

Optimism about the team's prospects evaporated dramatically after a 2–2 draw in October against 'easy' opponents Macedonia, the first full international to be played at Southampton's St Mary's Stadium. Macedonia scored first straight from a corner, a goal attributed to David Seaman's declining form. As Alan Smith put it in the *Telegraph*, when 'embarrassment and humiliation were flooding through England's ranks, one man stepped forward to drag England back, by hook or by crook. That man was David Beckham.' He rubbed out the deficit with a wonderful outfield goal. Paul Scholes played a delicate chip over the defender, which David controlled on his chest and in turn chipped over the goalkeeper's head. Then another defensive howler allowed Macedonia to retake the lead. A draw was salvaged by David's quick thinking. Scholes knocked the ball into the Macedonian penalty area, but it looked as if it was going out for a goal kick. Beckham, standing virtually on the goal line, headed it back for Gerrard to bring down and score with a magnificent volley.

The defeat by Australia in a friendly on 12 February 2003 gave the critics of Eriksson their opportunity, and the England manager was robustly defended by his captain in interviews against the charge that he was lacking in passion and could not motivate his team sufficiently. David was growing in confidence in the captain's role, and went on the attack. 'I heard the other day that he's not that passionate. But believe me he's one of the most passionate managers I've ever had. He may not be shouting and screaming, fists up in the air, but we understand him.'

Sven was even more direct. 'If you want someone shouting, you will have to change, because that's not my style.'

At the end of March and the beginning of April, England played the two games around which their campaign would hinge. 'Lowly' Liechtenstein were no threat on paper, but England put in a lukewarm performance to win 2–0. David started off the move which led to Michael Owen's first goal, then scored the second with another marvellous free kick, hit with a wicked swerve, which caused it to bounce off the inside of the post and into the net. Once that game had been negotiated, England faced their biggest rivals in the qualification group – Turkey – and beat them 2–0. The match was scrappy and ill-tempered. David, still fiery and prepared to stand up for himself on a football pitch, was booked for catching a Turkish player with his elbow. With the score at 0–0 as fifteen minutes remained, and a succession of English attacks having been thwarted by the Turkish goalkeeper, a floated corner from Beckham caused mayhem in the Turkish penalty area, and the ball was finally put in the net by Aston Villa's Darius Vassell. Kieron Dyer won a penalty which was hotly contested by the Turkish players. David slotted it right into the corner of the net, placing it beautifully so that the goalkeeper had no chance of saving it. In the post-match conference, David demanded better support and recognition for what the team had achieved. 'We knew we had it in us,' he declared, 'but people have got to have a little more faith in these players and in the manager.'

Though he was suspended for the next international game, against Slovakia at the Riverside Stadium on 11 June, Beckham was the name on everyone's lips. Sven was asked whether his transfer to a Spanish club would harm David's chances for selection for the national team. His reaction was polite, but showed that he thought the question completely ridiculous. When David did rejoin the team, for the match against Macedonia in Skopje, both goals came from long Beckham passes which floated into the opposition box. Wayne Rooney converted one to become the youngest-ever player to score a goal for England; the second won a penalty when Terry was fouled as he chested the ball down. David again tucked it into the net.

Less than two months after he had left, David was back at Old Trafford for the return game against Liechtenstein. In a nice touch the team played in an all-white strip at Beckham's request, a homage to Real Madrid. If they were successful in this game, the current side would break the record set by Sir Alf Ramsey's team of eight wins in a row. When Beckham was substituted in the second half, Sven mindful that if he collected a second yellow card he would miss the key game against Turkey, the crowd gave the footballer a standing ovation, which one reporter described as a 'royal salute'.

The task of qualification was completed with a hard-fought 0–0 draw in an intimidating and aggressive game against the Turks. The team had also been torn apart in the press for their support of Rio Ferdinand and their stand against the inconsistencies and ambiguities of the FA's disciplinary procedures. Once again, David was not prepared to walk away from a fight and from a mate. As captain he took the brunt of the criticism, and faced the media storm head on with dignity and wit. During a game which was described as 'brutal', David had a rare headed goal disallowed for offside, and when he took a penalty later in the game, he slipped as he took the shot and the ball ballooned embarrassingly into the crowd behind the goal. He lost his temper as well as his footing. The Turkish player Alpay taunted him over the penalty miss, and David pushed his forehead at him, in the semblance of a headbutt. As the players left the field at half-time, Alpay to all intents and purposes seemed to be trying to stick his finger up David's nose. At half-time there was a confrontation in the tunnel, involving several players, captured on video. But the draw was enough and David had triumphed over all distractions to lead his country to the finals in Portugal.

What lies even further in the future for David is impossible to predict. He has spoken of how he would like to run soccer schools for children all over the world when he finally gives up the game professionally, but there is still much football for him to play. Whether he can achieve his aims of concentrating on his football and bringing his family up to live as normal a life as possible is another question altogether. Jorge Valdano, Real Madrid's director of football, summarised this dilemma very neatly. 'On one hand he is the man with incomparable media power, and the other a fantastic player from head to toe who is captain of England ... He is so very important for the media and there is no way for the club to balance out that power. It is something that has worried us because we would like him to live a more normal life, but it is difficult to be Beckham and normal.'

EPILOGUE:
THE REAL DAVID
BECKHAM

The last time I saw David was on my birthday. I was in the Trafford Centre, and as I walked out of a clothes shop I walked straight into someone and dropped my bags. I was on the point of saying, 'Oh, I'm sorry!' when I saw that that someone was David. He was with Brooklyn and a minder; Brooklyn was holding the minder's hand.

David smiled at me. It was the old smile, the old David. I looked at him with no expression in my face, then bent down to pick up my shopping and walked away. We didn't say anything. I looked back, and saw the three of them disappear into the distance.

David and Victoria have presented their courtship and marriage as a fairy tale. Footballer sees gorgeous singer on TV and knows she is the one for him. Singer falls for the shy, romantic young man whose footballing talent is about to catapult him into superstardom. Despite long separations, their love grows ever stronger, sealed by the birth of their first son. Their storybook wedding and subsequent life together, despite its many tribulations, have done nothing to weaken the bonds between them. Victoria rocks David's world; David is the sexiest and most gorgeous man she has ever seen. But those who have observed the couple together and apart know that this fantasy masks the reality of what is becoming an increasingly difficult juggling act between the desire to lead some semblance of a normal family life and the demands of their joint careers.

My dad describes professional footballers as 'very basic people'. What they require is love and support, an ordered home which allows them to cope with the overwhelming pressures of playing at the highest level. They need to be able to let their hair down as one of the lads, but also to unwind with their families after the adrenaline rush of performing in front of thousands. You could also say the same about pop stars. Victoria seemingly cannot function without the constant presence of her mother, father and sister's family. They care for the boys and, as importantly, look after her, the princess of the family. She only feels comfortable living close to where she grew up. It almost seems as if she has never really left home. David has had to accept that, if he wants to play for Real Madrid, all his money and his fame cannot buy him the secure, ordinary family life he craves, and which he needs more than anything else.

Realistically, David only has at the very most six years left as a professional footballer, and his powers will start to decline when he reaches thirty-two. Victoria, slightly older than David, also has very little time left in which to reinvent herself before age catches up with her. She is not the Spice Girls' Robbie Williams, and I don't think she ever will be. Some commentators have suggested that she may trade upon public sympathy following David's supposed betrayal of their marriage vows by releasing a single which might make it to number one on the strength of her newly acquired victim status.

As for me, my life has moved on. I've grown up a lot in the last few years. I'm a lot more grounded and I know now what I want out of life.

My own personal experience leaves me in no doubt that the Beckhams need to ask not what is best for their careers, but what is best for their children. If David stopped playing tomorrow, if Victoria never sang another note, Brooklyn and Romeo would still face the challenge of carrying the enormous burden of their parents' fame in the future. Being part of a loving family will give them the emotional stability they will need to draw upon heavily as they grow up in the uncertain and often cruel world that all children of celebrities inhabit. For their sake, I hope that David and Victoria live up to the expectations of their fans.